Paul Orlowski

Teaching About Hegemony

Race, Class and Democracy
in the 21st Century

 Springer

Prof. Paul Orlowski
The University of Saskatchewan/Saskatoon
Campus Drive 28
S7N 0X1 Saskatoon
Saskatchewan
Canada
paul.orlowski@usask.ca

ISBN 978-94-007-1417-5 (hardcover)   e-ISBN 978-94-007-1418-2
ISBN 978-94-007-3881-2 (softcover)
DOI 10.1007/978-94-007-1418-2
Springer Dordrecht Heidelberg London New York

Library of Congress Control Number: 2011929656

Springer is part of Springer Science+Business Media (www.springer.com)

Preface

Anyone interested in contemporary educational issues must come to the realization that only certain aspects of schooling seem to preoccupy the minds of journalists employed by the corporate media. School rankings, boys being academically disadvantaged, voucher schools, charter schools, using tax dollars to support private schools, ending multicultural education, increasing teacher accountability, and implementing merit pay for teachers are only some of the myriad topics commonly found in media outlets today. Teacher unions in particular are regularly portrayed as the villain in matters pertaining to public education. As soon as the frontline public servants employed to teach children openly discuss school issues such as class size, special education assistants, state-wide testing, or school funding, the corporate media are very often quick to produce editorials and columns that denigrate the representative bodies of professional educators. Of course, it is not too difficult to see the political bias emanating from those who support tax cuts. Anyone with a political acumen understands that the corporate media have corporate interests.

A well-funded public education system is a very expensive undertaking for *any* society. Yet, research demonstrates that when schooling is properly funded, the benefits to the students, and to society as a whole, are great. Historians of education know that the struggle for a strong public education system is one of the great victories for common Americans and Canadians, those people who would have difficulty paying for their children to go to private schools. With excellent public schools, middle- and working-class families could expect to see their children get ahead from a very good academic grounding, as well as find meaning in their lives that comes from a decent liberal arts education.

So what happened? Since the 1980s in the United States and the 1990s in Canada, a massive transformation in collective thinking about public schools has occurred. The emphasis on critical thinking and liberal arts has been replaced by the human capital paradigm in which the focus is on filling the requirements of capital. Of course, developing properly trained workers for job openings has long been a consideration for governments and the captains of industry. Indeed, working class representatives have often touted similar philosophies for public schools. Of course, finding gainful employment is important, but something is profoundly different this time round. The constant media focus on academic "excellence" and international test score comparisons is new for the public to digest. We hear over and over how students in Finland are doing better than North American students in literacy and numeracy testing, but we never hear about how they fund their public school system. One wonders if the answer to this question might decrease the momentum the corporate media here have successfully generated for the current tax cut craze.

The biggest change that has occurred since the progressive schooling ideas of the 1960s and 1970s is that the economic doctrine known as neoliberalism appeared with such a force that to challenge it seems like pouring a bucket of water on a raging forest fire. Proponents of deregulation, union busting, and privatization of the commons are not interested in the egalitarianism of progressive politics. Indeed, the social welfare state is anathema to these people because of the financial commitment from the public purse. A concept like civil society does not even enter into any of their discourses.

One must ask, "How did this all come about?" After all, most people benefit from a well-funded public education system and a strong social welfare state. The economic elites touting their tax cut mantra are much fewer in number than everyone else. Because we do live in a democracy, the potential is always there to block these neoliberal forces and once again work to strengthen civil society, and stop the dismantling of it. Before this can happen, however, progressive educators must develop critical pedagogy with one collective goal, namely, to deconstruct the *false political consciousness* that has colonized the minds of many citizens from the middle and working classes. The recent rise of the American-based populist movement known as the Tea Party appeared shortly after the U.S. government gave over 1.4 trillion tax dollars to the very same financial institutions that caused a major economic crisis. This seemed hopeful until their refrain for more tax cuts made it clear that these concerned citizens had been successfully duped by hegemonic discourses deployed by the elites and their minions in the corporate media.

Teaching About Hegemony was written in response to neoliberalism and the false political consciousness of too many common citizens. In fact, the book is specifically written to have teachers understand political ideology, discourse, and hegemony so that they, in turn, can develop pedagogy specifically designed to educate their students about these important topics. The content of every one of the chapters in this book come from my almost 30 years of experience as an educator in high schools and university teacher education programs.

The conservative backlash has gone far enough. The gap between the rich and everyone else has grown to grotesque proportions. Racism has not been vanquished, so why has Arizona banned all forms of multicultural education? There is no more time to tolerate this widespread false political consciousness among the general public. When working-class people clamor for more tax cuts, they are saying that they have very little understanding of how and why a social welfare state exists and what it can do for them. Progressive educators have a responsibility to reverse this trend because a civil society is an ideal worth striving for. The alternatives offered by the corporate agenda point in the other direction, and these images are bleak indeed.

I say let us take neoliberalism on because we can win any rational debate about these issues. An informed and active citizen is required so that society can benefit from taking on racism through critical multicultural education, from supporting progressive tax reform in which the wealthy pay their fair share, and from an under-standing of why an enlightened society should help rather than denigrate its less fortunate members. The constant discourse now heard almost everywhere of blam-ing the victims of corporate capitalism for their misfortune is wrongheaded and mean-spirited. The time has arrived to put the blame for the current economic crises where it belongs – on those who want to sell off the commons so that a few can financially profit. After all, *everyone* benefits from living in a civil society.

Saskatoon   Paul Orlowski
SK, Canada

Acknowledgments

This book became possible because of the support of a number of people. I thank my friend and mentor Deirdre Kelly, the University of British Columbia; my friends and former colleagues Barbara Salingre and Sandy Hill, the University of the Fraser Valley in British Columbia; my friend and research specialist Terri Thompson, the Canadian Council of Learning. I lovingly thank my daughter Katrina for giving me the space to focus on this book during my spare time for the past three years. I express gratitude to the editors and staff at Springer, especially Bernadette Ohmer and Marianna Pascale, for their helpful tips and seemingly limitless patience. I give further thanks to all of the students I have had the privilege of teaching and learning from over the past three decades; to all of the participants in the educational research studies I have been involved with; to all of the scholars whose work has informed my thinking, my work, and my perspectives on the world and the society in which we live; to Ken Tobin and Shirley Steinberg for editing suggestions. And last but not the least I thank Joe Kincheloe for initially approaching me to write this book. I was always moved by Joe's encouragement and missed him when he left us. I still do.

This book was written in the hope that we can reverse the current neoliberal and neoconservative trends in our society. Every citizen deserves to have an accurate political consciousness rather than a false one. Developing a politically conscious teaching force engaged in critical pedagogy is the best way to educate for an informed and active citizenry. Our children and our children's children will appreciate these efforts.

Contents

1 An Introduction 1
So What Does Hegemony Mean? 2
    Chapter 1: An Introduction 5
Part I: Mostly Theory – Ideology, Discourse, Hegemony,
and the Curriculum 5
    Chapter 2: What's Ideology Got to Do with It? 5
    Chapter 3: The Power of Discourse, Of course! 6
    Chapter 4: The Purpose of Schooling: Ideology in the
    Formal and the "Enacted" Curriculum 6
Part II: Less Theory, More Applications
and Practice: Deconstructing Racial and Class
Discourses for a Stronger Democracy 7
    Chapter 5: Teaching About Race and Racism in Our Past
    and Present 7
    Chapter 6: Social Class: The Forgotten Identity Marker in
    Social Studies Education 8
    Chapter 7: Liberal Discourses About Aboriginal
    Students – A Case Study of Power Blindness 10
    Chapter 8: Ideology, Democracy, and the "Good" Citizen 11
    Chapter 9: Neoliberalism: Laissez-Faire Revisited? 12
    Chapter 10: Some Final Reflections: Dare the Schools Teach
    for a Fair Social Order? 12
A Few Words About Teacher Education 13
Questions to Ponder 14
Notes 15
References 15

**Part I   Mostly Theory – Ideology, Discourse, Hegemony,
and the Curriculum**

2 What's Ideology Got to Do With It? 19
Political Ideology in Its Historical Context 19
    Modernity 22

The Ideologies of Modernity   23
Liberalism   24
Socialism   26
Conservatism   28
Postmodernist Critiques of Modernity's Ideologies   30
Ideology Today   31
What Is Meant by Left Wing and Right Wing
in Today's Politics?   31
Suggestions to Further Comprehension   33
Questions to Ponder   35
Notes   35
References   36

3   **The Power of Discourse, Of course!**   37
Critical Discourse Analysis: A Brief Introduction   38
A Poststructuralist Approach to Understanding Power   39
Discursive Formations   40
Discourse and the Evolving Nature of Ideology   40
Discourse and Resistance to Power   42
Hegemony   42
Counterhegemonic Discourses   44
Social Positionality and Life Experiences   46
Locating Oneself in Our Racial Relations: Some Personal Reflections .   48
For Reflection   51
Questions to Ponder   51
Notes   51
References   52

4   **The Purpose of Schooling: Ideology in the Formal and
    "Enacted" Curriculum**   55
Teacher Accountability and a Relevant Curriculum   55
The Struggle over the Curriculum: A Brief History   58
Ideology and the Purpose of Schools: Then and Now   59
The Formal Curriculum and Political Ideology   61
Examples of Political Ideology in the B.C. Curriculum   64
The Enacted Curriculum and Race–Class Intersections   66
   Example 1: The Ludlow Massacre   66
   Example 2: Exploiting White Working-Class Racism in
   B.C.'s Coal Mines and Beyond   67
   Example 3: Women's Rights Across Space and Time:
   A Race–Class–Gender Intersection   70
Questions to Ponder   71
Notes   73
References   73

**Part II Less Theory, More Applications and Practice:
Deconstructing Racial and Class Discourses for a
Stronger Democracy**

5 Teaching About Race and Racism in Our Past and Present   77
Forms of Racism: A Narrative of a Teacher/Educational Researcher . .   78
A Few Words About Race and Racism in the Context
of North America   81
An Introduction to Racial Discourses   82
The Essentialist Discourse in Social Studies   83
The Color-Blind Discourse in Social Studies   87
The Race-Cognizance Discourse in Social Studies   89
Political Ideology and Multiculturalism   91
A Few Words on Contemporary Racial Discourses   93
Questions to Ponder   94
Notes   96
References   96

**6 Social Class: The Forgotten Identity Marker in Social
Studies Education**   99
A Waning Class Consciousness – Can Ideology Critique Help? 100
Ideology and Economic Issues 102
Public Education and Class Consciousness 103
Ideology in the Social Studies Curriculum 104
The Curriculum and the Individual 108
Ideology and Discourses of Working-Class Academic Performance . . 109
Ideology and How Veteran Teachers View Issues of Social
Class and Working-Class Students 111
How Teachers Think About Social Class 113
How Teachers Think About Teaching Social Class Issues 116
Summary and Conclusions 119
Implications: Can Social Studies Help Bring Social Class
to the Public Consciousness? 121
Questions to Ponder 123
Notes 123
References 124

**7 Liberal Discourses About Aboriginal Students – A Case
Study of Power Blindness** 127
Settings and Methods 129
Framing the Study 130
Racial Discourses 131
Canadian Multiculturalism – A Brief Overview 131
The British Columbia Social Studies Curriculum as Context 132
Teacher Attitudes 134
Teachers and the "One-Size-Fits-All" Color-Blind Curriculum 139

Summary and Conclusions 142
For Reflection 144
Questions to Ponder 145
Notes 145
References 146

8   Ideology, Democracy, and the "Good" Citizen 149
A Brief Discussion About Modern Democratic Concerns 149
American Democracy: Achieving Dignity for the Masses? 151
Ideology and Competing Visions of Democracy and Citizenship 154
Teaching For and About Democracy, Including Its Flaws 157
Hegemony and Counterhegemony 158
Teaching for a Political Consciousness 159
Ideology Critique 160
The Case for Critical Media Literacy 161
Teaching About the Flaws in Our Democracy 164
Reflections on Teaching for and About Democracy 166
Conclusions 167
Questions to Ponder 167
Notes 168
References 169

9   Neoliberalism: Laissez-Faire Revisited? 171
Neoliberalism: Is This a New Political "Ideology"? 174
If Not an Ideology, Then What is Neoliberalism? 176
From Laissez-Faire *to State Interventionism in the Economy* 176
Neoliberalism Finds Fertile Ground 178
Getting the Masses to Support the Neoliberal Project 180
Is Today's Globalization the Same as Yesterday's Colonization? 182
Neoliberalism On the Home Front 184
Neoliberalism and Its Implications for Public Education 187
The Neoliberal Attack on the Teaching Profession 189
Resistance to Neoliberalism: Where Hope Resides! 190
Questions to Ponder 193
Notes 194
References 194

**10 Some Final Reflections: Dare the Schools Teach for a Fair
     Social Order?** 197
Question to Ponder 204
Note 204
References 204

Index 207

About the Author

Paul Orlowski received his PhD at the University of British Columbia in Vancouver, Canada. His research interests are in Teacher Education, Social Studies Education, Sociology of Education, Aboriginal Education, Media Literacy, and Teaching for Social Justice. He has written several book chapters and journal articles, some of which have been published in the *Canadian Journal of Education*, the *Canadian Journal of Native Education, Democracy & Education, Scholar-Practitioner Quarterly*, and *Our Schools Our Selves*. Paul has 19 years of teaching experience in various high school settings in British Columbia, Canada. He has also taught for six years in UBC's Teacher Education Program, and for four years he was the department head of the Teacher Education Program at the University of the Fraser Valley in British Columbia. Paul is currently on faculty in the College of Education at the University of Saskatchewan in Saskatoon, Canada. The main goal of his teaching in all of these settings has been to develop a political consciousness in his students, so that they may become informed and active citizens focused on maintaining and even strengthening civil society.

Chapter 1
An Introduction

In both the United States and Canada today, anyone concerned with public education cannot help but notice the educational struggles reported in the mainstream media. These conflicts focus on a variety of aspects of schooling, including the curriculum itself, teachers' accountability, the agenda of teachers' unions, the voice of parents, school choice and voucher programs, school funding formulas, and even the expertise and basic character of contemporary teachers. Many of these important topics are not new – indeed, they have been part of educational debates since the dawn of the public education system in North America over a century and half a ago.

My own career as a veteran high school teacher and teacher educator in Canada has led me to a different set of questions, ones that do not often, if at all, make it into the public discourse. For example, it is very curious that most students enter high school without any conception of class consciousness and, despite several courses in social studies and history and perhaps even one in civics, graduate without one either. Why is this so? Why is it that so many working-class students see themselves as middle-class? Why do so few students understand the social ramifications of tax cuts? Why are liberal and pluralist versions of multiculturalism so entrenched in schools today? Why are these forms of multicultural education criticized from both the right and the left of the political spectrum? Why is it common to hear from adolescent female students that they have little or no interest in feminism or its goals? Moreover, why is the media focusing so much on the conservative backlash against a perceived influence of feminism and multiculturalism in our high school classrooms? Why are so many people uninterested in voting in elections or engaging in other forms of the democratic process? Indeed, why is it that so few people understand the obvious assumption that the corporate media support corporate interests? Most importantly, why are most people entering the field of education apolitical?

My experience in public education includes 19 years as a teacher in the high schools of British Columbia, Canada's most western province. These years were divided between urban and rural school settings, sometimes with predominantly working-class student populations, at other times with predominantly privileged students. In all of the classrooms where I have taught, the cultural diversity among the students was very significant, with very little resemblance to my own schooling in Toronto's east end of the 1960s and early 1970s. In addition, I have taught in teacher education programs for the past 11 years. These years have mostly been divided between the University of British Columbia and the University of the Fraser Valley in Chilliwack, where I was the department head of a Teacher Education Program. I am currently on faculty at the University of Saskatchewan in Saskatoon.

Teaching About Hegemony combines progressive theoretical perspectives with personal narratives from the classroom, as well as insights gleaned from my critical ethnographic scholarly research, in a manner that demonstrates effective ways to teach about hegemony in our society. I have spent almost two decades studying the theories of scholars in the fields of critical pedagogy, postcolonialism, and the sociology of education. For much longer than that I have been a high school teacher and teacher educator, refining pedagogical methods for teaching about hegemony based on these theories and reflections of my experiences in the classroom. In the writing of this book, I have drawn from all of these teaching experiences and scholarly inquiries.[1]

Teaching About Hegemony makes explicit the connection between critical theory and practice so that the contemporary school may be utilized for more progressive goals than conservatives and the corporate media want. The main purpose for writing this book is to help foster political consciousness in our educators, so that they, in turn, can help develop a politically conscious, informed, and active citizenry.

So What Does Hegemony Mean?

Hegemony refers to the ideal representation of the interests of the privileged groups as universal interests, which are then accepted by the masses as the natural political, and social order. My experiences as an educator have led me to believe that most people are unaware of this powerful dynamic. Hegemony explains, for example, why some women who are influenced by conservative discourses believe that men should make the important decisions, whether for a family or for a nation, because their own gender is, they come to believe, too emotional and irrational. Hegemonic processes are at work when masses of working-class people vote against their own best economic interests, preferring politicians who support tax cuts and oppose a publicly funded healthcare system. An understanding of hegemony enables one to grasp the reasons why racist and patriarchal attitudes increase during times when White working-class people are feeling insecure about their economic futures. In the context of the United States and Canada, a major factor in the apparent success of hegemonic processes affecting social relations is the massive influence of the corporate media on the public discourse itself.

Indeed, most students entering my classes still consider corporate media to be objective in their reporting of the news. The myth of media objectivity is one of the first issues I deal with in any classroom, at the high school level or in teacher education programs (Orlowski, 2006). Students come to understand why it is that in the months leading up to a federal election the media focuses on nativist concerns around jobs and immigration rather than on the loss of jobs caused by corporate decisions to downsize or relocate plants in less regulated countries. They get confused over matters of race instead of focusing on class concerns. Students in the classrooms where I teach come to see the corporate media as a hegemonic device in the service of the elites.

Moreover, when students see certain news events that challenge the status quo are mostly ignored in the mainstream media, they come to see *omission* as an effective hegemonic strategy. If the daily financial cost of the invasion and subsequent war in Iraq to the American taxpayer were juxtaposed with the subprime mortgage crisis or subsidies to the banks and financial institutions, the interests of the elites would be threatened. Moreover, following the March 2003 invasion of Iraq, if American newspapers had had front-page headlines that connected U.S. Vice President Dick Cheney to the price-gouging and war profiteering of Halliburton, Inc., it is possible, even likely, that the outcome of the 2004 presidential election would have been different. Before running for Vice President, Cheney was a CEO of Halliburton, Inc., a company that gave him over $30,000,000 when he left the company in 1999 (Bisbort, 2001).

All of these reasons should adequately explain the need to have citizens understand hegemony and the role of hegemonic devices, such as the corporate media, to further entrench the interests of the elites in the United States and Canada. Yet, it is also the case that wherever hegemony and power operate, there is also counterhegemony and resistance to power. *Counterhegemony* refers to the illumination of so-called universal interests as partisan interests that help the elites garner even more social, political, and economic power.

This book is about how teachers can create political consciousness in their students. As much as this book is about hegemony and power, it is also about counterhegemony and resistance to power. In order for counterhegemonic discourses to take root, apathy and hopelessness must disappear. The pedagogy described in the pages of *Teaching About Hegemony* is primarily about inspiring educators to see that a *very critical* form of critical thinking *is* possible to have in our schools, that the school could once again be seen as a site of resistance, and therefore, as a place of hope. An *informed* citizenry is a necessary step for our society to strengthen our democratic systems. But an *active* one is the next necessary step. This book proposes to do the first and, by way of narratives and critical exercises, inspires readers to strive for the second step, as well. The conservative backlash agenda for our schools and what is to be taught has gone far enough. The conservative backlash against the progressive social and economic policies that have been won since the 1930s has also gone far enough.

At the beginning of the book, I assume that the reader knows very little about hegemony or how to teach about it. By the end, the assumption is that the reader has a complex grasp of hegemony, political ideology, and how to teach about these concepts so that their students, in turn, will also be able to understand the complex ways that certain hegemonic devices in our society work to weaken our democratic processes at the same time that they further entrench the interests of the elites.

The main focus of the book is on subjects pertaining to race and social class, but similar analyses could be applied to issues of gender and sexuality, including the dominant constructions of masculinity and femininity, as well as the link between heteronormativity and homophobia. These are important topics for all progressive educators to consider as well, of course. Their exclusion from this book is only because there are many scholars and teacher practitioners much more knowledgeable about the various forms of feminism and queer theory than me.[2]

The book has two distinct parts. Chapters 2, 3, and 4 are more theoretical in nature, whereas the contents of Chapters 5, 6, and 7 are applications of the theories in the earlier chapters to various aspects of race and social class relations. These three chapters rely heavily on social science research that I have undertaken, primarily ethnographic studies of adolescents and social studies teachers, as well as critical discourse analysis of the formal social studies curriculum itself. I have always attempted to incorporate research findings into my lessons in high school social studies and civic studies, as well as in the teacher education courses. Chapter 8 relies on some of these theories to make a case for teaching for a stronger democracy in both Canada and the United States. Chapter 9 makes the case that the current forces fueled by discourses that support neoliberalism and globalization are somewhat similar to past forces pushing for laissez-faire economics and colonization.

The second half of *Teaching About Hegemony* is mostly the application of sociological research in deconstructing hegemony around issues of race and class. For several years, progressive scholars have argued for teachers to apply the latest research, especially from the field of cultural studies, into their pedagogical practice (Berliner & Casanova, 1993; Kincheloe, 2000). It has been my experience that many teachers are quite removed from the research in cultural studies, which is very unfortunate because this field, in particular, has provided numerous poignant revelations about the ways in which social power operates in Western nations. Joe Kincheloe (2000) explains how the latest research in the field of cultural studies can affect a stronger democracy:

> [C]ultural studies resists the canonization of knowledge. Because cultural studies proponents position culture as a lived activity, experienced within unequal power relations, that is still in the process of formation, culture can be democratically transformed. (Kincheloe, 2000, p. 97)

Kincheloe points out that knowledge is not reified; that is, it is always a dynamic entity that evolves over time. This also points to the contention that knowledge is socially constructed. This in itself implies that a kind of social power has been enacted in order to arrive at what stories or whose versions of events get put into the curriculum, and which ones do not.

Chapters 2, 3, and 4 provide the theoretical basis to answer these questions. Chapters 5, 6, 7, and 8 incorporate research from the social sciences, specifically the sociology of education, to add a cultural studies dimension to the analysis. A few of the chapters repeat what has been said in earlier chapters so that they can stand alone. For example, there are brief descriptions of the political ideologies that arose out of modernity in Chapters 5, 6, and 8. The descriptions of these chapters will give some idea about the manner in which these distinctions occur.

Chapter 1: An Introduction

This introductory chapter sets the tone for the book, namely, that this is a text-book for teaching that does not pretend to be politically neutral; rather, it promotes a progressive agenda for teaching rooted in critical pedagogy. For the main, this book will be of use to teacher educators and high school teachers of history and social studies, especially those working in Canada and the United States. It will especially appeal to educators in college and university teacher education programs that promote progressive education ideals. Additionally, this book should be useful to those in educational leadership positions who are committed to democracy and social justice, including school administrators.

Part I: Mostly Theory – Ideology, Discourse, Hegemony, and the Curriculum

Chapter 2: What's Ideology Got to Do with It?

This chapter provides the necessary grounding in political ideology and its influence on the ways people perceive and act in the world. It explains that every political ideology has three aspects: a *critique* of society, a *vision* of the best society, and *agency* to get closer to attaining that vision. Chapter 2 makes a case for the relevance of three political ideologies that arose out of modernity: liberalism, conservatism, and socialism. It explains the evolution of all three ideologies, in particular to the ways in which the *critical left* has taken the economic system of socialism and molded it into a less combative economic system called social democracy. This ideology shares the same social values as liberalism in terms of minority rights and anti-capital punishment. Social democratic governments accept capitalism but support legislation to help economically oppressed groups. Throughout the second half of the book, the term *critical left* refers to the most progressive ideas and proponents of those ideas that support racial minorities and working-class people.

Chapter 2 deconstructs ubiquitous use of political terms such as right wing and left wing by replacing them with a more sophisticated taxonomy that includes specific ideological positions on both economic and social issues. For example, this economic/social distinction explains why some Americans call the Democratic Party the left wing, whereas others consider it to be as supportive of the corporate agenda as the Republican Party. Both views are correct: on social issues, the Democrats are mostly progressive or left wing, whereas on economic issues they are clearly beholden to the right-wing agenda of the major corporations. The chapter includes questions that will help the reader develop a deep understanding of these ideologies and their positions on important social, economic, and political issues in the United States and Canada.

Chapter 3: The Power of Discourse, Of course!

This chapter builds on the previous chapter on ideology by explaining concepts such as discourse and hegemony from a poststructuralist perspective. Concerns around the power of discourse and hegemony are discussed in accessible ways that demonstrate how certain ideologies gain prominence, whereas others are dismissed. Discourse is always connected with desire and power. In this chapter, both discourse and power are explained in Foucauldian terms. Power is, therefore, conceived of as a set of social relations built seamlessly into daily relations and practices. In effect, this kind of almost invisible power acts as a social regulator in racial, class, and gender relations. Critical discourse analysis is effective in illuminating the ways in which social power is embedded in representation of text, such as in the school curriculum. Sometimes discourses come together to form discursive formations that are particularly powerful in affecting social relations. The chapter outlines the anti-liberal rhetoric in the discursive formation that helped propel George W. Bush into the White House for two terms.

Hegemony refers to the ideal representation of the interests of the privileged groups as universal interests, which are then accepted by the masses as the natural order rather than as a demonstration of the construction of power along lines of race, class, and gender. Sometimes discourses arise that are counterhegemonic in that they attempt to destabilize the status quo in some way. Chapter 3 examines the concepts of hegemony and counterhegemony from a mostly theoretical perspective, which also makes a distinction between a false political consciousness and a more accurate political consciousness.

This chapter also explains my own social positionality as a first-generation Canadian of working-class immigrant parents growing up in the 1960s and 1970s in Toronto with the support of a strong social welfare state. It explains how an individual's social location and experiences influence values and the perceptions of others. End-of-chapter exercises will give the opportunity for readers to personally reflect on their own social locations and values.

The notion of reframing social and economic issues from various ideological perspectives will be introduced in this chapter in an elementary manner. This pedagogical strategy of reframing will be further developed in Chapter 8 on understanding bias in the corporate media. Chapter 3 will outline the pedagogical approach I take in my own teaching about hegemony.

Chapter 4: The Purpose of Schooling: Ideology in the Formal and the "Enacted" Curriculum

Chapter 4 continues to develop the theoretical considerations that first appeared in Chapters 2 and 3, but it is focused on the school itself. It first addresses the longstanding question of what is the purpose of schooling. Should the school be used mainly to provide the necessary labor requirements for our capitalist system? Should the school be used to help students realize their own potential? Or should it be used in the way that American philosopher of education John Dewey envisioned it, namely, to develop critically thinking citizens who are able to address serious societal issues in a sophisticated manner?

The important issue of a culturally relevant curriculum is connected to these debates, as is its corollary, a common core curriculum. This chapter makes the argument that American and Canadian societies have changed too drastically to revert back to using a monocultural, Eurocentric curriculum that some conservative educators are calling for. It briefly discusses the early challenges over control of the school curriculum in both the American and Canadian contexts. The reader gains some understanding over the ideological struggles over the curriculum itself that have taken place for over a century, struggles that get to the heart of the purpose of schooling.

Apple's *Ideology & Curriculum* (2004) provides the analytical method used to determine how power can be embedded in the formal curriculum. In analyzing the evolution of the British Columbia Social Studies Curriculum, for example, readers can see how topics such as the trade union movement disappeared to make way for a focus on the individual. The question arises about the influence this curricular change in emphasis has had on progressive social movements being organized to resist the dismantling of the social welfare state.

Chapter 4 ends with a discussion of the *enacted* curriculum. This section describes what a passionate and knowledgeable educator can do with students who bring their own interests and meaningful life experiences into the classroom. The reader is introduced to examples of race/class intersections in the history of the United States and Canada. Hegemonic discourses figure prominently in these examples, which include The Ludlow Massacre of 1914, White/Chinese Coal Miners' Struggles of the 1870s and 1880s in British Columbia, and a more contemporary example of a race/class/gender intersection I have used in my social studies high school classroom in Vancouver's multicultural east end. Hegemonic discourses figure prominently in all three examples. The end-of-chapter questions ask readers to apply the concepts in the chapter to other historical examples in both Canada and the United States.

Part II: Less Theory, More Applications and Practice: Deconstructing Racial and Class Discourses for a Stronger Democracy

Chapter 5: Teaching About Race and Racism in Our Past and Present

Chapter 5 begins with a personal narrative of becoming slowly conscious of issues of race and discrimination in Canada. The formal curriculum is identified as a hegemonic device in creating myopia around, for example, institutionalized and systemic oppression of Canada's Aboriginal peoples. Such revelations led me to examine the role of the school in exacerbating racial tensions and certain forms of racism. I also provide a description of my burgeoning awareness of the effects of situating *whiteness* as the hegemonic norm in the school curriculum and corporate media, and how this results in an advantage for White people. In short, this strategy leads to an advantage for White people throughout almost all facets of society.

The United States and Canada are clearly among the world's most culturally diverse countries today. Yet, both are historically rooted in colonial projects that resulted in vastly different life experiences for people. The degree to which a person was granted a life of privilege or one of oppression depended on which side of the colonial divide they were born into. The legacy of these divisions lives on today. The history of the racial discourses used during the nation-building periods, the post–World War II period, and today will be discussed and presented in ways that teachers can use to explain both the past and the present in American and Canadian sociocultural relations. Also included here is a description of Frankenberg's (1993) taxonomy of racial discourses – essentialist, color-blind, and race cognizance – that more or less map onto the three political ideologies – conservatism, liberalism, and the critical left, respectively. The notion of *race* is fraught with complications and challenges, including blurred racial boundaries and persuasive arguments that race is but a social construction. Yet, no one can deny the existence of racism. Understanding the power inherent in racial discourses will help educators understand this complex topic and help them teach about it. The analysis of the formal social studies curriculum is based on Frankenberg's taxonomy of racial discourses and Apple's (2004) *Ideology & Curriculum*. These racial discourses are also apparent in the attitudes of White teachers toward racial minorities.

The chapter also discusses the various forms of multiculturalism outlined by Kincheloe and Steinberg (1997) and links them to political ideology, as well. The most common version of multicultural education is liberal pluralist, but teachers need to understand that placing posters of non-White athletes and other celebrities on classroom walls is only a baby step toward the disruption of racial power relations in society today. Readers will also come to understand that the conservative critique of multicultural education emphasizes a perceived watering down of the western canon, whereas the position of many in the critical left is that liberal pluralist forms of multicultural education do not do enough to combat racism.

The chapter demonstrates how the popular color-blind discourse supports the myth of meritocracy. The color-blind and the cultural-deficit discourses have greatly influenced the thinking of many teachers. Readers will develop a comprehension of how racial and cultural power structures are maintained within liberal power-blind conceptions of multicultural education. Exercises will focus on both personal and theoretical reflections on these concepts and research findings.

Chapter 6: Social Class: The Forgotten Identity Marker in Social Studies Education

As with the concept of race, the entire notion of social class is complicated. Yet, whether one defines social class in terms of social status or in more strictly Marxian terms, there is no denying its existence in Canadian and American societies. The glass ceiling may be harder to discern in the United States and Canada than in countries such as Britain, but it is still there.

Chapter 6 asks why it is that so many students enter high school without any class consciousness and graduate without any either. Much of this chapter is based on the analysis of two data sources: the evolving formal British Columbia Social Studies Curriculum and interview transcripts with veteran high school social studies teachers. It includes a discussion of how political ideology has influenced the curriculum developers and the teachers. This chapter demonstrates how omission as a hegemonic strategy is used to further entrench corporate interests in the United States and Canada. For example, topics such as the uses of taxes and the creation of the social welfare state had virtually disappeared from the British Columbia Social Studies Curriculum in the 1980s – could this be a factor in the recent rise of the tax cut discourse in both countries? Should it be any wonder that many working-class and middle-class citizens vote in favor of tax cuts and, therefore, vote against their own best interests? Might this be why so many people, such as many Tea Party members, seem to be motivated by a false political consciousness? Apple's contention of how power and ideology is embedded in the formal curriculum is made clear here.

I agree with Kincheloe's (2000) contention that teachers should be aware of the latest research in the social sciences and cultural studies, especially how it pertains to schooling. I have written this chapter in a format that is different from most of the other chapters because I want teachers and teacher educators to glimpse what the field of the sociology of education can address. Chapter 6 is mostly based on a sociological study of education I recently completed in Vancouver (Orlowski, 2008a). This study involved critical discourse analysis of both the social studies curriculum and the attitudes of teachers around issues of social class.

The historical analysis of the curriculum in itself yields many pedagogical ideas of how to supplement the curriculum so that the hegemonic middle-class norm is challenged. The formal social studies curriculum makes very little mention of class concerns, resulting in a middle-class bias as the hegemonic norm in much the same way that whiteness has been entrenched. Yet, very few teachers supplement the social studies curriculum in any significant way to counter this power blindness. There appears to have been a conscious decision on the part of curriculum developers to remove any concepts related to social class, while at the same time an emphasis on the individual appears. The chapter has a discussion on why this emphasis poses serious problems for civil society.

In the section that analyzes the attitudes of the teachers on issues of social class, Chapter 6 relies on the taxonomy of pertinent discourses developed by a group of Ontario scholars (Curtis, Livingstone, & Smaller, 1992). These discourses are also connected to the political ideologies, of course. It should be no surprise that the attitudes of social studies teachers mirror what can be found in the curriculum, namely, at best only an elementary understanding of how social class structures our society. This myopia will have major consequences. Indeed, it already has. As an example of what may happen if political awareness around issues of social class does not increase, Canadians may very well lose the universal healthcare system they fought so hard to create. Teachers have a responsibility to at least try to get as many students as possible to understand this struggle. They should also understand who benefits and who loses if public healthcare disappears. Critical pedagogy is urgently needed on this front.

Educators should emphasize a focus on social class issues in the curriculum and teacher education programs. In both countries, examples of the positive contributions of labor should be a mandatory part of every student's education. This chapter makes a case for all students to be given the opportunity to grapple with other important economic issues such as private versus public ownership, the anti-democratic effects of corporate political campaign donations, and the average income of CEOs versus laborers.

Chapter 7: Liberal Discourses About Aboriginal Students – A Case Study of Power Blindness

Canada often presents itself as a nation consisting of a population possessing progressive liberal values such as fairness and tolerance. The impetus for this image of Canada has been created to make a distinction with the United States (Mackey, 2002). But is this an accurate depiction of what has really transpired for those Canadians not part of the mainstream? How have these liberal discourses affected the relations between minorities and the dominant White society? These questions are answered with respect to the treatment of Canada's Aboriginal peoples, and how they continue to be treated in both the schools and in society in general. This chapter supports the position of those from the critical left who claim that the liberal ideology is adept at hiding social power.

The focus of Chapter 7 is mainly on examining how certain liberal discourses – in particular, the color-blind discourse and the cultural-deficit discourse – are to this day entrenched within the minds of veteran social studies teachers. This case study is also situated in Vancouver, British Columbia. It relies on the two data sources that formed the basis of the analyses in Chapters 5 and 6, namely, the British Columbia Social Studies Curriculum and interview transcripts with veteran social studies teachers. The teachers were asked two questions: first, why do you think that the British Columbia high school graduation rate for Aboriginal students is about half of what it is for non-Aboriginals? Second, do you or would you consider supplementing the curriculum with culturally relevant pedagogy? The assumption is that similar dynamics are at work with other minorities elsewhere.

To answer the first question, most of the teachers relied on variations of the cultural-deficit discourse. These same teachers did not want to supplement the curriculum with culturally relevant pedagogy. As one teacher put it, "That would be spoiling them." Their preference was to continue teaching the Eurocentric color-blind curriculum they had used for years. One progressive teacher suggested he would be open to altering the curriculum to reflect Aboriginal perspectives in addition to the mainstream historical narrative, but that he did not know enough himself in order to properly do so.

A brief look at the latest versions of the formal social studies curriculum indicates that this document has evolved to a more progressive place than the teachers have. The discourses used by the teachers are discriminatory in a subtle way, yet these are very significant obstacles for many Aboriginal students to overcome. Readers can reflect upon whether teachers in other regions of North America are similarly influenced by these power-blind liberal discourses in their attitudes toward Black and Hispanic students. The study described in this chapter indicates that there is much work to be done in teacher education programs in deconstructing the hegemony entrenched in liberal discourses.

Chapter 8: Ideology, Democracy, and the "Good" Citizen

Ever since the creation of public education systems in the United States and Canada, there has been much discussion in educational circles about the need for schools to develop the *good citizen*. This is not a new phenomenon. Yet, there is rarely any discussion about what constitutes a good citizen or its various conceptions. This chapter begins with a focus on concerns with democracy in the United States throughout history, including those raised by Alexis de Tocqueville and John Dewey, and in more contemporary works by Nancy Fraser (1997), Joe Kincheloe (1999, 2000), and Iris Marion Young (2000).

This discussion based on historical and philosophical considerations for the school is followed by a brief examination of the taxonomy developed by Joel Westheimer and Joseph Kahne (2004) that describes three different kinds of good citizens: the socially responsible citizen, the participatory citizen, and the justice-oriented citizen. Yet again political ideology can be applied to this taxonomy. In fact, if teachers are to have a clear understanding of what is meant by a good citizen, Westheimer and Kahne's work is crucial. Their work also guided me in my own teaching to develop the "good" social justice-oriented citizen, and the second half of the chapter moves away from theoretical considerations toward the practical aspects of teaching for a stronger democracy in both the United States and Canada. This section describes pedagogy I have developed to teach for a political consciousness.

My approach has three main components: first, students must understand political ideology; second, they must be made to realize that corporate media have corporate interests; and third, they should comprehend the inherent benefits for citizens in a strong democracy, and the flaws in our democratic systems. Today's students are being inundated with discourses that support corporate capitalism in the media and elsewhere. These discourses are hegemonic, rendering counterhegemonic discourses of class consciousness near invisible.

The final section of this chapter describes pedagogy that I have found to be successful in social studies methods courses. This strategy incorporates all three components and is based on the work by linguist George Lakoff (2004). This involves the reframing of political discourse from different ideological perspectives than what is normally included in the corporate media. In fact, if the schools are to be used to strengthen democracy, this chapter points to the crucial need for critical media literacy to become part of the enacted social studies curriculum, if not part of the formal curriculum. End-of-chapter exercises will further increase comprehension of the notion that corporate media support corporate interests.

Chapter 9: Neoliberalism: Laissez-Faire Revisited?

This chapter was written after the worst financial crisis in Western nations since the Great Depression of the 1930s. Media reports pointed to the deregulation of the American financial industry that first occurred in the 1980s as a major factor for the crisis. The response by the American government was to give over $1.4 trillion of tax dollars to the financial institutions of Wall Street. Given the general lack of class consciousness among the American citizenry (see Chapters 6 and 8), it is not surprising that the federal government determined that the best strategy to deal with the crisis was to give massive amounts of public monies to the very corporations that caused the crisis in the first place.

Chapter 9 outlines the major economic debates that occurred in Western nations, especially between the liberal John Maynard Keynes, the social democrat Karl Polanyi, and the nouveau laissez-faire economic theories of Friedrich Von Hayek. Unfortunately, the major economic theory guiding American economic policy since the 1980s was further developed by a disciple of Von Hayek, Milton Friedman. The main premise of this theory is that government should not intervene in the economy of the nation unless it is to protect private wealth or engage its military to support American interests in other countries.

The economic rationale underlying this philosophy is called *neoliberalism*, and its basic tenets are deregulation, privatization of the commons, and union busting. Neoliberalism is currently the biggest force to overturn the hard-won victories that helped build the social welfare state in western nations that occurred from the 1930s to the 1970s. Neoliberalism promotes the notion of the self-interested individual, a person who does not feel it is the responsibility of the state to help citizens in need. In this way, neoliberalism undermines democratic initiatives around the globe. This chapter also asks whether *globalization* is a contemporary version of the colonial projects of the past.

Neoliberalism has had a profound and deleterious effect on the public education systems of the United States and Canada. The chapter includes the strategies used by neoliberal politicians and journalists to undermine public education. The chapter ends on a hopeful note, however, as it points out that the neoliberal project is breaking down on the domestic and international fronts.

Chapter 10: Some Final Reflections: Dare the Schools Teach for a Fair Social Order?

It is my intention that all readers of this book will have a more sophisticated political consciousness, one that better explains what has been happening at the end of the twentieth century and early part of the twenty-first century. Educators will have some ideas for pedagogical strategies on how to deconstruct hegemonic discourses about race and social class issues, and how to teach for a stronger democracy. They will better understand hegemony and be better able to remove the blinders, so to speak, that work to impede the vision of their students.

A Few Words About Teacher Education

This book is for teacher educators and practicing classroom teachers, especially of social studies, history, and civic studies. I have written it with educators in both the United States and Canada in mind. After all, despite some differences, these two countries are more similar to each other than any other country is to either of them. It is my hope that educators who read this book will become inspired enough to use adapted versions of some of the pedagogical strategies in their own classrooms. Of course, in order for this to occur, there are many obstacles that progressive educators must overcome. A packed curriculum in tandem with state- or province-wide testing is clearly an issue. Determining the appropriate grade level, as with all pedagogy, is something that will improve only with experience.

Conservative ideologues – possibly school administrators, teacher colleagues, parents, or even school board trustees – may work to hinder the efforts of teachers committed to removing the hegemonic blinders. Yet, there are two reasons why I do not consider this to be a major obstacle. First, the formal curricula in high school social studies almost always has a prescribed learning outcome that encourages students to engage in the multiple perspectives approach to understanding reality. Epistemological questions arise from this over the ambiguity of "what is truth", and this is a topic that will be addressed to some degree in subsequent chapters. Second, I contend that most people influenced by conservatism will not object to any teacher committed to ideology critique on social issues. This has been my experience in the classroom, both at the high school level and with preservice teachers. Many students who ascribe to a conservative ideology appear to be pleased when the teacher explains the conservative position on various social and economic issues. This suits me just fine, because I have always been a person who is uncomfortable with overt tension and conflict in the classroom.

Teaching for Social Justice is a burgeoning field in Faculties of Education in both the United States and Canada, as well as in Britain and Australia. That said, there are almost as many approaches to teaching for social justice as there are sources and practitioners. *Teaching About Hegemony* is clearly a book with social justice aims. Yet, it differs from the others for two main reasons: first, it relies on students' understanding at more than a rudimentary level the complexities of political ideology; and second, I have spent 19 years in the high school classroom working on how best to develop a political consciousness in students, as well as over a decade doing the same thing with people on the verge of becoming teachers.

Teaching About Hegemony is a textbook for teaching that does not pretend to be politically neutral; rather, it promotes a progressive agenda for teaching rooted in critical pedagogy. This book sums up an approach that describes and demonstrates the possibilities of the school to help create a more progressive citizenry, to help people understand more progressive approaches and to organize a society other than the ones that have taken hold in recent decades. After all, there are very few progressives who support and respect a society that treats its vulnerable citizens as poorly as many poverty-stricken Americans and Canadians are treated today. Reflecting on the changing social conditions of one's own life is a good place to begin. Yet, in order to effectively do so, it is crucial that more and more people gain an understanding of how political ideology shapes the way we view our world. Teacher educators, social studies teachers, and educational leaders should be at the vanguard of this movement for understanding hegemony.

Questions to Ponder

1. What are some commonly held beliefs in our society that may be the result of hegemony? In your discussions, consider the variables of race, social class, gender, and government explanations for war.
2. Some early American educational theorists – such as John Dewey, Harold Rugg, and George Counts – wanted the schools to help develop students' critical thinking who would one day be citizens able to think through complex social problems. What do you think are some obstacles that current practitioners of such an approach would find?
3. (a) In 1969, a British rock group called The Kinks wrote and recorded a song called *Brainwashed* that attempted to highlight the insidious nature of hegemonic discourses around issues of social class. Can you think of any more recent pop songs that try to illuminate hegemony? Once again, consider the variables of race, gender, social class, and explanations for war. Which of these would you consider are appropriate for use in the high school classroom?
4. I often think of what a high school social studies teacher once said to me in a research project I was involved in. Here is his response to a question I asked about whether he would consider altering or supplementing the curriculum to help make it more relevant for students from marginalized groups:

> Teaching is not a vehicle to promote your agenda. You have a job, when you sign that piece of paper, to teach the curriculum. You are not there to create an army of followers. I think if you're a good social studies teacher you are facilitating diversity, you are facilitating different opinions and that's what it's all about, isn't it?... As a teacher, I think you should only facilitate. You have to understand that there are people who hold this perspective while there are other people who have that perspective. Teaching is not about trying to change any of that.

Discuss the teacher's quote above. Do you agree or disagree. Why?

Notes

1. The research projects I have been involved with are usually ethnographic studies pertaining to issues of social class and race. One examined how working-class youth from five different racial backgrounds perceive racism and economic inequality (Orlowski, 2001). Another involved both a critical discourse analysis of the formal high school social studies curriculum in its representations of race and class issues, and an examination of the attitudes of veteran social studies teachers around race and class issues (Orlowski, 2008a, 2008b). As well, I have been involved in qualitative research involved with Aboriginal peoples' agency when faced with economic changes from the dominant society (Orlowski & Menzies, 2004). Some of my work describes the experience of teaching civic studies to effect political consciousness (Orlowski, 2008c, 2009). For almost 20 years, I have been immersed in studying the theories of educators in the fields of critical pedagogy, postcolonialism, and the sociology of education. I have had the luxury of time to reflect on the practicality of implementing many of these ideas into classroom practice based on my own experiences.
2. Readers interested in these topics may want to look at the following:

   - Dalley and Campbell (2006).
   - Epstein and Johnson (1998).
   - Currie, Kelly, and Pomerantz (2009).
   - Youdell (2005).

References

Apple, M. W. (2004). *Ideology and curriculum* (3rd ed.). New York: Routledge-Falmer.

Berliner, D. C., & Casanova, U. (1993). *Putting research to work in your school*. New York: Scholastic Publishers.

Bisbort, A. (2001, April). Dick Cheney. *New Internationalist, 333*:30–33.

Currie, D., Kelly, D., & Pomerantz, S. (2009). *"Girl power": Girls reinventing girlhood*. New York: Peter Lang.

Curtis, B., Livingstone, D. W., & Smaller, H. (1992). So many people: Ways of seeing class differences in schooling. In B. Curtis, D. W. Livingstone & H. Smaller (Eds.), *Stacking the deck: The streaming of working-class kids in Ontario schools* (pp. 6–25). Toronto: Our Schools Our Selves Educational Foundation.

Dalley, P., & Campbell, M. D. (2006). Constructing and contesting discourses of heteronormativity: An ethnographic study of youth in a Francophone high school in Canada. *Journal of Language, Identity, and Education, 5*(1), 11–29.

Epstein, D., & Johnson, R. (1998). *Schooling sexualities*. Philadelphia: Open University Press.

Frankenberg, R. (1993). *White women, race matters: The social construction of Whiteness*. Minneapolis: University of Minnesota Press.

Fraser, N. (1997). *Justice interruptus: Critical reflections on the "postsocialist" condition*. New York: Routledge.

Kincheloe, J. (1999). Critical democracy and education. In J. G. Henderson & K. R. Kesson (Eds.), *Understanding democratic curriculum leadership* (pp. 70–83). New York: Teachers College Press.

Kincheloe, J. (2000). Cultural studies and democratically aware teacher education: Post-Fordism, civics, and the worker-citizen. In D. W. Hursh & E. W. Ross (Eds.), *Democratic social education: Social studies for social change* (pp. 97–120). New York: Falmer Press.

Kincheloe, J., & Steinberg, S. (1997). *Changing multiculturalism*. Buckingham, UK: Open University Press.

Lakoff, G. (2004). *Don't think of an elephant! Know your values and frame the debate*. White River Junction, Vermont: Chelsea Green Publishing.

Mackey, E. (2002). *The house of difference: Cultural politics and national identity in Canada.* Toronto: University of Toronto Press.

Orlowski, P. (2001). Ties that bind and ties that blind: Race and class intersections in the classroom. In C. E. James & A. Shadd (Eds.), *Talking about identity: Encounters in race, ethnicity, and language* (pp. 250–266). Toronto: Between the Lines.

Orlowski, P. (2006). Educating in an era of Orwellian spin: Making a case for critical media literacy in the classroom. *Canadian Journal of Education.* Special issue on *Popular Media, Education, and Resistance, 29*(1), 175–198.

Orlowski, P. (2008a). Social class: The forgotten identity marker in social studies education. *New Proposals: Journal of Marxism and Interdisciplinary Inquiry, 1*(2), 30–63.

Orlowski, P. (2008b). "That would certainly be spoiling them": Liberal discourses of social studies teachers and concerns about Aboriginal students. *Canadian Journal of Native Education, 31*(2), 110–129.

Orlowski, P. (2008c). Youth 'participaction' and democracy: Reflections on teaching Civic Studies 11 in British Columbia. *Our Schools Our Selves, 17*(2), 109–122.

Orlowski, P. (2009). Teaching for and about democracy, including its flaws. *Democracy & Education, 18*(1), 54–61.

Orlowski, P., & Menzies, C. (2004). Educating about Aboriginal involvement with forestry: The Tsimsian experience – yesterday, today, and tomorrow. *Canadian Journal of Native Education, 28*(1/2), 66–79.

Westheimer, J., & Kahne, J. (2004). What kind of citizen? The politics of educating for democracy. *American Educational Research Journal, 41*(2), 237–269.

Youdell, D. (2005). Sex-gender-sexuality: how sex, gender and sexuality constellations are constituted in secondary schools. *Gender and Education, 17*(3), 249–270.

Young, I. M. (2000). *Inclusion and democracy.* London: Oxford University Press.

Part I
Mostly Theory – Ideology, Discourse, Hegemony, and the Curriculum

Chapter 2
What's Ideology Got to Do With It?

> [A] ruling ideology does not so much combat alternative ideas
> as thrust them beyond the very bounds of the unthinkable.
> Ideologies exist because there are things which must at all costs
> not be thought, let alone spoken. How we could ever know that
> there were such thoughts is then an obvious logical difficulty.
> Perhaps we can just feel that there is something we ought to be
> thinking, but we have no idea what it is.
> (Eageton, 1991, p. 58)

Education in North America has always been a paradox. In both the United States and Canada, people look to the public school system as an instrument of social mobility. Yet, at the same time both countries have been very suspicious of too much education. The accepted position, especially today, seems to be that education is good if it gets you a better job, but bad if it makes you think too much. The early focus on a liberal arts education has given way to one that emphasizes the individual obtaining some skills that will lead to employment. I assume that the corporate sector is much happier with the current emphasis on preparing workers for employment at various levels of our capitalist system rather than on promoting critical thinking skills. For many citizens, however, the shift to a more utilitarian approach to schooling has not resulted in a better life.

Political ideology is at the root of most debates in our society on matters of social relations and of matters pertaining to the purpose of the schooling in Western society. Ever since the beginning of the public school system, this has always been the way it is, and is also the way it always will be in the future. It is best that the discussion around political ideology begins with a brief historical background on the use of the term *ideology*.

Political Ideology in Its Historical Context

The French philosopher Destutt de Tracy was the first to use the term ideology as a concept representing the "science of ideas" during the early period of the Age of Enlightenment. Yet, according to Henry Giroux (1981), an American theorist of critical pedagogy, it was Karl Marx who began to use the term to critique social relations

P. Orlowski, *Teaching About Hegemony*, Explorations of Educational Purpose 17, DOI 10.1007/978-94-007-1418-2_2, © Springer Science+Business Media B.V. 2011

of domination. Marx conceptualized ideology in political terms both as a critique of consciousness and as possibilities within consciousness. John Schwarzmantel (1998) restates Marx's conceptualization in a clearer manner by explaining that each ideology consists of three elements: a critique, an ideal and agency (p. 2). In other words, each ideology has a response to the prevailing social conditions, either favorable or not, depending on to what extent an individual's perspective agrees with the dominant ideology. Moreover, each ideology has an articulation of the ideal society.

Ideology is about the "thought-production of human beings" (Giroux, 1981, p. 19). A political ideology contains "a specific set of assumptions and social practices" that leads to various "beliefs, expectations and biases" (p. 7). In other words, a political ideology socially constructs its own knowledge. This has important implications for teachers and students, particularly of social studies. The political ideologies that inform teachers' attitudes and beliefs are at the root of the ways in which they relate to and teach their students (Bartolome, 2008; Orlowski, 2008; Sleeter, 2004).

All political ideologies function to provide the framework for political action designed to produce the good society, a term that is highly contested and at the root of many if not most political struggles today. The basic notion of ideology, and one that is of utmost importance to educators, is that it is possible to transform society and change human nature so that people are prepared to become suitable members of the new society. It is important to bear in mind, therefore, that the conceptual basis of ideology is filled with optimism. Current political ideological debates are often around inclusion and exclusion because, as Slavoj Zizek (1994) puts it, ideology "regulates social visibility and non-visibility" (p. 3). As an example, the current social conservative movement in the United States is fueled by a backlash of angry White (mostly male) people against immigration, feminism, and the liberal responses to these changes, such as affirmative action programs. White defensiveness can be viewed as a reaction to what is for White people the novel experience of having to argue for one's beliefs rather than simply assuming their acceptance. Sometimes, the cause of this conservative reaction may simply be experiencing new situations of being in a minority. Might this be the underlying basis for the vociferous attacks by Fox News commentators toward liberals and the liberal ideology? This will be discussed in Chapters 8 and 9.

Although the terms ideology and perspective are often used interchangeably, for me there is a crucial difference. I interpret the meaning of political perspective to be the coupling of critique and ideal. In other words, perspective refers to the lens through which an individual sees the world, or a critique of consciousness. The second aspect of this conception of ideology, "possibilities within consciousness," addresses notions of action on the part of the individual as well as the collectivity. Perspective does not include this aspect. This prescription for ideology also clearly separates perspective from ideology by including the notion of *agency*, most meaningful for political and social activism, of course, and the major reason why this book was written in the first place.

Before I outline the core characteristics of each of the main ideologies, it is necessary to explain why I have chosen to use conservatism, liberalism, and radicalism (i.e., the critical left) for my analysis.[1] The radical ideology that has most informed my own understanding is related to a Marxist articulation of socialism. I am familiar with feminist, multicultural, and environmentalist concerns with Karl Marx's work. Yet, I agree with feminist political philosopher Nancy Fraser's (1997) contention that it is best for those who subscribe to a radical ideology to rework socialism by incorporating these valid concerns to make it an even stronger ideology than it was in its original form or any time since. The major difference between the class-based Marxist interpretation of the radical ideology and my interpretation of the radical ideology is that I am considering class as much more heterogeneous than Marx. After all, the multicultural metropolis that many cities in the United States and Canada have become renders the classic Marxist notion of class somewhat inadequate. It is the ways that race and class are part of the social hierarchies in both countries and the ways that they are represented in curriculum and thought about by teachers that is germane to deconstructing hegemony.

But one may ask why we need to use the concept of ideology at all anymore, that it has served its useful purposes and needs to be discarded. In *Beyond Left and Right* (1994), Anthony Giddens, at one time considered a sociologist with a socialist perspective, makes a case that the old ideologies of conservatism, liberalism, and socialism have been turned inside out by powerful social, environmental, and technological forces to the point that today's socialists are conservative and today's conservatives seem to adhere to an extreme brand of radicalism. To some extent, a case could be made that the New Democratic Party (NDP) in Canada is a social democratic movement trying to conserve the hard-fought struggles won by the common people, such as public healthcare and welfare, against corporate intrusion and demands for privatization. There is also a strong case to be made that the former U.S. administration led by George W. Bush was an extreme brand of radicalism even though it presented to the masses as driven by conservatism. Clearly, Giddens is onto something. That said, I will refrain from changing the usage of these terms, if mainly to be in harmony with the vast amounts of scholarship that use conservatism to describe a type of right-wing politics and radicalism to represent a left wing politics. That said, throughout this book, I usually use the term critical left, rather than radical, to label the positions to the left of the ideological spectrum of social and economic ideas in the North American context.

In cultural studies, as well as in the mainstream media, there are many important examples of language that confuse people. As many readers know, George Orwell predicted the deliberate manipulation of language by those in power. A simple example of this is in the unfortunate situation of soldiers killed by weapons fired by soldiers on their own side; the media refers to this as "friendly fire." We will discuss more examples of this kind of linguistic manipulation in the section on media literacy in Chapter 8.

Quite often the confusion is no one's fault; rather, it is the result of people working through the meanings of complex social theory. Describing what is meant by left wing politics is one such area where there are myriad terms that refer to similar concepts. For instance, on economic issues, the left-wing position that gained currency in the second half of the nineteenth century and first half of the twentieth century is socialism. This ideology evolved in most Western countries into social democracy, which is liberal on social issues and somewhere between socialism and liberalism on economic issues. In the United States, similar leftist movements have been called progressivism and the reformist left.

In a similar fashion, there are words used in political economics that often find their way into school textbooks and the media that could be better explained to the general public. For example, many high school students have come to understand the French term laissez-faire to refer to a discredited economic theory primarily utilized during the British Industrial Revolution. This term meant that the free market of capitalism should not have to abide by state interventionism, and that the state's role was mainly to ensure the protection of property rights and the so-called natural order. In today's discourse, such noninterventionist economic policies are part of neoliberalism. Neoliberalism basically refers to a fairly similar philosophy that underlays laissez-faire economics. It is ironic that the global economic crisis that began in 2008 has been attributed to a lack of state regulation of monetary policy that began in the 1980s under the Reagan administration. This will be briefly discussed later in this chapter in the section on libertarianism.

Poststructuralist and postmodern theorists have attacked modernity and its political ideologies on several fronts (Foucault, 1980; Laclau & Mouffe, 1985). Stanley Aronowitz (1988) makes the contentious suggestion that we abolish the concept of ideology altogether, in education and everywhere else. I resist the decision to do away with the concept of ideology because an understanding of political ideologies offers the language to debate and discuss social hierarchies, economic policies, trends, and social movements. This will need to be discussed further, of course, but the argument will be clearer if at this time I briefly describe the conditions and traits that have allowed the three major political ideologies to develop in the ways that they have.

Modernity

Modernity itself is a period that began with the Enlightenment and was furthered by the American and French revolutions in the late 1700s. In *Lectures on the Philosophical Discourse of Modernity* (1987), Jurgen Habermas interprets Hegel, whom he considers to be "the first philosopher to develop a clear concept of modernity" (p. 4), to claim that there were two features that separated the new period from what was before. First, the notion of individual freedom or emancipation, contained in the idea of subjectivity, meant that individuals were free to apply their own thinking to making a new social and political order. Not only were people responsible for their own individual actions, but society itself was the result of collective human action rather than a God-given creation. Second, ties between the state and the economy must be completely severed. Taken together, these two features led to radically altered social relationships during the period of modernity. Traditional ascribed roles that once ensured people remained in their station throughout their entire lives became destabilized, enabling some commoners the opportunity of social mobility and the pursuit of happiness.

The essential state of the individual and of human nature itself, considered flawed by the conservative authorities of divinity, were, for the most part, outright dismissed by philosophers of the Enlightenment. Indeed, progressive thinkers have always had difficulty with essentialism, which is the belief that there is no hope for changing a person's behavior or personality characteristics. Yet, these same philosophers could not find a solution to the problem that has dogged modernity since it began, namely, the possibility for a society of autonomous individuals to collectively unify. This is a very important tension that currently plagues sociopolitical relations in the United States and Canada. To put it succinctly, the issue is how to reconcile individual rights with some version of the common good. This will be discussed further in Chapters 8 and 9.

Some philosophers worried that the new society "might fall into decadence and corruption, because commerce could loom so large in people's lives that they would neglect the public and political spheres" (Schwarzmantel, 1998, p. 33). The recent neoliberal trend in North America, as well as in many other countries, indicates that these concerns have some validity. Certain ideologies, such as conservatism, nationalism, and socialism, developed responses to this tension of individual free-dom versus social cohesion, a tension that continues to destabilize the liberal project to this day.

Modernity also ushered in the notion of *progress*, tied as it was to the control of nature, and a term that has been highly contested by postcolonial scholarship. In recent decades, there has been a considerable attack on the idea of inevitable or tele-ological progress, especially the manner in which early liberal and socialist thinkers portrayed it. My position is that the term still holds some validity, although more for the purposes of guiding the path toward the ideal society in social terms rather than as something inevitable. Throughout this book, the reader will come across an important binary I utilize: all cultural issues are placed on either an economic scale or a social scale. This is crucial for students to gain an understanding of political ideology.

Two other concepts that first arose during this period seem to have lasting endurance, namely, citizenship and the nation state. Citizenship is important to this entire book, linked as it is to democracy, inclusion, power, and social justice. In fact, democracy is so important to the period of modernity that many of the tensions and struggles throughout the entire period are centered around it. As flawed a system as it is, and there are many valid criticisms of its shortcomings, I feel it is still the best system humans have developed for a nation's power to be divided, and for the rights of its citizens to flourish.

This book is about ideology and teaching for social justice in twenty-first century North America. I think it is pertinent to describe the reasons why and how the major political ideologies originated.

The Ideologies of Modernity

The ideologies of modern politics functioned to provide the goals and framework for polit-ical action designed to produce 'the good society'. Ideology as a concept thus took as its basis the notion that it was possible to transform society and change human nature to make people into suitable members of this new society. (Schwarzmantel, 1998, p. 63)

The concepts of democracy and emancipation are central to most notions of social justice. Both democracy and emancipation were also central to the tensions within the politics of modernity that led to the competing political ideologies. Many philosophers of the Enlightenment, even those who believed that human happiness was possible, "had doubts about all human beings sharing in the benefits" (Schwarzmantel, 1998, p. 23). There was major debate around who should profit from the new society with its burgeoning economies, who should be included, and what role should be given to the "vulgar masses" in the democratic republic that the "cultured elite" was attempting to create (p. 23). That the working classes of Europe were thought of in this contemptuous manner sheds light on the even worse treatment that the indigenous peoples of the empire-building territories were subjected to. Despite these obvious contradictions in Enlightenment philosophy, several political ideologies emerged out of these struggles, each one made up of many situations that are grounded in social and material reality (Zizek, 1994). The first ideology to articulate a new way of perceiving the world and organizing society through human reason during this period was liberalism.

Liberalism

The two social cornerstones of liberalism in its classic form are "the supreme value of the individual and the need for a political system that was suitable for an emancipated and rational population" (Schwarzmantel, 1998, p. 68). Hence, it can be argued that the concepts of *emancipation* and *democracy* are the progeny of liberalism. But initially, liberals were quite happy to engage in the pursuit of wealth through laissez-faire economic policy and the conquest of nature. An economic system based on free-market principles became dominant as the newly emerging bourgeoisie refined the economically successful but racist mercantile system that had existed for at least a century prior to these revolutionary times. Adam Smith's *Wealth of Nations* became the source of rational liberal principles. Smith's belief in free-market capitalism was based, in part, on what he also thought to be the best way to free as many people as possible.[2] Yet, Smith also advocated government intervention to counteract the destructive forces inherent in the free enterprise system (Chomsky, 1999, p. 39).

Liberalism became entrenched to some extent in France, Britain, its colonies, and the United States. A growing populace of small property owners began to create social stability and allow democracy (in its representative form) the opportunity to flourish. Yet, some liberal thinkers such as Alexis de Tocqueville worried about the effects of excessive privatization (Heffner, 1956, pp. 209–213) and excessive individualism (pp. 192–194) because they would work to undermine any concern with common citizenship, public values, and collective benefits. Others, like John Stuart Mill, were concerned with who would be granted citizenship rights and what negative effect giving non-propertied White men (i.e., laborers) the vote would have on the "tone of political discourse" (Schwarzmantel, 1998, p. 80). The concerns with American democracy will be discussed in more detail in Chapter 8. At this point in history, it is significant that there was very little thought given to any notions of emancipation for those who had been colonized or enslaved. Yet, recent public debates in the United States during the Obama administration, such as around the public healthcare option, suggest that Tocqueville and Mill had very valid concerns.

Eventually, liberalism developed civil, political, and consumer rights for all White men, regardless of wealth and status, and in this way it was successful in integrating these masses into the new society. By the late 1800s, classical liberalism evolved into progressive or reform liberalism in which a more state-interventionist approach developed in part to appease the growing discontent of the working classes. Reform liberalism also included a "tempered" individualism, which developed out of the inevitable tension between an ideal of liberty and an ideal of equality.

Over the course of the twentieth century, a color-blind racial discourse became part of liberalism, and with this came another cornerstone of this ideology, namely, *meritocracy*. Meritocracy refers to the social system whereby each individual reaches a social and economic status commensurate with their individual talents and how hard they have worked. It is also used to explain why some individuals excel while others flounder. At the same time that meritocracy reinforces the inequalities in our society, it makes people unconscious of any notion of privilege. In other words, meritocracy works as a hegemonic device. This was a central part of the socialist critique of liberalism. Yet, both ideologies had not developed any serious thought to notions of justice for those who were not of European extraction. Neither would the significant number of Europeans who had a more conservative vision of the ideal society be concerned with the welfare of non-White people. In other words, the original versions of the ideologies of modernity were premised on an ethos of White supremacy. Yet, for the first time, there was a new way of discussing what kind of society was best, with a language that included a conceptual framework based upon universal emancipation, citizenship, and other democratic rights, and above all, the primacy of the individual. They merged together to form what is likely the first discursive formation that addressed social justice issues in a profound way (in Eurocentric history, at least).

A related ideology that is a spin-off of liberalism is called *libertarianism*. Adherents of this ideology believe that people should be free to do what they want, as long as they do not infringe on the rights of others. In general, libertarians believe that human nature is selfish and competitive rather than cooperative. In other words, self-interest is the motivation for human activity, according to libertarians. Libertarianism has come to refer to the view that human activity in general and economic activity in particular should be released from all regulation by the state other than what is required to maintain social order. One of the most famous proponents of this ideology is Alan Greenspan, the 13th Chairman of the Federal Reserve in the United States from 1987 until 2006. Greenspan replaced Paul Volcker, who was at odds with President Reagan because he favored regulation of American financial lending institutions. Reagan named the libertarian Greenspan as Volcker's successor precisely because of his view that the free markets, including the financial industry, should not be regulated. There are many today, including Nobel Prize–winning economists Joseph E. Stiglitz (2003, 2008) and Paul Krugman (2005, 2008), who contend that much of the devastating problems associated with a deregulated financial industry should be attributed to Alan Greenspan and his libertarian policies.[3] We will focus on the economic aspects of libertarianism, often called neoliberalism in the current context, in Chapter 9. Until then, the focus will be on the ideology it sprang from, namely, liberalism.

Much of what liberalism spoke of Karl Marx agreed with. His major criticism of the liberal position was what he saw as an unsolvable contradiction: the rights of the individual in an economic structure based on inequality. All of his work addressed this contradiction. For Marx, the prime social unit was not the individual. It was social class.

Socialism

A product of both the industrial revolution and the French Revolution, the original idea of socialism was that human beings could control and master "the forces of nature and production to achieve a common happiness of mankind" (Schwarzmantel, 1998, p. 88). Socialism can be seen as a spin-off ideology from liberalism, another attempt to realize the goal of emancipation. The original socialist tradition was in agreement with the liberal idea of a rationally controlled society that could be made even better, that is, progress through conscious human action. Both ideologies dismissed the notion of divine guidance as the underlying source of rules, roles, and regulations in industrially advanced societies.

Contrary to popular misconception, Karl Marx had little difficulty with the liberal idea of democracy and its potential to engage and deliver power to the masses. Indeed, Marx approved of the demand for universal suffrage made by Chartist working-class organizations in Britain in the 1830s. Moreover, he commented that its "inevitable result . . . the political supremacy of the working class" was only a matter of time (Schwarzmantel, 1998, p. 22). Yet, democracy in action proved itself to be different from democracy in its ideal form. The same people Marx referred to as the working classes were called the unenlightened or even the vulgar masses by many bourgeois liberal thinkers. Marx became convinced that liberalism was, at best, a naïve attempt to bring freedom to the masses.

The failure of liberalism became especially clear to Marx after the 1851 Third Republic election in France, a test for liberal democracy in which the bourgeoisie ended up supporting the elites rather than the workers. A major tension within the liberal philosophy was made clear: the desire for universal rights coupled with the fear of the unenlightened masses holding the reins of power. For these so-called unenlightened masses, however, power was still beyond their reach, traditional community support networks were breaking down, and working conditions for the laborers of the industrial revolution were abominable. Historian Eric Hobsbawm explains the dilemma the working classes of Europe faced.

Three possibilities were therefore open to much of the poor as found themselves in the path of bourgeois society, and no longer effectively sheltered in still inaccessible regions of traditional society. They could strive to become bourgeois; they could allow themselves to be ground down; or they could rebel. (Hobsbawm, 1962, p. 245)

As Hobsbawm suggests, the Marxist critique of liberalism cogently expressed the discontentment of the masses and their potential for revolution. For Marx, liberalism's major flaw was its emphasis on the individual as the most important unit in society. In the Marxist interpretation of the social relations of that period, it was social class that was the crucial aspect of a person's identity. This was because of the great disparities in wealth and opportunities with which the working classes had to contend.

It is beyond the scope of this book to go into any depth about the Marxist prescription for freedom based on a violent confrontation over the means of production between the proletariat and the bourgeoisie. It is paramount to understand, however, that the original socialist ideology also articulated a vision for a socially just world in a similar vein as its liberal predecessor. As Marx and his early supporters viewed the liberal ideology as naïve and flawed, similar critiques of socialism have been launched by feminists, antiracists, and environmentalists. At this point in the discussion of the role of ideology, suffice to say that Marx predicted, indeed, saw as inevitable, a worker-led revolution that would finish the bourgeois project of liberalism, namely, the emancipation of everyone. Yet, adherents of both liberalism and conservatism were appalled at the notion of what kind of society the laboring masses would construct. A violent revolution was a frightening prospect; yet, so was the idea of the working classes gaining power through the mechanism of universal suffrage, that is, the vote. Marx gained very few allies from opposing ideologies, given his view of the inevitable clash between social classes.

As the capitalist system demonstrated its metal by surviving the crisis of the almost decade-long Great Depression of the 1930s, and knowledge of the atrocities of the Stalin-led Soviet Union became known to people in Western nations, the popularity of the socialist ideology began to wane. Over time, a new leftist political ideology gained currency, a hybrid of socialism and liberalism merging together to form *social democracy*. The basic tenets of social democracy include an acceptance of capitalism and an objective to help those social groups that have little hope to better their economic standard of living. It also shares with liberalism a respect for the rights of the individual, something that most forms of socialism do not value to the same extent. Social democratic parties have grown in every Western nation except the United States.[4]

In fact, it is Marx's essentialist view of history with which many people disagree. Human destiny is not predetermined, say liberal critics; rather, it has all to do with our agency in constructing what it is we truly want. Yet, it is precisely this position that the conservatives took exception with; for them, human reason is flawed. A central tenet of conservatism is that society should be led by a stable group of people who, through past experience, would have the ability to do so wisely. Its spin-off ideology, nationalism, is positioned even further to the Right on the Left-Right spectrum. Because it is only a matter of degree that separates these two ideologies, and because the criticisms leveled by liberals and socialists are similar for both, I will discuss them in a single section.

Conservatism

The conservative ideology developed as a reaction to modernity and the revolutionary fervor it spawned. According to Schwarzmantel (1998), "[c]onservatism was critical of modernity while at the same time being its product" (p. 111). Early conservatives believed that the commercial forces unleashed by the liberal project were tearing apart the bonds needed for social cohesion. Moreover, conservatives considered the notion of progress, central to both liberalism and socialism, as unsettling and threatening to tradition and community. A central theme of conservatism is that tradition gains strength from the long held views inherent in the common sense of the community. Conservative theorists believed in "the idea of an organic and hierarchical society, in which people knew their place yet are related to each other as part of a totality" (p. 110). The idea of each person understanding their place in society at least partially explains why there has been a vociferous backlash against feminism, multiculturalism, and the trade union movement in recent years. Tradition and progress are directly at odds with one another; conservatives cherish the former while fearing the latter.

Conservatism shared with socialism a fear of the fragmentary atomistic processes in the individual-obsessed philosophy of liberalism. Both were fearful of liberalism's unchecked economic policies, processes that might render all familiarity unrecognizable. The similarities between the two ideologies end there, however, as traditional conservative thought was focused on how to maintain the status quo in the face of economic, political, and social upheaval. As mentioned already, the idea that society must depend on human reason repulsed conservatives, who focused on divine guidance in this life to get people to the after-life.[5] By corollary, conservatives such as Edmund Burke were staunchly opposed to involving the masses in the political realm. For Burke and many other conservatives, the idea of giving the working classes the opportunity to vote was appalling.

In its original form, conservatism was adamantly opposed to democracy. Yet, there were some conservative theorists who attempted to encourage the engagement of the masses into politics through the use of referenda and plebiscites. Conservatism in this form often uses populist sentiments to give people a false sense of participation as authoritarian policies are entrenched. As Richard Rorty (1998) points out, progressive legislation brought about through the painstaking agency of various groups is easily and quickly extinguished.

Strands of conservatism venture even further to the right on the Left-Right political spectrum, of course. In the 1930s, European fascists seized the opportunity presented by the onward rush of modernity to claim that rational human thought is flawed, that an all-powerful leader is required to forge a strong sense of community in the face of social forces brought on by democratic, liberal thought. Fascism contains a central element of the ideology of *nationalism*, namely, the use of revisionist history and myth to foster racial or ethnic pride. As we near the end of the first decade of the twenty-first century, there are once again signs pointing toward fascist threats in several Western nations.

Most forms of nationalism also rely on scapegoating vulnerable groups in order to mobilize the masses to move toward a more authoritarian political and social structure. For example, on October 26, 2001, a few weeks after the terrorist attacks of September 11, 2001, the George W. Bush administration passed the U.S.A. Patriot Act. This act expanded the state's ability to legally employ surveillance techniques on many domestic groups and movements. It has been criticized by many for limiting the civil rights of American citizens. There are more progressive forms of nationalism, but for our purposes, the discussion on nationalism focuses on its more common and regressive form.

Nationalism is much more likely to survive social crises because of its chameleon-like qualities. As well, its critique of the universalism espoused by liberals and socialists allows it to mobilize large groups of people opposed to the concept in these postmodern times, allowing groups to be pitted against one another, as currently seen throughout many parts of the world, including North America. For example, mainstream media outlets such as Fox News are wont to pit conservatives against liberals under the guise of determining who is a "real American." The so-called Tea Party demonstrates how this discourse can resonate in the political culture of a nation. Nationalism is able to better guarantee "a sense of inclusion and citizenship" (Schwarzmantel, 1998, p. 147), most often by excluding others from the rights and benefits of citizenship. (A most frightening situation can arise with what Tocqueville called the "tyranny of the majority.")

The critiques of both conservatism and right-wing nationalism from both the liberal and socialist camps are clear and succinct and based on several principles of social justice. To begin, they believe that a society constructed by rational human-thought makes more sense than one based on divine principles (which most on the Left would claim to be open to multiple human interpretations anyway). Moreover, and especially germane to this book, traditional communities are most often nonegalitarian with entrenched social hierarchies and, therefore, clearly anti-democratic. Traditional hierarchies by definition take exception with the discourse for the emancipation of the masses, a situation that can lead to the oppression of many for the benefit of the few. Lastly, the focus on tradition and the past often seems to lead to the exclusion of certain groups from attaining citizenship. Even more disturbing, there is a tendency within extreme conservatism and right wing nationalism to scapegoat vulnerable groups of people.

In these brief descriptions of the political ideologies of modernity, it is clear that both liberalism and socialism include principles of social justice. Both couplings – liberalism/socialism and conservatism/nationalism – work, to a large extent, in opposition to each other. This binary produces tensions around the issues of engaging the masses politically, of inclusion and citizen rights, of equality, and of progress. The critical left considers much of liberalism to be power-blind, a contention I examine in Chapter 7. According to postmodern theorists, however, all of the ideologies that arose out of modernity are flawed and mostly irrelevant for today's society.

Postmodernist Critiques of Modernity's Ideologies

It is the claim to universalism by the major ideologies of the Enlightenment, particularly liberalism and socialism, that leaves them open to attacks from the post-modernists. Because of the diverse pluralist nature of Canada and the United States, especially in urban centers, much of what each of the major political ideologies promises cannot be delivered. Relatively new ideologies such as certain versions of feminism, environmentalism, and multiculturalism have articulated well-developed critiques of the older ideologies, which they see as metanarratives incapable of addressing the social problems inherent within a diverse and pluralistic society.

The political conditions during this emerging postmodern period are vastly different from those that led to the creation and development of the Enlightenment. The erosion of the powers of the nation state, one of the cornerstones of modernity, has added to the social fragmentation and disappearance of community for many people. The indisputable and undeniable destruction of the environment proves that liberals and socialists were wrong in thinking that nature could simply be controlled. In fact, the problematic status of any social movement or collective agent powerful enough to claim to speak on behalf of society about general grievances has added to the conviction among many that no grand metanarrative can speak for all social groups. The postmodern critique of modernity is that there can be no universal emancipation in this postmodern world, there can only be a politics of identity and difference. Shifting subjectivities, they contend, make social movements based on any one marker of identity suspect.

Progressive social movements, most of which "protest structural inequalities that they perceive unfairly privilege some social segments and oppress others" (Young, 2000, p. 92), are obviously at variance with conservatism's axiom of knowing your place in traditional social hierarchies. The postmodern critique of socialism is that a person's identity includes several markers, social class being only but one. The postmodern critique of liberalism is centered around the notion of the primacy of the individual, that the individual is a rational and autonomous subject of agency. In short, postmodern theorists question the idea that any one group is capable of developing an emancipatory political agenda as both the liberals and socialists espouse. Each ideology is limited because it speaks to and benefits only a partial population in society, blocking any hope of realizing its ideal through agency, as well as making any claims to universality unsustainable.

Ideology Today

> If democracy and emancipation are to be more than pious aspirations, the ideologies must once again be linked to social movements and political parties that are putting them into practice. (Schwarzmantel, 1998, p. 12)

These postmodernist critiques are included to address the frequent and often valid attacks on any conceptual discussions of the political ideologies that developed in response to the sweeping changes transforming Western societies during the period of modernity. There is no question that the ideologies of emancipation – liberalism and socialism – have to take into account the postmodern critiques in order to have relevance. In particular, socialism has to find the political space and will to take into account the diversity along axes of race and gender and not only social class.

The political ideologies of the Left-Right spectrum are still highly relevant in the politics of today's postmodern society. Political ideologies are necessary to comprehend in order for a truly democratic politics to develop. The concern is that if we do not have political ideologies that political parties ascribe to, then we get power for the sake of power.[6] These ideologies enable debate and discussion to flourish with a backdrop of common understanding. In terms of social justice, a Marxist notion of a collective entity that includes race and gender is better positioned to build sustaining coalitions in order to confront the major obstacles. Yet, it will be difficult to overcome these obstacles because of ideological differences and the powerful influence of the corporate media.

Some people do not agree with the principles of social justice, of course. Conservatives do not accept the notion of equality, believing that traditional social hierarchies are required for social cohesion. (In academic terms, they generally prefer tradition to progressivism.) The liberal vision of an ideal world differs from the social democratic vision. Much of this variance can be attributed to differing levels of support for the corporate agenda. Yet, it is still important for critically minded citizens to know how adherents of each ideology think about conceptions of social justice, the individual, and the common good.

The ideologies of modernity will be revisited in the second half of this book, especially their positions on race, social class, and the "good citizen."

What Is Meant by Left Wing and Right Wing in Today's Politics?

As mentioned near the beginning of this chapter, there are many people who call for the dismissal of talk of political ideology. It is as though to refrain from talking about it will make things work better. All things considered, this must be viewed as a naïve proposition.

In a similar fashion, there are numerous calls by politicians and media pundits stating that the old political terms of left and right have outworn their usefulness, that it is long past time to put these terms to rest. If common people were to forget the political meanings of left and right, there is no question that the elites would benefit from this myopia. Even if people were to have a basic political understanding with some semblance of what is meant by the left and the right, they would also possess the rudimentary basics of a political consciousness. This is necessary in order for resistance to hegemony to develop. By this reasoning, it is important for citizens to know what is meant by these terms.

The political meanings of left and right also have their origins in France. Prior to the French Revolution of 1789, within the legislative chambers of the French Estates General, the nobility sat on the King's right while the "third estate" – a conglomerate of peasants, working people, and the bourgeoisie or middle class – sat on the King's left. As time passed, other European legislative chambers took up this practice. These seating arrangements have come to mean that the representatives of the elite are usually – but it is important to note that not always – influenced by right wing policies, while the representatives of common citizens are influenced by certain left wing policies.

In more specific terms, left wing ideas in Western democracies are rooted in a sense of freedom, equality, egalitarianism, and social justice. In the main, these ideas champion the rights of women, gays, and non-White peoples, and a strong social welfare state. The ideas of the right wing, on the other hand, have evolved to include policies that encourage the individual to advance economically and socially on their own accord, without help from the state. As well, the right wing is dismissive of claims by various minorities that the system is inherently unfair. In other words, the Right, which includes conservatives and right liberals, has co-opted the notion of meritocracy in order to maintain privilege in current day social, political, and economic hierarchies.

An effective way to have students understand what is meant by the left and the right in political terms is to consider all issues as either economic or social. Economic issues are those that represent significant amounts of money, while social issues do not. For example, capital punishment is a social issue while tax reform is an economic issue. The case can be made that some issues are both social and economic – healthcare is a case in point – yet, to save on getting mired in semantics, the basic economic/social distinction is useful (see Fig. 2.1).

With political ideologies and political issues divided into the economic and the social, students are able to make headway around why certain media are called left wing by some, and the very same media outlets are called right wing or right leaning by others. For example, during the past few federal elections in Canada, leaders of the federal Liberal Party appeal to social democrats (that is, supporters of the New Democratic Party) as having values that have appeared out of the same concerns for justice, and that their vote should switch to the Liberals. The truth of the matter is that on social issues, they are correct. On economic issues, however, the two parties diverge significantly – the Liberals are to the right of center, closer to where the Conservative Party are positioned, while the NDP are to the left of center. Yet, this distinction of the Liberal Party being left wing on social issues and right wing on economic issues is rarely mentioned in the corporate media.

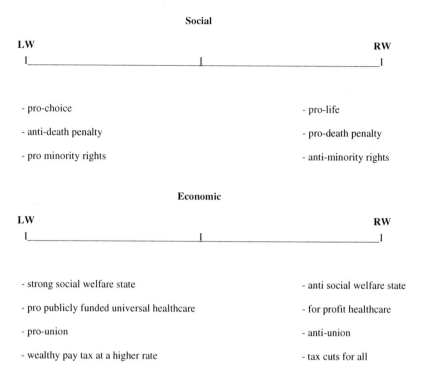

Social

LW   RW

- pro-choice   - pro-life

- anti-death penalty   - pro-death penalty

- pro minority rights   - anti-minority rights

Economic

LW   RW

- strong social welfare state   - anti social welfare state

- pro publicly funded universal healthcare   - for profit healthcare

- pro-union   - anti-union

- wealthy pay tax at a higher rate   - tax cuts for all

Fig. 2.1 Left and Right on the Social and Economic Spectra

In the United States, the media usually refer to the Democrats as left wing, and on social issues they do champion the rights of minorities. Yet, on economic issues, both parties develop policy supported by the corporate sector and most wealthy individuals. In other words, neither of the two major American parties would be considered left wing on economic issues.

All of the adherents to the political ideologies discussed in this chapter, whether on the left or on the right, compete to garner support for their way of seeing the world and their plans to organize society through discourse. This term will be the main focus of the next chapter.

Suggestions to Further Comprehension

(a) Research the platforms of the following American political parties:

- The Republican Party
- The Democratic Party
- The American Green Party

(b) Research the platforms of the following Canadian political parties:

- The Liberal Party
- The Conservative Party
- The New Democratic Party
- The Bloc Quebecois
- The Green Party of Canada

(c) Use the social scale or the economic scale to place the various political parties. Be prepared to explain why you placed each one where you did.

```
                          Economic Scale
      LW                                                   RW
      I-----------------------------------I------------------------------------I


                          Social Scale
      LW                                                   RW
      I-----------------------------------I------------------------------------I
```

(i) The three American political parties
(ii) The five Canadian political parties
(iii) Using a separate set of axes to represent the economic and social scales, place the letter representing each of the following issues on one of the scales. Be prepared to explain why you placed each one where you did.

A – capital punishment
B – increased rights of gay people
C – gun control
D – tax cuts for all
E – increased funding for public education
F – pro-life
G – pro-choice
H – regulating the financial industry
I – increased military spending
J – increased social welfare spending
K – publicly funded healthcare system
L – subsidized daycare
M – the UN Declaration of Human Rights
N – "pull yourself up by the bootstraps" philosophy
O – support for unions
P – free trade with Mexico
Q – increased rights for Aboriginal land treaties
R – martial law
S – progressive tax reform
T – support for replacement workers during a strike

Questions to Ponder

1. What are some commonly held beliefs in our society that may be the result of hegemony? Consider the variables of race, gender, social class, and government explanations for war.
2. Some early American educational theorists – such as John Dewey, Harold Rugg, and George Counts – wanted the schools to be used to develop critical thinking students who would one day become citizens able to think through complex social problems. What do you think are some obstacles that practitioners of such an approach would come up against?
3. Social democratic parties have grown in every Western nation except the United States. Speculate as to why the social democratic option did not appear on the American federal scene after World War II, as it did in other Western countries. Why do you think a viable social democratic party has not appeared in the United States in recent years?
4. The conservative idea of each person understanding their place in society at least partially explains why there is often a vociferous backlash against feminism, multiculturalism, and the trade union movement. Discuss this aspect of contemporary conservatism in the United States and Canada.

Notes

1. Throughout much of this book, I will refer to the radical ideology as the *critical left*. Yet, the vast body of academic literature uses the term *radical* to refer to a more leftist orientation toward society.
2. In recent decades there has been a resurgence back toward the notion of positioning the market as the organizing principle of a society. It is called *neoliberalism* and it is the focus of Chapter 9. As Chomsky (1999) points out, Adam Smith was in favor of government action only if it helped the workers, not the capitalists (p. 39).
3. It is noteworthy that President Reagan and Federal Reserve Chair Greenspan were Republicans, the American political party most closely associated with conservatism. It is also worth noting that President Clinton, a liberal Democrat, kept the self-proclaimed libertarian Greenspan in the position of Federal Reserve Chair. Since the 1980s, both parties while in government have supported the economic policies of neoliberalism.
4. The relatively new but small American Green Party has many policies in common with Canada's social democratic party, the New Democratic Party (NDP).
5. In the United States today, neoconservatives want to "re-Christianize" the state by, for example, bringing prayer back into the public school classroom.
6. In Chapter 8, I describe a teaching experience in 2006 in which the students were involved in a Civics unit on "Flaws With Democracy." Toward the end of the unit, there was a federal election in which the government changed from the Liberals to the Conservatives. A few days after the election, David Emerson, a Liberal cabinet minister, crossed the floor and immediately became a Conservative cabinet minister, telling the media that the ideological lines between the two parties had "blurred."

References

Aronowitz, S. (1988). *Science as power: Discourse and ideology in modern society*. Minneapolis: University of Minnesota Press.

Bartolome, L. I. (Ed.). (2008). *Ideologies in education: Unmasking the trap of teacher neutrality*. New York: Peter Lang Publishing.

Chomsky, N. (1999). *Profit over people: Neoliberalism and global order*. New York: Seven Stories Press.

Eageton, T. (1991) *Ideology: An introduction*. London: Verso.

Foucault, M. (1980). *Power/knowledge: Selected interviews and other writings, 1972–1977*. London: Harvester Press.

Fraser, N. (1997). *Justice interruptus: Critical reflections on the "postsocialist" condition*. New York: Routledge.

Giddens, A. (1994). *Beyond left and right: The future of radical politics*. Stanford, CA: Stanford University Press.

Giroux, H. A. (1981). *Ideology, culture, and the process of schooling*. Philadelphia: Temple University Press.

Habermas, J. (1987). *Lectures on the philosophical discourse of modernity*. Cambridge, MA: MIT Press.

Heffner, R. D. (Ed.). (1956). *Democracy in America (by Alexis de Tocqueville)*. New York: The Penguin Group.

Hobsbawm, E. (1962). *The age of revolution, 1789–1848*. London: Sphere Books.

Krugman, P. (2005, February 18). Opinion: Three-card maestro. *The New York Times*. Retrieved on 9 June 2011, from http://nytimes.com

Krugman, P. (2008) *The return of depression economics and the crisis of 2008*. New York: Norton publishers.

Laclau, E., & Mouffe, C. (1985). *Hegemony and socialist strategy: Toward a radical democratic politics*. London: Verso Books.

Orlowski, P. (2008). "That would certainly be spoiling them": Liberal discourses of social studies teachers and concerns about Aboriginal students. *Canadian Journal of Native Education, 31*(2), 110–129.

Rorty, R. (1998). *Achieving our country: Leftist thought in twentieth-century America*. Cambridge, MA: Harvard University Press.

Schwarzmantel, J. (1998). *The age of ideology: Political ideologies from the American revolution to postmodern times*. New York: New York University Press.

Sleeter, C. E. (2004). Context-conscious portraits and context-blind policy. *Anthropology & Education Quarterly, 35*(1), 132–136.

Stiglitz, J. (2003). *The roaring nineties: A new history of the world's most prosperous decade*. New York: W.W. Norton.

Stiglitz, J. (2008, September 17). How to prevent the next Wall Street crisis, *CNN*. Retrieved on 9 June 2011, from http://www.cnn.com/2008/POLITICS/09/17/stiglitz.crisis/

Young, I. M. (2000). *Inclusion and democracy*. London: Oxford University Press.

Zizek, S. (Ed.). (1994). *Mapping ideology*. London: Verso.

Chapter 3
The Power of Discourse, Of course!

> *[A]t the heart of ideology is the problem of social relations of domination made intelligible through discourse.*
> *(Leonardo, 2003, p. 204)*

Whether critical educators are attempting to illuminate the political ideologies underlying the formal state-sanctioned curriculum or CNN newscasts, one of the most effective ways of doing so is through an understanding of *discourse*. In elementary terms, discourse can be seen to be a social theory in which repeated usage by certain experts, for instance, in the media or the academy, result in increased social power for some people usually at the expense of others. For example, ever since September 11, 2001, the general public has heard an oft-repeated attempt to explain these attacks: They hate our freedoms. This discourse of oppositional civilizations helped justify an attack on both Afghanistan and Iraq, benefiting the military-industrial complex and subsidiary companies, at the expense of moderate and fundamentalist Muslims the world over, as well as the soldiers of allied forces.

Discourse is always connected with desire and power. Yet, these links must be hidden if desire and power are to manifest themselves in language. As Norman Fairclough (1989) puts it, "[d]iscourse can never be 'neutral' or value-free; discourse always reflects ideologies, systems of values, beliefs, and social practices" (p. 21). In other words, discourses can work toward either sustaining unequal relations of power or challenging them. Using an historical example to make the point more clear, the discourse of White supremacy worked to justify to White people both the enslavement of Black peoples and the reservation system for Aboriginal peoples. An overt discourse of White supremacy today would be unacceptable to most White Americans and Canadians. The color-blind discourse that rose to prominence after the Second World War worked to disrupt some aspects of racial inequality in North America. The famous speech by Reverend Martin Luther King that began with "I have a dream..." is laced with the color-blind discourse. The result of this disruption is that by the second half of the twentieth century, the essentialist discourse that postulated a genetic advantage for White people had been successfully marginalized.

Yet, there are still powerful dominant discourses today that support the agendas of economic, social, and political elites. Of significance to critical educators is the manner in which these discourses operate in the public realm. Hegemonic discourses must be covert in the contemporary context because, for the most part, the elites are in a minority in both Canada and the United States. Otherwise, there would be more resistance to the desired goals of the elites. For example, the powerful discourse of "taxes as burden" would lose much of its influence on the public's collective consciousness if journalists and educators deconstructed it in terms of who benefits and who suffers with repeated tax cuts. Not all discourses work in the interests of the elites, of course. At this point in the discussion, however, it is important to understand that discourse is how "ideology is understood, perpetuated or challenged" (Leonardo, 2003, p. 207).

Critical Discourse Analysis: A Brief Introduction

In order to understand discourse and its relationship to power/one must engage in an analytic combination of ideology and discourse, or what Jay Lemke (1995) calls "the ideological functioning of discourses" (p. 12) and many others call critical discourse analysis. This concept is very similar to what French philosopher Jacques Derrida (1978) calls deconstruction. Deconstruction, or critical discourse analysis, is an alternative approach to interpreting texts. Instead of focusing on the author and the overt meaning of a work, the deconstructionist approach attempts to grasp the implicit meanings of texts by exposing their underlying and hidden assumptions.

The results of deconstruction and critical discourse analysis are often referred to as ideology critique. Leonardo (2003) contends that "ideology critique lifts the veil of common sense in order to arrive at underlying interests and agendas structured in language" (p. 208). The importance of this statement cannot be overstated, and critical educators need to understand this. This idea is also at the root of this entire book.

Critical discourse analysis is a useful strategy for educators to analyze school related text. For example, the knowledge contained in the state-sanctioned curriculum is interwoven with power. First, it is seen as official knowledge upholding authority (Apple, 2004). Second, the "knowledge" contained in the curriculum is what the students learn about. Whatever topics are excluded do not become part of the classroom discussions; nor do they engage in structuring society and its social relations. What is included in the curriculum eventually becomes normalized, as if this was inevitable, natural, perhaps, even invisible. Both exclusion and inclusion are examples of hegemonic strategies. Chapters 5, 6, and 7 include detailed examples of using the critical discourse analysis approach to expose the hidden assumptions implicit in the formal social studies curriculum.

Traditionally, discourse and discourse analyses are thought of in mechanistic terms and within the realm of linguistics. Rather than thinking of discourse in this way, I have used it in a more poststructuralist sense of the term, that is, as a critical tool enabling the illumination of the political ideologies underlying educational texts. The formal social studies curriculum and the attitudes of teachers toward issues of race and social class captured in interview transcripts are examples of educational texts I have analyzed in my own research. Critical discourse analysis is a powerful technique to determine the political ideologies underlying these educational texts. In terms of locating the nexus of power in American and Canadian society, there is much potential in this poststructuralist approach to ideology critique.

A Poststructuralist Approach to Understanding Power

Australian educator R. W. Connell (2004) emphasizes that "[p]oststructuralism represents an important creative resource for the social sciences and the humanities" (p. 22). I contend that it is also useful in preparing preservice teachers. A poststructuralist understanding of language in the representation of social life demonstrates its importance with discourse, discourse analysis, and ideology. Language itself has clearly stopped being solely within the domain of formal linguistics. As Leonardo (2003) puts it, "language is a tool not only for communication, but also for domination and liberation" (p. 205). The theoretical work of Michel Foucault (1970) is particularly effective in demonstrating the usefulness of viewing the connections between language, discourse, and power.

Foucault reconceptualized language as a sociopolitical entity, as the means by which certain social relations can actually be created. For Foucault, knowledge itself involves social, political, and historical conditions under which various statements come to count as true or false. In other words, power is always at the root of discourse and which discourses gain currency as official knowledge. Foucault is not saying that there is no truth. On the contrary, he is in agreement with postmodern theorists that there can be many truths of the same event, each with its own rationality. What is important for Foucault is this: *which* interpretation of the truth, at any given period, becomes the official discourse and *how* does this occur? Two further important questions stemming from Foucault's theory of discourse are: first, "How does an interpretation get to be told as truth?" and second, "What can be said?" To ask such questions involves the notion of power. Questions such as these emanate from a critical left perspective.

Power is the underpinning of Foucault's theory of discourse. Yet, power is conceived very differently from commonsense and sociopolitical interpretations: "Power is everywhere, not because it embraces everything but because it comes from everywhere" (Foucault, 1979, p. 93). In the Foucauldian sense, power is conceived as a set of relations of force, relations that are local and historically contingent. Power is seamlessly built into daily relations and practices, rather than as something imposed from the top down. Discourse is not so unidirectional.

A comprehension of the role discourse plays in sustaining or resisting dominant ideologies is of paramount importance to understanding the ways in which political ideology shapes our perceptions. Leonardo (2003) concurs, arguing that "a discursive understanding of ideology critique" has huge "potential as an analytic tool" (p. 204). Such an understanding forces a person to appreciate the role that language plays in the representation of social relations, and in the way language engages with power. Within this framework, ideology is not reified; rather, this demonstrates the evolving nature of ideology. This makes sense when one considers how the ideologies discussed in Chapter 2 change as the social conditions change. Quite often, it is important to note, differing emphases of certain discourses can effect change in social conditions. An example of this can be seen in the repeated usage of the dominant hegemonic discourse of tax cuts that emanated out of corporate media outlets in both the United States and Canada in the 1980s and 1990s. Once the tax cuts were implemented, cuts to social programs and public education followed, thereby causing social conditions to change, especially for working families and the poor.

Discursive Formations

Not all ideas or discourses take hold to form an ideology on their own, of course. At the risk of oversimplification, an ideology rests at the pinnacle of certain sets of discourses that have formed into powerful discursive formations. Stuart Hall states, "It is not the individual elements of a discourse that have political or ideological connotations, it is the ways those elements are organized together in *a new discursive formation*" (cited in Grossberg, 1986, p. 143, emphasis mine). Across time, the discourses change, as do the discursive formations, thereby forcing ideologies to adapt, always in response to changing material and social conditions.

The dominant discourses in a society often work in concert, that is, as discursive formations, to maintain the status quo and further the interests of the privileged. For an historical example, in the period of White settlers populating the western regions of North America, the dominant discourses of White supremacy, Christianity, capitalism, the dying race (i.e., Aboriginal peoples), and the yellow hordes (i.e., East Asian peoples) all worked in concert to increase economic, social, and political power for the White middle class at the expense of the Other (mostly Aboriginal and Asian). Once White hegemony was entrenched, this particular discursive formation was not required anymore and was, therefore, abandoned.

For a more contemporary example of a discursive formation, attacks on the social welfare state in the United States and Canada included discourses about the need for tax cuts, immigration and the swelling welfare ranks, the evils of feminism, big public sector unions (such as teacher unions), the high costs of public education, and the most important one of all, the free hand of the market. Considered together, by the late 1980s, these discourses set in motion a neoliberal agenda that progressives have found very difficult to counteract. Corporate media repeated these discourses in various ways and in different combinations that left very little space for dissent. This example also demonstrates how the corporate media is a hegemonic device in the service of elite groups.

Discourse and the Evolving Nature of Ideology

Discourse is engaged with the representation of our world. It is also engaged with shaping our consciousness of the world. Yet, interwoven with power as it is, discourse is placed in a material condition or in a set of material conditions which, in turn, place boundaries on the socially productive imagination. Returning to the same historical example, the discursive formation of White supremacy and capitalism, in tandem with the dying race discourse, worked to rationalize the theft of Aboriginal lands and subsequent legislation forbidding status Aboriginal people from owning land or starting a business in the province of British Columbia from the 1850s until the 1950s. The discourse at the root of this example of institutional racism, that is, a racist law, was the dying race discourse. The rationale for this discourse stated that if the Native Indians were dying out, then "we" might as well use the land.[1] Discourse, in this sense, engages in power relations with definite material consequences. It also supported a political ideology, in this case, an earlier version of conservatism.

Ideologies evolve over time. In Chapter 2 the discussion included a brief description of classical liberalism evolving into progressive or reform liberalism which allowed for a more state-interventionist approach to appease the growing discontent of the working classes. Ideological evolution can be seen more recently with many Western governments. Many political followers will remember Republican president Richard Nixon famously declaring, "We are all Keynesian now" (Harvey, 2005, p. 13). Since the 1980s, however, the dominant approach dismissed Keynesian economics in favor of the neoliberal theories of University of Chicago economist Milton Friedman. Friedman favored industry deregulation and eschewed government intervention in the economy. In fact, another change in this corporate approach toward governance can be seen with the Republican administration led by George W. Bush creating record-breaking deficits year after year, something that was particularly avoided by Republican administrations throughout most of the history of the United States. The situation is much the same in Canada. The federal Conservative government led by Prime Minister Stephen Harper, first elected in 2006, promoted the idea of fiscal responsibility and no-deficit budgets. Yet, with the economic crisis that began in 2008, this same government produced a budget with a large deficit. In other words, even conservative politicians have reverted back to the more centrist economic theories developed by John Maynard Keynes when they have no other choice.

It is important to understand, however, that ideology does not fall prey to relativism or to a form unrecognizable from the original version. This is because there are core characteristics, discussed in the preceding chapter, that are unique to each ideology. To return to our example from the American and Canadian nation-building periods, conservative discourses included the dying race discourse to rationalize taking over the land of the Aboriginal peoples. As well, the yellow hordes discourse enabled the White settlers to exclude Chinese laborers from receiving citizenship. Both discourses supported the notion of race-based social stratification that dominated White hegemony in North America and elsewhere. Neither of these discourses is used anymore because they are no longer required. Moreover, liberal sentiments in the general public of both countries would deem such discourses as distasteful and unacceptable. The current discursive formation in support of neoliberalism and neoconservatism includes anti-affirmative action and the poor-are-lazy discourses that work to fuel a White backlash. The Tea Party is a manifestation of this backlash.

Discourse and Resistance to Power

It is crucial that we see discourse as more than ideological manipulation emanating from those in power. Without specifically referring to Foucault, Apple (1989) succinctly states a Foucauldian premise, "[w]herever there is power, there is resistance" (p. 182). In other words, dominant discourses can fail because human beings are also agents capable of changing the conditions under which they live. History is replete with examples of discourses that run counter to the interests of the privileged, sometimes gaining enough currency because of the way they explain material conditions to foster social movements that actually succeed in transforming major segments of society. The gains created out of feminism, anti-racism, and trade unionism – movements that continue to fight against various forms of oppression – attest to this. In short, the dominant discourses are about power; the counterhegemonic discourses are about resistance to power.

It is the elements of various discourses, as part of discursive formations, which are involved in the dynamics of constructing political ideologies. It is often difficult for certain discourses that have the best interests of significant numbers of people to take hold because the dominant ideology influences these same people to perceive the world in ways that work to oppress them. In other words, discourses do not compete as equals. Whereas some are considered to be authoritative, others are quickly marginalized, even by those who might benefit from the ideas contained within them. Roland Barthes "proposed the notion of ideology as the 'naturalization' of the symbolic order" (cited in Zizek, 1994, p. 11). At this point, a more detailed discussion of hegemony will be helpful in explaining this naturalization of the symbolic order. After all, hegemony is the connection between ideology and discourse.

Hegemony

It is often astounding to learn of people who act in ways that are neither in their best interests nor in the best interests of the social groups to which they belong. A few examples will make this statement more concrete. First, there are some teachers in the union to which I used to belong, the British Columbia Teachers' Federation (BCTF), who want the union to disappear, to be replaced by loosely affiliated associations. For another example, during the last two elections in British Columbia, a province in which most populace is considered working class, 58% of the popular vote went to the neoliberal and virulently anti-union B.C. Liberal Party rather than to the pro-labor New Democratic Party. To understand why it is not uncommon to witness people acting with a contradictory consciousness, it is helpful to utilize the Gramscian notion of hegemony.

Hegemony refers to the ideal representation of the interests of the privileged groups as universal interests, which are accepted by the masses as the natural order. Antonio Gramsci (1971) developed the Marxist conception of hegemony as the principal manner in which social order is maintained within capitalist societies. Force is not required in a society in which the masses freely give their consent to the existing order and social hierarchies, (although the possibility of force is ever present). In the context of British Columbia during the last few election campaigns, a bourgeois or middle-class hegemony permeated almost the entire public space for debate so that even the working classes considered the notion of severe tax cuts as being in their own best interests. The subsequent massive funding cuts in social services, public education, and healthcare, in tandem with a record-breaking deficit and an agenda of privatization, left the masses reeling (Beers, 2005). Once again, it is clear that there are material consequences to these ideological struggles. Understanding the role of hegemony can explain how situations like this occur.

The effects of hegemony are so difficult to combat because hegemony itself "constitutes the limit of commonsense for most people" (Williams, cited in Apple, 2004, p. 4). In other words, hegemony shapes how people view life itself through organizing values, rituals, and meaning. Further, hegemonic discourses can eventually become self-fulfilling prophecies. Returning once again to the historical example of Europeans settling in Canada, imperialism required that White people take the land away from the Aboriginal peoples. Discourses on capitalism, Christianity, and White supremacy formed a rationalizing discursive formation to aid in this theft. Smallpox wreaked death and destruction upon the original inhabitants of the land. The White settlers saw these peoples as inferior and treated them accordingly. After some time, this oppressive process led to increased dysfunction in Aboriginal communities, reinforcing notions of European superiority and the racial hierarchies that emanated from them.

Consider the following example that demonstrates the media's role in promoting these discourses of White supremacy from the middle of the nineteenth century. In 1861, future B.C. premier Amor de Cosmos, formerly named William Smith, summed up the growing racist sentiments of the colonists toward Aboriginal people in an editorial he wrote in the British Colonist newspaper:

> Shall we allow a few vagrants to prevent forever industrious settlers from settling on the unoccupied lands? Not at all ... Locate reservations for them on which to earn their own living, and if they trespass on White settlers punish them severely. A few lessons would enable them to form a correct estimation of their own inferiority. (cited in Barman, 1991, p. 153)

With the help of the newspapers, racist conservatives put increasing pressure on the colonial government to pass legislation to segregate Aboriginal peoples from the "more respectable" all-White Christian neighborhoods (p. 110). A few years later the colonial government in British Columbia forced Aboriginal peoples to live on tiny reserves. Even a century and a half ago the role of the media was very powerful in promoting certain discourses that eventually result in material changes for various groups of people. The case will be made in Chapter 8 that in order to develop an informed and participatory citizenry, critical media literacy in high school social studies is required.

Giroux (1981) describes this form of hegemony, which he and others term "cultural hegemony," as "the successful attempt of a dominant class to utilize its control over the resources of the state and civil society, particularly through the use of the mass media and the educational system, to establish its views of the world as all inclusive and universal" (p. 23). Indeed, both Giroux and Apple (2004, p. 5) interpret hegemony mostly around issues of social class, or how one class consciously imposes its values on another class. As the historical example in the previous paragraph indicates, however, it is the same dynamic at work with race relations, as well.

In Gramscian terms, Giroux is claiming that the state operates in a much broader framework than what is commonly thought of as the public sphere, namely, the government, political parties, and the military. The state, according to Gramsci, also includes the private sphere of civil society, including church, the media, and of great significance for this project, public education (Gramsci, 1971, p. 261). The state can be seen as a social relation in much the same way that Foucault conceptualized power. Rather than thinking of the state as a distinct institutional category, it is more profound to think of it as a form of social relations that enables capitalism and other dominant discourses to find expression. This broader conception of the state also allows for a better understanding of the hegemonic devices employed in the service of maintaining the status quo.

Gramsci noted that the success of the hegemonic function of the state depends on the "organic intellectuals," a group composed of educators, journalists, and experts within various fields. These organic intellectuals play a hegemonic role in the way that they can control and further entrench certain discourses that support the dominant ideology. In short, their role is to manufacture consent. Yet, this group is not a monolithic entity sharing exactly the same views. This is where hope resides.

Counterhegemonic Discourses

It is possible to destabilize the dominant role of the organic intellectual. In particular, the role of the autonomous educator offers promise for counterhegemonic discourses to develop and effect positive change. Counterhegemony includes the notion that, for example, a working-class culture with its own values and norms would arise to confront bourgeois hegemony. Of course, a counterhegemonic movement can also struggle against White supremacist hegemony, patriarchal hegemony, or heteronormativity. The organic intellectuals who promote counterhegemonic discourses might hold down any job, from within the trade union movement to community work and, especially pertinent to this book, to the high school social studies teacher.

Before Gramsci's time, much Marxist discourse involved the notion of a false consciousness, or the idea that many people adhere to one or more political ideologies, whether or not they are able to articulate it, that does not work in their best interest. False consciousness attempts to explain why some people, for instance, the working classes, consider themselves to be politically conscious and yet vote against their best interests. Working-class votes for the Bush administration in the 2004 election serve as an excellent example of a false political consciousness.

Gramsci, however, preferred the idea of a contradictory consciousness, which, according to Giroux (1981), means that "human beings view the world from a perspective that contains both hegemonic forms of thinking and modes of critical insight" (p. 25). Jean Anyon (1981) developed a theory of contradictory consciousness in a slightly different manner. She postulates that most people are influenced by a consciousness that is made up of a practical component and a theoretical component. The practical component involves the "everyday attempts to resolve the class, race, gender and other contradictions one faces" (p. 126). In other words, it is about how people understand the system to work. Theoretical consciousness, on the other hand, is mostly developed by ideologues of the dominant political ideology in a manner that attempts to thwart serious dissent through the use of an array of hegemonic devices. An example of this is evident in contemporary corporate media outlets around the labeling of conservative values as American values, and liberal values as elitist or un-American.

For a significant number of people, the practical and the theoretical do not sit well with each other. This undoubtedly occurs for some workers who have been downsized, hard-working, and long-serving employees who have been laid off because of something out of their control such as technological innovations, corporate mergers, or free trade agreements. The blame-the-victim discourse that has become commonplace in North American media outlets in the past 20 years or more must conflict with the practical realities of this newly unemployed individual. This contradictory consciousness may allow for counterhegemonic discourses to find resonance in their new way of seeing the world.

There is another way of explaining the formation of a contradictory consciousness. It is probably the case that significant percentages of exploited populations in western countries today believe in some version of the economics within capitalism. There are two basic reasons why these groups hold onto these values and political ideas: first, simply trying to survive, as with much of the working classes; and second, attempting to enjoy themselves as consumers within capitalism. Looking at public education, a critical left teacher may see a contradictory consciousness as an opportunity to develop a counterhegemonic discourse. For example, I have found that the anti-consumerist philosophy found in the popular Vancouver-based *Adbusters* magazine, used in tandem with the Canadian documentary *The Corporation*,[2] can provide the resources for effective lessons that help students question consumerism from the perspective of an environmentalist or a sweat-shop worker. Students can have the opportunity to deconstruct the extremely powerful pro-capitalist discourse at the same time that they understand the enjoyment they may experience from living within a capitalist society. Students can weigh the pros and cons, realize the contradictions involved in such a lifestyle, and decide to make changes if they are moved to do so.

Yet, Tony Whitson (1991) makes a key point about counterhegemonic efforts:

> The concept of hegemony would be superfluous if it meant nothing more than domination through the combined effects of diverse ideological and coercive factors. The essential and unique contribution of hegemony is its revelation of how the program of dominant groups is advanced, not simply by excluding oppositional programs, but by locating the opposition

within the total ideological and sociopolitical structure in places where the opposition may
be harmless or even supporting to the structure's viability. (pp. 78–79)

Whitson is warning those who critique the dominant relations that simply to offer
a counterhegemonic discourse may not be enough. Capitalism has proven time and
again that it has the capability of co-opting oppositional forms. Moreover, capitalism
might lead other oppositional forms to places where they support the system they are
trying to change. In the 2000 American presidential election, the emergence of the
Green Party led to an extremely close race that allowed the Florida Supreme Court to
essentially hand over the presidency to George W. Bush. Indeed, ultra-conservative
corporate media outlets such as Fox News were not an obstacle to the growth of the
Ralph Nader-led Green Party in 2000 for precisely the reasons Whitson suggests.

Bearing Whitson's point of caution in mind, I still see a vital role for public education to be a site of fostering counterhegemonic discourse. The social reproduction
theorists, such as Samuel Bowles and Herbert Gintis (1976), postulated that the
schools were the main instrument used by the state to ensure that the factories and
offices had enough workers and managers. If they were proven to be correct in their
essentially determinist view of the school as a site of social class reproduction, then
there would be little point in writing this book. Many scholars have since dismissed
much of the work of the reproduction theorists because it is too deterministic and
precludes the possibility of agency in the form of progressive and influential counterhegemonic discourses, in schools and elsewhere. I still find that the main thesis
of the reproduction theorists to hold some merit, however.

The notion of hegemony can be further developed by incorporating human
agency into the dynamics of ideological manipulation. Critical left teachers who
manage to find the space in the curriculum to deconstruct hegemonic discourses are
examples of such agency. Apple's (2004) assertion that "wherever there is power,
there is resistance" is evident throughout the American and Canadian public school
system.

As a veteran teacher, I have experienced teachers and students working together
to create and develop counterhegemonic discourses that serve to undermine or destabilize the dominant economic and social relations. In other words, there is room in
the classroom to help manufacture dissent rather than consent. It helps to have a
politically conscious teacher, of course. Yet, it is also helpful to have more than a
few students in the classroom who are able to reflect on their own social location
in the myriad social hierarchies that they must navigate through. In particular, the
second half of Chapter 8 describes such a classroom.

Social Positionality and Life Experiences

A person's experience is a major factor influencing the perspective they develop for
looking out at the world. Each individual's social positionality is extremely influential in the way a person views gender relations, race relations, and relations of
social class, as well as other forms of social relations. Indeed, an argument can

easily be made that social positionality is at the base of what a person experiences, and is, therefore, extremely important in determining how certain discourses, either hegemonic or counterhegemonic ones, are received.

My use of the term *positionality* involves the idea that people from differing social backgrounds often have different ways of perceiving the world, constructing knowledge, and making meaning. In other words, each individual's social positionality is influenced by the social groups to which they belong, either by birth or by choice. A person's experience is central to their positionality, and vice versa. As well, one's positionality is always in relation to others. In other words, a person's experience combines with other attributes, either ascribed or socially constructed, to create their *shifting* positionality. In my own case, I have learned to reflect on my own social positionality and how this has influenced what I have experienced in my life, and how I see the world. In the research projects I have been involved with, I have had to contend with certain biases that may at least be the result of my social positionality. For example, I must be aware of the influence that being a veteran, White, middle-aged male teacher researching the perspectives of other veteran White male teachers either a few years older or a few years younger than me has on the data itself. As many have said before, what is the relationship between the word and the world? Would another researcher's social positionality affect what data is collected and how it is analyzed? These same questions are applicable to the classroom teacher. Teachers should pay attention to these different ways of knowing. A teacher's beliefs, values, and interests shape the topics they select, the questions they ask, and even the assessment tools they use. Most importantly, they can affect attitudes toward the students and expectations of their academic performance.

Political ideologies affect the ways that I see and act in the world, of course. Moreover, my own social positionality undoubtedly leaves certain traces upon any text I produce, a process Edward Said (1978) so eloquently described in *Orientalism*. How I teach any topic in any of the social studies courses I have taught has been shaped by the values I hold onto, values that are from the ideologies that have influenced me. But why do some ideologies directly influence me while others do not? It is difficult to speculate as to why, but one thing for certain is that my own experience has been a factor. In fact, reflecting on one's own experience, especially in terms of social relations, is extremely helpful in understanding the binary of privilege and oppression.

In any society there are social hierarchies that to varying degrees involve the categories of gender, race, ethnicity, social class, religion, sexuality, age, and ability. You may have considered such factors in your own education when the teacher was emphasizing an individual's identity construction. In the field of cultural studies, the phrase *social positionality* is used to connote the degree of privilege or oppression one experiences because of the connection to each of these categories. In this way it becomes a more powerful analytic tool than identity construction. Let's look a little closer at why a person's social positionality is so important.

In a patriarchal society, males have more social power than females. In Eurocentric societies, White people, in general, have more social power and privilege than non-White people. In capitalist societies, the upper and upper middle

classes enjoy much more power than other people do – in fact, their power extends to
social, economic, and political matters. In every social studies course I have taught,
either at the high school level or in Teacher Education programs, the first assignment the students are required to do is one in which they reflect on their own social
positionality. It makes teaching all of the other concepts – such as hegemony, discourse, and ideology – so much easier. The next section, which describes my own
social positionality in some detail, is an example of what I require from the students
in teacher education programs.

Locating Oneself in Our Racial Relations: Some Personal Reflections

I grew up in the east end of Toronto in a neighborhood filled with working-class
European immigrants displaced by the Second World War and many working-class
White Canadians who often resented our presence. Yet, despite these tensions, I was
fortunate to be part of a generation who enjoyed the benefits of the social welfare
state, including sufficiently funded public education and public healthcare systems.
My experience as the child of working-class immigrants living in a social welfare
state was positive and clearly beneficial for me. I am concerned with the current
trend toward privatization because I fear others from similar or less privileged backgrounds will not have the opportunities I had. Consequently, I am a social democrat
and tend to see the world through a progressive lens. Although I am a liberal on
social issues, I feel that social democracy is better suited to contend with poverty in
North America.

I still recall learning in my all-White sixth grade classroom about the history of
slavery in the United States. (It is noteworthy that we were not taught about the
legal institution of slavery in Canada's past, even though it was part of the Canadian
economic system until a quarter century before it ended in the United States) From
what we were taught, it seemed only a matter of time before racism would be completely eradicated from the few places where it still might exist, places far away
from Toronto like Texas, Alabama, and Georgia. This is how naïve we sixth graders
were. I do not blame myself for this myopic view; nor do I blame the teachers. After
all, their consciousness was also a result of their own schooling.

Yet, somehow young Canadians were led to believe that our society was morally
superior to all other nations, including our neighbors to the south. Indeed, this
has been a strategy of the Canadian state since confederation in 1867 (Mackey,
2002). Students across Canada found the resistance to the American Civil Rights
Movement repugnant in the extreme, as did many teachers. Throughout my entire
schooling from kindergarten to grade 13,[3] I was never made aware that the Canadian
government had forced Aboriginal families to "give" their children to authorities in
residential schools, a racist policy that led to much psychological, physical, and sexual abuse among the young students at the hands of their teachers. What is even more
disturbing is that I had graduated from high school in 1975, yet the last residential

schools for Aboriginal children in Canada did not close until the 1980s. Omitting this part of the Canadian past and present from the school curriculum enabled young non-Aboriginal Canadians to go about their day thinking that Canada was a near perfect nation. This is an example of employing omission as a hegemonic strategy.

Growing up in an almost all-White urban metropolis like Toronto was during my childhood was another factor in my naivety around issues of race and racism. We simply did not know anything about it. Of course, being the son of immigrant parents with an obviously eastern European name led me to be the brunt of some "Polack" jokes. It has only been in recent years that I have come to understand where I was situated in terms of the ethnic hierarchies operating in Canada during that period. Being of Polish descent automatically placed me below the White Anglo-Saxon Protestants, a group that dominated positions of economic, social, and political power throughout most of Canada's history. These ethnic tensions gave way to more overtly racist ones when the largest Canadian cities – Toronto, Montreal, and Vancouver – became the destination of peoples from various parts of the world, especially Asia, Africa, and the Caribbean.

In "There Is No 'Race' in the Schoolyard: Color-Blind Ideology in an (Almost) All-White School", Amanda Lewis (2001) found that most of the teachers and parents she interviewed in an American Midwestern city felt quite strongly that the school curriculum did not need to incorporate any forms of multicultural education. As one parent put it, "I'm very strongly into 'we're in America, now be an American" (p. 794). My own schooling was very much the same, except "Canadian" was substituted for "American," of course. Yet, this color-blind discourse was ineffective when Toronto's racial demographic went through a massive shift in the 1980s. Today, there are around half a million Black people living in Canada's largest city, mostly from the Caribbean islands, as well as myriad peoples from parts of Asia. The newspapers are filled with articles about racial tensions, especially between the non-White residents and the police. Indeed, in 2008 the Toronto School Board passed a motion emanating from the Black communities to build an all-Black school in the hope of helping Black students succeed academically without the hindrance of systemic racism holding them back (Rushowy, 2008). It is not difficult to extrapolate from my own experience in Toronto that the parents and teachers in the Lewis study were incorrect to assume that their children in the almost all-White neighborhood did not need a multicultural education. Many of these students will undoubtedly come into contact with people from other races through work and sports, and other routes, as well.

Indeed, because of my school experience, I was completely unaware of the privileges that my status as a White person, albeit one from a less than desirable background, gave me that were not granted to my fellow non-White Canadians. This is the hegemonic function of situating *whiteness* as the hegemonic norm, a concept that will be discussed more fully in Chapter 5. Yet, my whiteness is not the only variable that influenced my identity construction.

In the past twenty years or so, I have become aware of the erosion of public institutions, and have often heard the mantra touted in today's daily newspapers that the solution is either to privatize or to develop private-public partnerships, that an infusion of corporate money will help slow down the dismantling of the social welfare state. To me, this is nothing but a Faustian agreement; as such, I dismiss these P3s, as they have come to be called, as yet another way for shareholders to benefit from tax dollars, a policy to which I am politically opposed. After all, the gap between the wealthy and the poor has been steadily increasing since neoliberal discourses rose to prominence in the 1980s in Canada and the United States. The massive bail-out packages for the American financial industry in 2008 and 2009 I find particularly distasteful – after all, it was this same industry that collaborated with various federal administrations to deregulate it in the first place (Weissman & Donahue, 2009).

In terms of social justice, I believe that the Enlightenment with its liberal principles of equality and universal emancipation are noble goals that denoted a profound shift in European consciousness. Yet, I agree with Marx that classic liberalism and neoliberalism are incapable of delivering on their promises. (The increasingly unequal distribution of wealth in Canada and the United States can lead me to no other conclusion.) But liberalism has been successful in one extremely important aspect of North American life, namely, social inclusion and, by corollary, tolerance for difference. Because of the entrenchment of the liberal ideology within the Canadian mainstream, cultural struggles have been fairly successful for certain social groups. Indeed, liberalism has informed my own social views around difference.

I agree with those contemporary conservatives who claim that liberalism is incapable of solving today's social problems. Yet, I completely disagree with their reasoning. The current blame-the-victim discourse I find inaccurate and quite repugnant. Nor do I believe that there was once a mythic period of bliss in North America that was ruined by feminists, trade unionists, civil rights, and visible minorities. Discourses on privatization and tax cuts are surprisingly effective in getting the support of those who are harmed by such policies. In order for the tide to turn against these regressive measures, counterhegemonic discourses must find a way into the public's collective consciousness. Because the Canadian corporate media has moved so far to the right of mainstream public thought (Martin, 2003), I contend that it is left to teachers in the public school system to help develop these counterhegemonic discourses.

As a veteran teacher, I feel I have experienced some success in helping students reflect upon their worlds in critical ways, especially around race, class, gender, and sexuality issues. The social studies courses I teach are based in an ideological critique of our society, both past and present. Yet, as Leonardo points out (2004), "[i]deology critique is not merely criticism" (p. 14). My focus is on helping to facilitate student learning of "the ways that capitalism discourages, at the structural level, a materialist analysis of social life" (p. 14). Ideology critique, media literacy, and other ways of deconstructing hegemonic discourses are pedagogical strategies I employ.

Students are expected to understand the ideological positions posited by conservatives, liberals, and the critical left on both the social scale and the economic scale. As well, they are expected to do a series of assignments and engage in discussions that highlight the inevitable tensions and contradictions within a capitalist, demo-cratic society. My pedagogical goal is to "assist students not only in becoming comfortable with criticism [of society], but adept at it" (Leonardo, 2004, p. 12). In my teaching experience, this has proven to be the best vehicle to enable students in my classes to become informed about current political debates, knowledgeable about the insidiousness of power, and aware of what is in their own best interests. This type of education holds great transformative potential, as I will describe in Chapter 8. At the least, it seems to me that many students in courses I have taught undergo a transformation along these lines.

I know that I am not alone in believing in the capacity of public education to make it a better world for everyone. Indeed, John Dewey and early Social Reconstructionists such as Harold Rugg and George Counts have left some sort of progressive legacy in public education circles, even in British Columbia. Their vision, like mine, is a utopian vision, but one that I feel is worth striving for.

For Reflection

Describe your own social positionality. Use some or all of the following categories: race, ethnicity, gender, social class, religion, sexuality, and nationality. Reflect upon how your social positionality has influenced your values around economic and social issues.

Questions to Ponder

1. Deconstruct the following discourse used by former President George W. Bush: "If you are not with us, you are with the terrorists." Who benefits from the accep-tance of this discourse? Which groups lose from acceptance of this discourse? Explain.
2. In March 2003, the United States led a military alliance in the invasion of Iraq. Try to recall the discourses used before and after the invasion that justified both the invasion and the occupation after the Iraqi government was overthrown. Use the Internet to help you recall these discourses, if need be. When taken together, do these discourses constitute a discursive formation? Explain.
3. Can you think of any other discursive formations in American politics, either in the social, economic, or military realms, that the public has endured over the past decade? Explain.

Notes

1. A crucial omission in this story is that significant percentages of Aboriginal peoples were dying, in some communities with a fatality rate of over 60%, because of a smallpox epidemic caused by contact with White settlers. See Campbell, Menzies, and Peacock (2003).

2. See www.adbusters.org and www.thecorporation.com.
3. The Ontario high school system went to grade 13 until 2003. It is now in line with almost all other jurisdictions in Canada and the United States with graduation occurring with the successful completion of grade 12.

References

Anyon, J. (1981). Elementary schooling and distinctions of social class. *Interchange, 12*(1), 118–132.

Apple, M. W. (1989). *Teachers & texts: A political economy of class & gender relations in education*. New York: Routledge.

Apple, M. W. (2004). *Ideology and curriculum* (3rd ed.). New York: Routledge-Falmer.

Barman, J. (1991). *The west beyond the west: A history of British Columbia*. Toronto: University of Toronto Press.

Beers, D. (2005). *Liberalized: The Tyee report on British Columbia under Gordon Campbell's Liberals*. Vancouver: New Star Books.

Bowles, S., & Gintis, H. (1976). *Schooling in capitalist America: Educational reform and the contradictions of economic life*. New York: Basic Books.

Campbell, K., Menzies, C., & Peacock, B. (2003). *BC First Nations studies*. Vancouver: Pacific Educational Press, UBC; Victoria: British Columbia Ministry of Education.

Connell, R. W. (2004). Encounters with structure. *International Journal of Qualitative Studies in Education, 17*(1), 11–28.

Derrida, J. (1978). *Writing & difference*. New York: Routledge.

Fairclough, N. (1989). *Language and power*. London: Longman Group UK Limited.

Foucault, M. (1970). *The order of things: An archaeology of the human sciences*. New York: Random House.

Foucault, M. (1979). *The history of sexuality, volume one: An introduction*. London: Allen Lane.

Giroux, H. A. (1981). *Ideology, culture, and the process of schooling*. Philadelphia: Temple University Press.

Gramsci, A. (1971). *Selections from the prison notebooks of Antonio Gramsci*. New York: International.

Grossberg, L. (1986). On postmodernism and articulation: An interview with Stuart Hall. *Journal of Communication Inquiry, 10*(2), 45–60.

Harvey, D. (2005). *A brief history of neoliberalism*. Oxford, UK: Oxford University Press.

Lemke, J. L. (1995). *Textual politics: Discourse and social dynamics*. London and Bristol, PA: Taylor & Francis.

Leonardo, Z. (2003). Discourse and critique: Outlines of a post-structural theory of ideology, *Journal of Educational Policy, 18*, 203–214.

Leonardo, Z. (2004). Critical social theory and transformative knowledge: The functions of criticism in quality education. *Educational Researcher, 33*(6), 11–18.

Lewis, A. (2001). There is no "race" in the schoolyard: Color-blind ideology in an (almost) all-White school. *American Educational Research Journal, 38*, 781–811.

Mackey, E. (2002). *The house of difference: Cultural politics and national identity in Canada*. Toronto: University of Toronto Press.

Martin, L. (2003, January 23). It's not Canadians who've gone to the right, just their media. *The Globe & Mail*, p. A8.

Rushowy, K. (2008, January 17). School board to discuss Black-focused schools. *Toronto Star*, p. A1.

Said, E. (1978). *Orientalism*. New York: Random House.

Weissman, R., & Donahue, J. (2009, January/February). Wall Street's best investment: Ten deregulatory steps to financial meltdown. *The Multinational Monitor*. Retrieved on 28 January 2011, from http://www.multinationalmonitor.org

Whitson, A. (1991). Post-structuralist pedagogy: Can we find the baby in the bathwater? *Education and Society, 9*, 73–86.

Zizek, S. (Ed.). (1994). *Mapping ideology*. London: Verso.

Chapter 4
The Purpose of Schooling: Ideology in the Formal and "Enacted" Curriculum

> *Those who tell the stories also hold the power.*
> *(Plato)*

In May 2010, the Governor of Arizona, Jan Brewer, signed a bill banning public schools from offering courses that are designed for students from certain ethnic backgrounds. The Arizona Superintendent of Public Instruction, Tom Horne, a Republican candidate for state Attorney-General, said the bill "was written to target the Chicano, or Mexican American, studies program in the Tucson school system" (Santa Cruz, 2010). According to Horne and other advocates of the bill, the goal was to block any courses that support ethnic solidarity over treating students as individuals. The supposed purpose of this conservative backlash to critical multicultural education is to inhibit teachers from creating resentment among Latino students toward the White majority for past and present injustice. Clearly, these conservatives are very clear about the inherent power in the school curriculum.

Since the early 1990s much has been made in the media about teacher accountability. Indeed, one of the major underlying reasons for state and provincial testing appears to be teacher accountability. There is nothing unethical about holding teachers accountable for the work they do with our children. The unexamined question, however, is: Who exactly should teachers be held accountable to? Should it be the captains of industry? Should it be society itself? Should it be to the dominant groups in society? Or should it be the students themselves?

Teacher Accountability and a Relevant Curriculum

Beginning in the mid-1980s, I taught for 19 years in various high school settings in British Columbia, most of which were in the city of Vancouver. Toward the end of these years, I was forced to accommodate the growing public pressure to hold teachers accountable for what it is they teach. Province-wide testing became more and more the norm, just as state-wide testing had become the norm a few years earlier throughout much of the United States. This shift clearly altered the way teachers focused on teaching the curriculum. Of course, initially I despised this policy of surveillance, but over the years my position has softened somewhat.

It became clear to me that a significant proportion of the general public was buying into the media-driven argument that teachers need to be held accountable, which is part of the neoliberal assault on public education. There was not very much teacher unions could do to counteract this pressure without appearing to be self-serving, especially with the corporate media leading the charge. My position evolved to the point where I begrudgingly accepted the idea of a common curriculum, and that certain important ideas must be covered and then tested across the state or province. But where I differed was to the extent the curriculum was to be so tightly controlled. Perhaps as much as 60% of any high school social studies courses, I argued, should be open to exams set by people working in the Departments or Ministries of Education. The remaining 40% should be used for topics that are relevant to the particular context that most students in that particular classroom find themselves living in. There is little doubt that a curriculum based on local concerns and conditions would prove more interesting to students than other more abstract topics. In other words, 40% of the curriculum should be decided by the profession-als who actually do this work, namely, the teachers. Since the 1990s, however, the professionalism of teachers has been under attack.

There are two reasons for distinguishing between the two sets of knowledge. First, state- or province-wide testing is most effective in testing for recall of facts. By extension, the results of this form of testing are not indicative of *higher order* thinking skills such as synthesis and analysis. Second, leaving a significant percentage of the time in the classroom for the teacher to engage in higher order thinking pedagogy creates space for the teacher and students to immerse into topics that are much more relevant to the students' lives. This means that the common curriculum many conservatives call for contains topics that are mostly irrelevant for students from social backgrounds that are not part of the White middle class.

The discussion around social positionality in the previous chapter points to the various categories involved with these differing social backgrounds. For example, if a classroom is filled with mostly immigrant youth from working-class backgrounds, the teacher would do well by developing pedagogy pertaining to the historical experiences of people from similar backgrounds attempting to get settled in the United States or Canada. From a similar point of view, a teacher who includes the concerns of Canada's first peoples with English-French relations during Canada's nation-building phase will clearly notice an increased interest in their Aboriginal students, and likely many of their classmates, too. This approach incorporates two important techniques for the progressive teacher to employ, namely, *culturally relevant pedagogy* and the *enacted curriculum*.

The notion of culturally relevant pedagogy, most famously developed by Gloria Ladson-Billings (1994, 1995), is crucial to making the school experience meaningful for students. Because of the increased cultural diversity in both nations, calls for a common curriculum put forth by conservatives such as E. D. Hirsch, Jr. (1996) and Diane Ravitch (2000) in the United States and Jack Granatstein (1998) in Canada need to be challenged. The demographics in both societies have changed too much to ever accept reverting back to using a monocultural, Eurocentric curriculum. Moreover, the common curriculum makes it very difficult for the teacher to use the constructivist approach to developing unit and lesson plans. Constructivist pedagogy makes use of the differing experiences of the students in the classroom so that the actual content is more meaningful, and therefore, the learning is at a deeper level and more relevant to the lives of the students.

Making the curriculum relevant for students is the main criteria for creating a space for counterhegemonic discourses to develop. Catherine Cornbleth (1990) emphasizes the importance of choosing relevant topics for the students in any particular sociocultural context:

> Sociocultural context includes demographic, social, political, and economic conditions, traditions and ideologies, and events that actually or potentially influence curriculum. (p. 6)

Cornbleth calls for contemporary and historical conflicts to be brought to the fore in the *enacted* social studies curriculum (p. 34). What Cornbleth calls the enacted curriculum is the pedagogy created out of the interests and passions of the teacher and the interests and passions of the students based on their life experiences and the context in which they live. She states that "curriculum is contextually shaped" and "always mediated by students" (p. 53). Part of what Cornbleth means by *contextually shaped* is the sociocultural aspects of the local population. For example, if most students in a classroom are from the working classes, then the social studies curriculum should reflect this. Any progressive teacher in such a classroom would do wise to include labor struggles, past and present, in the curriculum. Toward the end of this chapter, I will describe some examples of the enacted curriculum in my classrooms that led me to realize the possibilities for hope in emphasizing relevant topics for students that may not be in the formal curriculum.

Culturally relevant pedagogy and the enacted curriculum are two reasons for my contrary position to a common curriculum that supposedly covers everything the student needs to know to do well on a state- or province-wide test. It is next to impossible for curriculum developers to create prescribed learning outcomes that students in diverse cultural and socioeconomic settings will find reflective of their daily experience. Yet, there is one more very important factor.

In response to the conservative call for a common curriculum, I also believe that the so-called golden time for American and Canadian citizens, specifically in the school experience, but also for life in general, to be nothing but a myth. There has never been a perfect time that we should strive to recreate or emulate. My own understanding of the history of schooling in North America suggests that there has always been a gate-keeper role for the school and other institutions to exclude certain groups of people from improving their standard of living. If there is any doubt of the truth in this claim, I suggest discussing this with elders of Aboriginal, African or Asian ancestry. A reading of Howard Zinn's (1980) *A People's History of the United States: 1492 to the Present* will also demonstrate the power of omission as a hegemonic strategy to any American social studies teacher unfamiliar with the struggles along axes of race, class, and gender. In light of my position that perhaps 60% of any social studies curriculum should be open to state-wide examination, even the content of this common curriculum should be negotiated between the various groups.

The quote by Plato at the beginning of this chapter holds true, but the question today that is more relevant is this: who exactly is holding the power today? In the past, there was no question that the educated, White, middle-class, Christian male represented a privileged position in our society, the kind of person who filled most positions of influence in educational policy and curriculum development, as well as myriad other important positions in society. Yet, in recent decades the universal norm has been destabilized in academic circles by scholars developing theories in postmodernism, postcolonialism, feminism, and neo-Marxism. Proponents of the Eurocentric curriculum can argue all they want – despite their efforts, the answer they will get is that it is unlikely that the Eurocentric common curriculum will ever be acceptable again.

Anyone interested in the state of public education has to wonder about the veracity of these struggles. Why do so many people get up in arms about what goes into the curriculum? Some historical context will help shed some light on this.

The Struggle over the Curriculum: A Brief History

In *The Struggle for the American Curriculum: 1893–1958*, Herbert Kliebard (1986), an American historian of education, describes four different positions toward the American school curriculum during the late nineteenth and early twentieth centuries. First, there were the *humanists* who believed that all children, regardless of background, should have an equal opportunity to develop an appreciation for the best of what western civilization has to offer. Second, there were the *developmentalists* who pushed for the streaming of students so that society would not waste any extra effort on the "great army of incapables", as one proponent put it. Third, a group Kliebard calls the *efficiency educators* wanted standardized curriculum and a business model to run the school system, a position that resonates with what conservatives are calling for today. Fourth, the *social meliorists* were against the Social Darwinist philosophy entering the school system via streaming. As it has turned out, for well over a century, Americans have struggled over tensions around egalitarianism, the needs of the individual and the needs of the society at large.

The situation was not very different in Canada, as the following quote indicates:

> The school promoters of the late nineteenth and early twentieth centuries were clear that schools were needed as much for political as educational reasons. The curriculum had to be shaped, textbooks written, teachers trained and inspected, and children compelled to attend school, in order to preserve or create a particular social order. (Osborne, 1995, p. 16)

It is clear that there are many who viewed what goes into the curriculum and the purpose of schooling to go hand in hand. Moreover, it is evident that in both countries, the school was viewed as an instrument to "create a particular social order," as Osborne contends.

John Dewey, the noted American philosopher of education, waded into the curriculum wars being fought by the four groups Kliebard describes. Dewey sought to take the best from the humanists and the developmentalists and forge a new philosophy of education, one that acknowledged individual rights and supported increased life chances for all in combination with the notion of the common good: "For Dewey, then, a curriculum built around fundamental social occupations would provide the bridge that would harmonize individual and social ends – what for him was the central problem to be resolved in any educational theory" (Kliebard, 1986, p. 61). A curriculum developed along these parameters would respect the needs and interests of the child, a position favored by the developmentalists, with the liberal educational aims of the humanists. This complex arrangement would lead to each child becoming part of "a miniature community, an embryonic society" (p. 68).

Political ideology was at the root of these tensions, as well. Struggles centered around who was to be included in the privileged sectors of society and who was to be excluded. During this era, John Dewey's educational philosophy was the most inclusive. Yet, since the Reagan era of the 1980s, Dewey's influence on education has been under attack. The conservative agenda often points to Dewey's theories of progressive education as the cause for almost all the ills befalling our schools today (Hirsch, 1996). Many blame Dewey for the loss of a common curriculum. Of course, such positions are in keeping with the traditional conservative view toward schooling.

Ideology and the Purpose of Schools: Then and Now

The early conservative view toward schooling was focused on placing each student on a path that fit with their station in life, which was ascribed at birth. The push for tracking, sometimes called streaming, espoused by Kliebard's developmentalists, is an example of this sort of conservative view toward schooling. Females, especially from the working classes, were encouraged to take domestic science or home economics courses. Working-class males were slotted into shop and trades courses. Of course, non-White people often had to contend with segregated schools, and in the case of Aboriginal students, residential schools that attempted to erase their cultures. Traditional conservatism emphasized the maintenance of social hierarchies along axes of race, class, and gender in order to maintain social cohesion. This focus enabled the school to work for the advancement of students who belonged to groups inside the power nexus, and work against those students who were outside of it.

As the liberal ideology gained strength in both countries after the Second World War, conservatives had to adopt some liberal discourses in education. One of these is *meritocracy*, which posits that each student will arrive at their natural station in life through their intelligence, talents, and work ethic. Conservatives have accepted meritocracy from the more individual-oriented liberal ideology. The reason for this shift was most likely because of more progressive attitudes toward people from marginalized groups across Western nations. The school could no longer overtly work against students who belonged to groups mostly excluded from the mainstream. Consequently, and this is an important point, exclusion had to occur in a more covert manner.

Conservatives accept student tracking as a most efficient way of placing students on paths that they perceive to be headed toward their likely end goal in terms of employment. As mentioned above, working-class boys deemed unlikely to become part of a profession, were slotted into trades courses; similarly, working-class girls went into the domestic sciences.[1] The decisions around which students go into these less academic streams underscore the gate-keeper role that school personnel have in society. These decisions most often have the effect of masking and perpetuating social and economic inequalities.

Society's acceptance of the discourse of meritocracy as truth and the practice of tracking should not be surprising when one considers the demographics of students streamed into less academic programs. These students are most often from immigrant and poor families (Oakes, 2005; Kelly, 1993; James, 1990); after leaving school, they are also more likely to become members of the working class (Curtis, Livingstone, & Smaller, 1992). It is clear that adopting meritocracy in the contemporary context is an effective way to maintain the conservative desire for social hierarchy. As Oakes (2005) points out, the practice of streaming or tracking structures societal inequality because most modified school programs are filled with students from economically and socially marginalized families. I spent several years teaching in alternative programs in Vancouver and can attest to Oakes' premise from my own experience. Only a small percentage of these students came from middle-class backgrounds.

Liberals also see the role of the school as providing social skills and training for the demands of work. They differ from the conservatives in that they emphasize the importance of the school to ensure equal educational opportunity for each student, regardless of background. This is consistent with the emancipation-of-all discourse in classic liberalism that developed during the Enlightenment. The liberal view toward schooling is that it should level the playing field for each student to succeed in life. Guided by the idea of meritocracy, school personnel differentiate based on ability and effort as to the roles each individual will fill once they have left school. Yet, because of liberalism's focus on the individual, its version of meritocracy ignores the fact that most modified high school programs are filled with students from economically and socially marginalized families. In sum, liberals view public education as the best vehicle for "redressing social inequalities through the equalization of educational opportunity" (Apple, 2004, p. 18). Yet, their focus on the decontextualized individual ignores the ways that power works to privilege students from certain backgrounds while oppressing others. The neoliberal agenda for public education, which will be discussed in Chapter 9, makes use of the "equalization of educational opportunity" discourse to garner support for voucher and charter schools.

Critical left educators, on the other hand, view the liberal notion of "equality of opportunity as an illusion" (Sadovnik, Cookson, & Semel, 1994, p. 9). Whether a conscious political strategy or not, both discourses, equality of opportunity and meritocracy, serve to placate the working classes into thinking that "they have been given a fair chance, when in fact they have not" (p. 9). This is the case regardless of racial background (Oakes, 2005).

Reproduction theory stresses that to a large extent schools have almost always been used to reproduce the unequal social and economic relations endemic to capitalist society (Bowles & Gintis, 1976). Reproduction theory is used to explain, for example, why most working-class students grow up to become members of the working class. Critical resistance theorists (Willis, 1977; Giroux, 1983) have countered that schools are also the sites for agency on the part of students and teachers engaged in counterhegemonic discourse formulation. Often, this requires an alteration of the formal curriculum into the enacted curriculum, which as I said earlier involves the extent to which teachers and students engage with and veer from the course content. Of course, the very idea of a book like this indicates that I position myself with the critical resistance theorists. This position is so much more hopeful than the determinism of reproduction theory.

Typically, critical left educators are against the practice of *tracking*. This stance is because of the association between the practice and the future life chances of students. Tracking serves to more or less entrench students into certain pathways with varying degrees of opportunities. It is important for teachers to remember that, in terms of race and class, less academic streams are most often filled with students from less privileged backgrounds. Most of these students will experience limited life chances because of being tracked into these modified school programs (Oakes, 2005).

The Formal Curriculum and Political Ideology

Recognizing the importance of historical context, Apple (2004) states that the entire field of school curriculum "has its roots in the soil of social control" (p. 47). As mentioned earlier, Osborne (1995) states that the situation is not very different in Canada: the curriculum was immediately seen as an important instrument in the molding of the population. Privileged White people hoped that the masses would accept a set of social relations that granted certain groups, especially themselves, more privilege at the expense of others. In other words, the elites viewed the curriculum to be a powerful hegemonic device. Plato's quote at the beginning of this chapter is once again instructive as to why this is the case. For example, if workers held the power in our society, the formal curriculum would look a lot different than it does today. It would most likely be replete with stories of labor's battles with capitalists rather than an almost total omission of these struggles, as is the case with almost all of the provincial- and state-mandated social studies curricula. Similarly, if non-White people held the reins of power, the curriculum would most surely reflect this. It would undoubtedly be less Eurocentric.

David Tyack and Larry Cuban (1995) claim that one of the biggest impediments to implementing a progressive curriculum in the United States is the long entrenched view that this is not what "real schools" do (p. 88). Osborne (1991) concurs that this is also the case in Canada (p. 80). But should "real schools" be used for social control? Is this a better role for schools and the school curriculum rather than the Dewey prescription of developing critically thinking citizens? Obviously, there are conflicting ideologies here. The position of the critical left is that schools should not be used for purposes of social control. This is understandable, especially if one considers the curriculum to be a microcosm of the clash of cultural values throughout the histories of both the United States and Canada.

As mentioned in Chapter 2, each political ideology socially constructs its own knowledge. By corollary, school knowledge is not objective and value-free either but is a social construction tied to the interests, experiences and perceptions of those who produced and negotiated its meaning. As Ann Manicom states (1995), the school curriculum is "the result of conscious and unconscious ideological choices, exercised within an explicitly political arena and mediated by the state" (p. 51). Stated more bluntly, the official knowledge in the formal curriculum is political and most often serves the interests of those with the power to decide what gets into these documents.

Apple (2004) points out the irony in recalling that during the Cold War it was common to hear the American refrain that communist ideology was embedded in Soviet school curricula; yet, very few bothered to ask how political ideology was influencing American curricula (p. 8). In both societies, it is the selection and organization of knowledge that is most influenced by the dominant political ideologies. Connell (1993) explains how and why the selection and organization of knowledge is hegemonic:

a) it marginalizes other ways of organizing knowledge (and other perspectives)
b) it is integrated with the structure of power in educational institutions (and in society)
c) it occupies the high culture ground, defining most people's common-sense views of what learning ought to be. (p. 38)

Connell calls for the curriculum to be altered to reflect the "standpoint of the least advantaged" (p. 43), or that educational matters be considered from the perspective of the oppressed rather than the privileged. Implementation of such a progressive curriculum, however, would be difficult in the current cultural context. The aforementioned Arizona school legislation passed in 2010 demonstrates the validity of this point.

It is highly unlikely that the elites and their supporters in the media, in government, and in the public education system would allow Connell's perspective to infiltrate the curriculum on a large scale. In fact, long before the Arizona law of 2010, there has been a powerful conservative backlash against progressive educators and social historians, particularly in the United States. American historians Nash, Crabtree & Dunn (1997) attempted to include the voices of marginalized groups in the early 1990s in a national curriculum, unleashing an incredibly vitriolic attack on his own credibility and his "biased agenda" from very powerful conservatives. One of the most outspoken critics of Nash's progressive agenda for high school history was Lynn Cheney, the wife of former American Vice-President, Dick Cheney. Here is a quote that she had published in the Wall Street Journal as the chair of the

National Endowment of the Humanities a few days before the work by Nash and his colleagues was made public:

> Imagine an outline for the teaching of American history in which George Washington makes only a fleeting appearance and is never described as our first president. Or in which the founding of the Sierra Club and the National Organization for Women are considered noteworthy events. (October 20, 1994)

Cheney went even further, inciting American conservatives to block Nash, who she claimed wanted American youth to learn about the Ku Klux Klan and McCarthyism rather than the wonderful accomplishments of (White) Americans (Nash, Crabtree, & Dunn, 1997).

The situation is similar in Canada. In *Who Killed Canadian History?* (1998), Granatstein demands a return to the Eurocentric and pro-British curriculum of the past. Granatstein, the president of the conservative Dominion Institute of Canada, chastises any teacher whose lessons make immigrant children and their families feel bad about the country they worked so hard to live in. Granatstein attacks progressive educators, whom he claims see "history [as] boring, irrelevant, and fit only for the slag heap, except for small nuggets ... useful for current concerns about racism, gender equity, and the plight of native peoples" (p. 26). It is clear that to try to sell the Canadian public on a state-sanctioned curriculum based on social history would be unleashing a conservative backlash much like the American example. At this historical moment, the most that progressive educators can do is find ways to teach for social justice on an individual basis. They must always be wary, however, of conservative colleagues, administrators, parents, and members of the media and the public opposed to those aims.

Apple (2004) claims that "education [is] not a neutral enterprise" (p. 1). By corollary, I contend that the curriculum is not an apolitical or neutral document. Indeed, I maintain that the formal social studies curriculum can be viewed as a set of discourses, or a discursive formation, connected to power. Epistemologically, this notion assumes that knowledge is socially constructed and that school knowledge has a political dimension. This assumption is clearly positioned within the critical left ideology.

Apple's *Ideology and Curriculum* (2004) has been very influential in my work involving deconstruction of the curriculum. Apple's method of relational analyses focuses on the ways in which the content of the school curriculum, seen as official knowledge, supports the economic and political interests of the most powerful people in our society. What gets told, how it is represented, and how everyone else is represented are crucial factors in the social relations of any society. Toward the end of this chapter, historical examples of importance and relevance will be included that will illuminate the power of omission as a hegemonic strategy. Each one of these examples will be focused on race–class intersections.

Yet, before the discussion moves in that direction, a brief but detailed examination of the formal social studies curriculum will make clear what is meant by the ideological influences in a curriculum. Because so much of my own research is based in the British Columbia school experience, the examination will specifically involve the British Columbia Social Studies Curriculum as it has evolved since the 1950s. I encourage readers from other parts of North America to engage in similar studies of the social studies curriculum in their jurisdictions.

Examples of Political Ideology in the B.C. Curriculum

Apple's theory about the relationship between curricular content and economic and political interests is straightforward. Schools do not exist in a social vacuum. They are inextricably linked to the values of the surrounding communities. An example of Apple's theory in a historical context can be seen in the 1956 version of the British Columbia Social Studies Curriculum. By the mid-1950s, both the American and Canadian economies were robust, healthy and growing. Canada's westernmost province was no exception as the B.C. government constructed massive infrastructure projects, especially in transportation and hydroelectricity (Barman, 1991). As concerns of a crashing economy subsided, so did fears of a Bolshevik revolution. The senior level high school course of the late 1950s, History 91, was filled with learning objectives that reflect a decreasing influence of the conservative ideology on the curriculum: the legalization of trade unions, social security programs, and even cooperatives were included in the prescribed learning outcomes. Significantly, however, and consistent with the liberal ideology, the conflict between labor and capital, so much a part of British Columbia's history, does not appear at all. The learning objectives are worded in such a way that a student might be inclined to believe that the legalization of trade unions, for instance, came about out of the benevolence of capitalists and right-wing provincial governments rather than out of intense struggle.

The resistance posed by B.C.'s working classes has most often been led by its critical left elements articulating the need for the capitalist system to be reformed or even destroyed in order for social justice aims to be realized (Leier, 1990; Palmer, 1992). This was clearly the situation during the first half of the twentieth century. Speculation leads me to conclude that the 1956 curriculum developers consciously omitted any historical or current references to the critical left ideology or its proponents. Society would not benefit, they might have surmised, if students learned about these class struggles. Or perhaps they thought that the captains of industry would not gain very much from such a curriculum. It is also noteworthy, of course, that this curriculum was published at the height of the Cold War.

A liberal school curriculum is less overt in the way social relations are presented. From the discussion in Chapter 2, it is clear that the individual is the main social unit of the liberal ideology. It should not be surprising, therefore, that a liberal-influenced social studies curriculum would focus on the individual rather than on any notion that hints at our social interdependence. As Apple (2004) states, the curriculum "does not situate the life of the individual, as an economic and social being, back into the unequal structural relations that produced the comfort the individual enjoys" (p. 10). If we can assume that the curriculum does, indeed, influence society, then this aspect of the curriculum can only help to create a legion of individual consumers who despise the social redistributive aspects of progressive taxation. Moreover, we are not able to clearly see how our comforts are produced, or who is producing them. Consequently, we get situations of race–class intersections in which White nativist angst is aroused around the issue of illegal immigrants (Archibold, 2010), especially in the United States, who work at low-wage jobs, sometimes even in sweatshop conditions. By rendering the connection between material production and consumption invisible, unethical aspects of capitalism also remain hidden. In this way, the liberal-influenced curriculum acts as a hegemonic device.

Liberals claim that there is a level playing field in the school system and that every child has equal access for educational opportunity. Yet, their focus on the decontextualized individual ignores the way that power works to privilege students from certain backgrounds while oppressing others. The liberal focus on meritocracy leads them to believe that the school system has led each student to their role in life once they leave school in a fair manner. Although I did not know the word, I was raised in Toronto believing that meritocracy was a fair and equitable system. But I was not a female, nor was I a visible minority, and this undoubtedly influenced my perspective on what was fair.

A social studies curriculum influenced by a critical left political ideology is rarely seen in North American public education systems. If we assume that Althusser (1971) was correct in labeling the school as part of the ideological state apparatus, this situation is understandable, especially from the standpoint of the privileged. That said, it is still possible to articulate what a critical left social studies curriculum might look like. If, for instance, North American history is taught as a series of conflicts between social groups, a better understanding of our present tensions and hostilities throughout the entire population would result. As Gerald Graf (1994) states, "[w]hen a country is little known, fabulous and monstrous tales readily circulate about it" (p. 4). A near absence of the history of labor struggles and class antagonisms, such as how the liberal curriculum looks, puts all the gains made by the struggles of working-class people in jeopardy. Not surprisingly, both Canadians and Americans are currently experiencing a concerted attack on the vestiges of the social welfare state. We can only speculate about how much more difficult this would be for today's economic elites if most people were aware of past struggles. A social studies curriculum designed from the standpoint of the critical left would rectify this omission. For example, it would have to include the benefits to each group under various taxation schemes.

In order for such a social studies curriculum to be accepted and implemented, however, large segments of society must recognize the legitimacy of the numerous social struggles. Protest and civil disobedience have been productive avenues of dissent in the history of both countries. Yet, conservative and right-liberal elements do not support the idea of schools teaching about these struggles. It is ironic that the mainstream media considers race, class, gender, and sexuality conflicts to be legitimate topics for popular culture and public hearings to address. These same media outlets, however, will produce catastrophic visions and help to create a public backlash should the public school social studies curriculum attempt to address similar topics. As mentioned above, part of the problem is the commonly held belief that the role of the school is not for these purposes. This belief has become so widespread because of vested interests in maintaining the status quo. A critical left curriculum would go far to help sway the public in understanding how power is involved even in the dissemination of views around the role of the school in general and the curriculum in particular.

In Chapter 3, I discussed the power of discourse, or how power is entrenched in the language and ideas emphasized by organic intellectuals often made up of educators, media pundits, and politicians. In this chapter, the discussion has focused on the purpose of schooling and the formal curriculum itself. At this point, the focus of the discussion shifts to resistance to the hegemonic strategy of omission.

The Enacted Curriculum and Race–Class Intersections

The discussion on ideology and the curriculum has thus far emphasized a few general facts: first, those who hold the power tell the stories; second, the knowledge included in the curriculum is socially constructed; third, the entire document is imbued with power. As well, I have stated the potential for counterhegemonic discourses to become part of the enacted curriculum. Freire (1970), Ladson-Billings (1994, 1995) and Cornbleth (1990) contend that it is important for the curriculum to be relevant to the students so that the learning that takes place resonates with their day-to-day experience. In this section, I would like to give three examples of several race–class intersections in American and Canadian history that are not in the formal curriculum in any state or province. Yet, in terms of the enacted curriculum, students find them very enlightening as to how the past influences the present.

Example 1: The Ludlow Massacre

Several years ago I heard the late social historian Howard Zinn recount his surprise when he listened to a Woody Guthrie song describing an event in American history referred to as the Ludlow Massacre. What surprised him was that despite several years studying history in high school and at university, he had never heard of this event, one that Zinn considers to be particularly important in understanding worker exploitation and in illuminating the alliance within privileged circles to brutally suppress nonviolent dissent. One interesting aspect to this sad and tragic event was that it occurred with the U.S. government using the military to protect corporate profits on American soil.

In April 1914, the murder of a coal miner union organizer led to 11,000 miners in southern Colorado going on strike. They were employees of the Colorado Fuel & Iron Corporation, which was owned by the Rockefeller family, and most were born in Greece, Italy, and Serbia. The strike was against "low pay, dangerous conditions, and feudal domination of their lives in towns completely controlled by the mining companies" (Zinn, 2003, p. 72).

The chain of events of led to the actual massacre of men, women, and children included the arrest of union organizer and a powerful voice for social justice, Mother Jones. As well, after the miners were evicted from their homes they set up a tent colony in the nearby hills, prompting hired gunmen to use Gatling guns and rifles on the tents, killing many miners in the process. The Colorado governor called on the National Guard to help quell the situation.[2] At first, the miners cheered the arrival of the Guard, thinking they had been called to protect the miners and their families from the hired guns. They quickly discovered that the Guard was there to protect the interests of the mine owners, especially after many miners were beaten and arrested.

The stalemate included the Guard bringing in strikebreakers, inviting a leader of the miners into their camp to discuss a truce only to be murdered, and the tragic climax – torch-carrying Guardsmen going into the miners' camp and setting their tents on fire, resulting in eleven children and two women being burned alive. Workers from the United Garment Workers Union, the Denver Cigar Makers Union, and other miner unions went to the site of the murders to lend support. The *New York Times* responded with an editorial that said, "With the deadliest weapons of civilization in the hands of savage-minded men, there can be no telling to what lengths the war in Colorado will go unless it is quelled by force" (Zinn, 2003, p. 75). Woodrow Wilson complied with the request from the media to take action against the miners and sent federal troops to end the miners' resistance, a resistance that resulted in the deaths of 66 miners and their families, and not one militiaman or mine guard being indicted.

The Ludlow Massacre illuminates the vulnerability of workers, especially those from cultures not considered desirable, in countries perceived to be progressive such as the United States and Canada. Moreover, it casts a light on the alliance between the various levels of government, the military, the capitalists, and their mainstream media outlets, an alliance formed to protect the massive profits of the capitalist class over the human and working rights of laborers. It also highlights the very effective strategy of hiding the partnerships between capital and the state apparatus. After all, Professor Zinn learned of the Ludlow Massacre not from one of the many books he had read or from myriad history classes he had taken, but from a song by the folksinger Woody Guthrie. The questions that progressive educators should speculate upon are these: What effect does keeping such knowledge from the public have on their sense of patriotism, on their class consciousness, on their respect for government and related institutions? Why are tragic events kept out of sight from American citizens? In this situation, do the ends justify the means? Why?

Example 2: Exploiting White Working-Class Racism in B.C.'s Coal Mines and Beyond

In English Canada, migrant labor was specifically used for nation-building purposes, as well as for "the consolidation of political and economic power by the Anglo-Saxons and Scots" (Ng, 1993, p. 55). When British Columbia joined Confederation in 1871, one of the conditions politicians in British Columbia demanded from their federal counterparts in Ottawa was the construction of a railway across the country. Despite protests from British Columbians, the federal government allowed migrant laborers from China to be brought to Canada in order to complete this "herculean" task (Tan & Roy, 1985, p. 7). Ng (1993) has described the indentured labor system that resulted in thousands of Chinese men being brought to Canada to build the railway system in the 1870s and 1880s, a project that would enable the new Canadian nation to expand from the Atlantic to the Pacific. In order to maintain White hegemony in Canada, the Chinese men were forbidden to bring their wives or children. Moreover, they were not allowed to engage in "sexual relations with White women, for fear of spreading the 'yellow menace' " (p. 56). In that era, White authorities on both sides of the 49th parallel approved of anti-miscegenation sentiments.

Anti-Asian sentiments, however, were especially strong in British Columbia (Barman, 1991). White laborers in particular feared for their own economic well-being by competing against Chinese laborers. Yet, some capitalists were aware that profits could be significantly increased by pitting one race or ethnic group against another. For instance, the extremely virulent anti-unionist Robert Dunsmuir ran most of the coal mines on Vancouver Island in the 1870s with his sons. He was also adeptly opportunistic in exploiting White working-class racism. According to Barman (1991):

> The Dunsmuirs' total concern with profit extended to their treatment of employees ... Dunsmuir & Sons sought workers least likely to rock the boat. Chinese were hired at the lowest possible wages ... Knowing no English, newcomers could not communicate with other employees to fight against poor working conditions. (p. 121)

One example of the Dunsmuir attitude to profit by exploitation will illuminate the complex tensions between the White (mainly) British capitalists and the different groups making up the working class. According to labor historian Bryan Palmer (1992), when the Chinese miners tried to improve their situation through collective action, they received no support from their White colleagues (p. 123). Moreover, when management demanded increased productivity, the White miners decided to use the Chinese as "beasts of burden" to increase their own pay checks. This arrangement, which was nothing short of a Faustian agreement between White labor and White capital, was doomed to be temporary.

As class conflict between these unlikely bed fellows erupted in the mines during the late 1870s, Dunsmuir hired the Chinese to do the bulk of the mining. This relentless drive for profit resulted in the Chinese being branded as scabs, a label that had the effect of fragmenting worker solidarity for over half a century in British Columbia. The Dunsmuirs continued to exploit White racism and Chinese economic need by increasing the number of Chinese miners each time the White miners attempted work stoppages throughout the 1880s. In 1883, the Knights of Labor came to the B.C. mines to help stop the Chinese workers from doing "White man's work," invoking what David Roediger (1999) and others refer to as a *herrenvolk* labor system, which was common in antebellum America (p. 94). Fortunately for the Dunsmuirs, the discourse of White supremacy seemed to blind White labor groups to class concerns.[3]

Even as the trade union movement grew across Canada during this period, most White workers were opposed to Chinese memberships in the unions. White labor blamed the Chinese workers for their decreasing standard of living rather than put the blame where it belonged, namely, on White capital. (This same dynamic, rooted in an attitude of White defensiveness, exists in contemporary British Columbia.) When Robert Dunsmuir's son James became the premier of British Columbia in 1900, "his mines continued to maintain their justly deserved reputation as the most dangerous in the world, with a death rate of three to four times that of elsewhere in the British Empire" (Barman, 1991, p. 122).

An estimated 15,000 to 17,000 Chinese came to British Columbia from either China or San Francisco between 1881 and 1884 (Barman, 1991, p. 107; Tan & Roy, 1985, p. 7). Most came to do the dangerous work of building the Canadian Pacific Railway. When it was finally completed in 1885, connecting British Columbia to the rest of Canada, the railway immediately became the great symbol of national pride. Yet, it is sadly ironic that the people who labored to make the railway a reality, with significant numbers dying in the process, became the victims of racist legislation almost from the day the railway was completed. The discourse of White supremacy aided in the passing of legislation that would force Chinese immigrants to pay a head tax as they arrived in Canada. Those Chinese workers who re-entered the labor market with the completion of the railway in the mid-1880s had to contend with the Knights of Labor, whose "history on the west coast is . . . interwoven with a racist working-class attack on Oriental workers" (Palmer, 1992, p. 124). The appearance of a different labor group in British Columbia caused an even bigger ruckus, however, especially among the owners of big business.

In the year 1906, B.C. capitalists got a serious scare: the Industrial Workers of the World (IWW), sometimes called the Wobblies or One Big Union, moved up from Chicago and became active in British Columbia. According to historian Mark Leier, the IWW "fought for immediate improvements in working conditions and organized visible minorities and recent immigrants, women, and 'unskilled' workers" (in Laut, 1913/2003, p. iii). This was the first significant appearance of the socialist ideology in British Columbia. Moreover, the IWW seemed to be an extreme threat because of the radical insight they had developed – that race should not be an issue in who can join a union – thereby negating the most effective strategy capitalists in British Columbia had for increasing profit margins.

This ideological clash between conservatism and socialism was not taken lightly by the capitalists. IWW members practiced nonviolent civil disobedience; the B.C. government responded by removing the strikers at rifle point (Laut, 1913, p. 31), putting many away in the "overflowing prisons." According to Leier another common scenario was "[w]hen workers resisted, capitalists hired thugs or had the government send in the police to smash strikes and heads" (in Laut, 1913/2003, p. vi). Even the middle class in British Columbia was becoming concerned at the presence of the growing working class. After all, the workers "did not share its ethnicity, race, views or mores" (p. vii).

Support for the crushing of the Wobblies came from eastern Canadian capitalists and its pro-British middle class, both groups being terrified at the prospect of losing power to an organization led by "uneducated" eastern Europeans who also spoke of the rights of Asians, Aboriginals, and Blacks. After the IWW led a strike of 8,000 railway workers in 1912, the capitalists used all their power, including hegemonic instruments such as the media and the school, in tandem with the physical force of the police and strike-breaking "thugs," to stamp out this radical threat that attempted to join the working classes across race and ethnicity (Leier in Laut, 2003). Shortly thereafter, the IWW and its progressive agenda for class over race had all but disappeared in British Columbia.

The pedagogy I employ around this historical event inevitably results in the students coming to see how working-class racism works against their own interests. Students come to the understanding that a class consciousness is beneficial in being able to withstand potential exploitation. If I have time, I often have linked this B.C.-based narrative to similar situations in the contemporary context. For instance, students are asked for their thoughts on why unions are not as strong or as popular in areas Where white supremacist attitudes are more prevalent, such as in the American South.

Example 3: Women's Rights Across Space and Time: A Race–Class–Gender Intersection

Despite the grandiose sound of the name of this example, I only want to describe some pedagogy I have tried on several occasions in high school social studies courses I have taught.

Classrooms in east Vancouver are very multicultural, as they are in many cities in Canada and the United States. Students in my classroom have been from diverse cultural backgrounds such as Salvadorean, Vietnamese, Serbian, Iraqi, Ethiopian, Indian, Chinese, and Chilean, often at the same time. One assignment that I have the students engage in is for them to interview women from different generations on the different roles of females in the family.

The students ask their grandmother, their mother, or a sister in their immediate family a series of questions designed to inquire about the changing role of women in the family structure. Those students who do not have a grandmother, a mother, or a sister to interview fulfill this requirement by asking a female family member from the same generation as the missing member such as a great aunt or an aunt or cousin. The inevitable analysis leads to a very similar conclusion, namely, that over time the roles of women have increased quite significantly. The most striking differences occur for families who have moved to Canada from countries with conservative views toward women. It becomes apparent that most countries are far less liberal than Canada in views toward women. Even families who have come from western European countries or the United States, or those families who have spent several generations in Canada, have experienced an increase in a more liberal view toward women over time. As well, all of the students come to see that women today are able to strive for much more variety in terms of employment. They learn that although in general men still make more money, women today often have a larger income than in the past.

One of the benefits from this assignment is that students come to see the dynamic nature of cultures and that roles and values seemingly written in stone are influenced by outside factors at play in the society in which they live. Views toward women have become more liberal in the twentieth century, especially with the burgeoning feminist movement that began in the 1960s. Yet, another benefit for students often occurs. Comments I receive from the parents on Parents Night or from the students themselves indicate that many of the mothers and grandmothers are pleasantly surprised by the interest the students show in their lives. I often wonder if this assignment plants seeds that helps the students respect their elders for the experiences they have endured and the wisdom that comes from these experiences. This is mere speculation, of course, but the awareness that comes from understanding how time and space are integral to the dynamism of culture, especially around the issue they have explored, is unmistakably real.

These three examples are indicative of the limitless possibilities of what a teacher can do to help students understand the dynamic nature of culture. Students come to understand the epistemological underpinnings of knowledge, and by corollary, the social construction of racial, class, and gender relations. Social hierarchies that seemed inevitable, universal, and essentialist are seen to be what they are, namely, exercises in power that work to privilege some groups at the expense of others. The enacted curriculum, especially when based in culturally relevant pedagogy, can be very powerful in deconstructing hegemonic attitudes. It has been my experience as a teacher educator that focusing on the possibilities of the enacted curriculum offers preservice social studies teachers an exciting source of optimism. Moreover, the high school students themselves come to appreciate social studies a lot more than if the teacher sticks to the formal curriculum, oblivious to the experiences and concerns of the students and their families.

Questions to Ponder

1. The movement in support of teacher accountability has influenced the current trend toward state- and province-wide testing. How has this trend affected the ability of teachers to engage in an enacted curriculum that seeks to uncover structures that govern social relations of race, class, and gender?
2. Kliebard and Osborne claim that throughout the history of public education in the United States and Canada the school and the curriculum have been used for purposes of social control.

   (a) Do you think this is true of the school social studies curriculum today? Explain.
   (b) Discuss the pros and cons of using the curriculum for this purpose.

3. If the social studies curriculum included labor struggles within capitalism, what effect do you think this might have on society in general? What about if it included struggles around Aboriginal rights?
4. During federal election campaigns, the media is often filled with concerns around immigration and employment. This often results in tensions arising between various racial and ethnic groups, rather than tensions between the social classes.

   (a) How do you think the teacher could best deconstruct the tension between immigrants and people born in the United States or Canada?
   (b) Do you think that a citizenry with class awareness would result in less tension between racial and ethnic groups? Why?

5. During the first half of the twentieth century, the International Workers of the World, also known as the IWW or The Wobblies, made a serious attempt to unite all workers regardless of race, gender, religion, etc. (See Zinn, 2003, pp. 41–52.) They were active in both the United States and Canada. Why do you think such an important and progressive movement is not part of the school curriculum?
6. On September 2, 1885, in the present-day city of Rock Springs, Wyoming, in Sweetwater County, a violent confrontation occurred along racial lines. This event is known among certain labor historians as the *Rock Springs Massacre*. The riot between Chinese immigrant miners and White, mostly immigrant, miners was the result of racial tensions and an ongoing labor dispute over the Union Pacific Coal Department's policy of paying Chinese miners lower wages than White miners. When the rioting ended, at least 28 Chinese miners were dead and 15 were wounded. Rioters burned 75 Chinese homes resulting in approximately US$ 150,000 in property damage. It is noteworthy that tensions between White and Chinese immigrants in the late nineteenth century American West were particularly high, especially in the decade preceding the violence. The massacre in Rock Springs was the result of years of an anti-"coolie" discourse prevalent in many parts of western United States. In the immediate aftermath of the riot, federal troops were deployed in Rock Springs. They escorted the surviving Chinese miners, most of whom had fled to Evanston, Wyoming, back to Rock Springs one week after the riot. Reaction came swiftly from the newspapers of the day. In Rock Springs, the local newspaper endorsed the bloody outcome of the riot, while in other Wyoming newspapers, support for the riot was limited to sympathy for the causes of the White miners. The massacre in Rock Springs touched off a wave of anti-Chinese violence, especially in the Puget Sound area of Washington Territory.

   (a) Discuss the role of the media in exacerbating racial tensions among the working classes of Rock Springs, Wyoming. What purpose does it serve to highlight racial tensions rather than the working conditions that all of the coal miners had to contend with?
   (b) Does the corporate media engage in similar strategies today? If so, what are some examples?

Notes

1. A study in the United Kingdom (Dunne & Gazeley, 2008) found that teachers' identification of underachieving students overlapped with, and were informed by, their tacit understanding of the students' social class background. This was the case even though most of the teachers in the study wanted to "abdicate agency in the construction of educational and social hierarchies" (p. 460).
2. The wages of the National Guard were paid for by the Rockefellers.
3. The power in the discourse of White supremacy has ironically been the main obstacle to advancing the rights of workers, both White and non-White, in the American South today. The trade union movement has had difficulty gaining traction in this region.

References

Althusser, L. (1971). Ideology and ideological state apparatuses. In P. Bourdieu & J. P. Passeron (Eds.), *Lenin and philosophy and other essays* (pp. 127–186). New York: Monthly Review Press.

Apple, M. W. (2004). *Ideology and curriculum* (3rd ed.). New York: Routledge-Falmer.

Archibold, R. C. (2010, April 23). Arizona enacts stringent law on immigration. *The New York Times*. Retrieved on 9 February 2011, from http://www.nytimes.com/2010/04/24/us/politics/24immig.html

Barman, J. (1991). *The west beyond the west: A history of British Columbia*. Toronto: University of Toronto Press.

Bowles, S., & Gintis, H. (1976). *Schooling in capitalist America: Educational reform and the contradictions of economic life*. New York: Basic Books.

Connell, R. W. (1993). *Schools and social justice*. Toronto: Our Schools Our Selves Educational Foundation.

Cornbleth, C. (1990). *Curriculum in context*. London: The Falmer Press.

Curtis, B., Livingstone, D. W., & Smaller, H. (1992). So many people: Ways of seeing class differences in schooling. In B. Curtis, D. W. Livingstone & H. Smaller (Eds.), *Stacking the deck: The streaming of working-class kids in Ontario schools* (pp. 6–25). Toronto: Our Schools Our Selves Educational Foundation.

Dunne, M., & Gazeley, L. (2008, September). Teachers, social class and underachievement. *British Journal of Sociology of Education, 29*, 451–463.

Freire, P. (1970). *Pedagogy of the oppressed*. New York: Seabury.

Giroux, H. A. (1983). Theories of reproduction and resistance in the new sociology of education: A critical analysis. *Harvard Educational Review, 53*, 257–293.

Graf, G. (1994). Beyond the culture wars: How teaching the conflicts can revitalize American education. In W. E. Cain (Ed.), *Teaching the conflicts: Gerald Graf, curricular reform, and the culture wars* (pp. 3–16). New York: Taylor & Francis.

Granatstein, J. L. (1998). *Who killed Canadian history?* Toronto: HarperCollins.

Hirsch, E. D. (1996). *The schools we need and why we don't have them*. New York: Doubleday.

James, C. E. (1990). *Making it: Black youth, racism and career aspirations in a big city*. Oakville, ON: Mosaic Press.

Kelly, D. M. (1993). *Last chance high: How girls and boys drop in and out of alternative schools*. New Haven, CT: Yale University Press.

Kliebard, H. (1986). *The struggle for the American curriculum: 1893–1958*. New York: Routledge & Kegan Paul.

Ladson-Billings, G. (1994). *The dreamkeepers: Successful teachers of African American children*. San Francisco: Jossey Bass.

Ladson-Billings, G. (1995). Toward a culturally relevant pedagogy. *American Education Research Journal, 32*, 465–491.

Laut, A. (1913/2003). *Am I my brother's keeper? A study of British Columbia's labor & Oriental problems*. Reprinted by M. Leier (Ed.), (2003). Vancouver: Subway.

Leier, M. (1990). *Where the Fraser river flows: The industrial workers of the world in British Columbia*. Vancouver: New Star Books.

Manicom, A. (1995). What's health got to do with it? Class, gender, and teacher's work. In M. Campbell & A. Manicom (Eds.), *Knowledge, experience, and ruling relations* (pp. 135–148). Toronto: University of Toronto Press.

Nash, G. B., Crabtree, C., & Dunn, R. (1997). *History on trial: Culture wars and the teaching of the past*. New York: Alfred A. Knopf.

Ng, R. (1993). Racism, sexism, and nation-building in Canada. In C. McCarthy & W. Crichlow (Eds.), *Race, identity, and representation in education* (pp. 50–59). New York: Routledge.

Oakes, J. (2005). *Keeping track: How schools structure inequality* (2nd ed.). New Haven: Yale University Press.

Osborne, K. (1991). *Teaching for democratic citizenship*. Montreal: Our Schools/Our Selves Education Foundation.

Osborne, K. (1995). *In defense of history: Teaching the past and the meaning of democratic citizenship*. Toronto: Our Schools/Our Selves Press.

Palmer, B. (1992). *Working-class experience: Rethinking the history of Canadian labour, 1800–1991*. Toronto: McClelland & Stewart.

Ravitch, D. (2000). *Left back: A century of failed school reform*. New York: Simon & Schuster.

Roediger, D. R. (1999). *The wages of whiteness: Race and the making of the American working class* (rev. ed.). New York: Verso.

Sadovnik, A. R., Cookson, P. W., & Semel, S. F. (1994). Perspectives in education: Conservative, liberal, and radical visions. In A. R. Sadovnik, P. W. Cookson & S. F. Semel (Eds.), *Exploring education* (pp. 21–37). Toronto: Allyn and Bacon.

Santa Cruz, N. (2010, May 12). Arizona bill targeting ethnic studies signed into law. *The Los Angeles Times*. Retrieved on 29 January 2011, from http://articles.latimes.com/2010/may/12/nation/la-na-ethnic-studies-20100512

Tan, J., & Roy, P. E. (1985). *The Chinese in Canada*. Ottawa: Canadian Historical Association.

Tyack, D., & Cuban, L. (1995). *Tinkering toward utopia: A century of public school reform*. Cambridge, MA: Harvard University Press.

Willis, P. (1977). *Learning to labour: How working-class kids get working-class jobs*. New York: Columbia University Press.

Zinn, H. (1980). *A people's history of the United States: 1492 – Present*. New York: HarperCollins.

Zinn, H. (2003). *The twentieth century*. New York: HarperCollins Publishers.

Part II
Less Theory, More Applications and Practice: Deconstructing Racial and Class Discourses for a Stronger Democracy

Chapter 5
Teaching About Race and Racism in Our Past and Present

As a naïve child growing up in the east end of Toronto during the 1960s, I lived under the delusion that racism was on the verge of being a thing of the past, that before too long it would be something that would be discussed in historical terms only. To be sure, at times I was the recipient of an Anglo-Saxon peer yelling "You Polack" in the schoolyard, and some of my Italian friends were sometimes referred to in derogatory terms based on their ancestry. At that time, Toronto was almost completely a city made up of European Canadians. Yet, no matter which European country we claimed as our heritage, we were all in the same classroom, learning the same Eurocentric curriculum, trying out for the same sports teams, and more or less being influenced by the same trends in pop culture. To me, racism did not seem to be a part of the Canadian experience, because it didn't resemble anything like the racism we heard about in the American South. After all, these were the years in which the American Civil Rights movement led by Dr. Martin Luther King dominated much of the news we were getting.

Now, after four more decades of life experience, I look back with embarrassment at my naivety toward the ideology of racism and how it operates, how it always changes its form and level of intensity as social conditions change. Of course, the Toronto of my youth only faintly resembles what it has become today. There is no question that the racial and ethnic makeup of Toronto and Vancouver, as well as many other large cities in Canada and the United States, has been drastically altered in recent years, as they transform from centers of Western society into multicultural postmodern Meccas. At the same time, the American and Canadian economies have also rapidly changed, mainly because of the neoliberal agenda of globalization and increased corporate power, and mainly affecting the working classes.

Of course, there is a reason why I was so oblivious to issues of race and racism. I am White, and as I mentioned, the neighborhoods of my youth were filled almost completely with White residents. In fact, I had never even met an Aboriginal person, a Muslim or a Jew until I went to university in Ottawa in the late 1970s. And although in high school I had been made aware of the Nazi Holocaust, I had not been taught how Israel came to be in 1948 in a region that had previously been called Palestine. No teacher ever made mention of the Canadian government's residential school policy that resulted in the forced attendance of Aboriginal children in schools designed to engage in destroying their traditional cultures. Moreover, this policy that

P. Orlowski, *Teaching About Hegemony*, Explorations of Educational Purpose 17,
DOI 10.1007/978-94-007-1418-2_5, © Springer Science+Business Media B.V. 2011

began in the 1870s was still in effect while I went to high school, with the last one closing in the 1980s! None of my teachers ever mentioned any of these things.

In retrospect, it is clear that the curriculum developers had engaged in omission as a hegemonic strategy. Not one of the teachers in my own schooling had ever led me to question the ethical dimensions of empire and the effects of colonization. In short, because of its expected role of maintaining traditional racial hierarchies, the school had failed to properly educate me so that I would develop into a critically thinking citizen able to contend with complex issues of race. The journey I undertook to become aware of historical and contemporary racial injustice took place in spite of the schooling I had received.

Forms of Racism: A Narrative of a Teacher/Educational Researcher

Several years ago, in my role as a teacher in an east end Vancouver working-class high school, I was walking across the campus when a grade 12 student, unaware of my presence, yelled out to some grade 8 students of East Asian ancestry, "Go home, ya immigrants!" The subsequent conversation he and I had did nothing to quell the disturbing feelings I had when he first demonstrated his racial prejudice. This student was quite strident in his opinions of East Asian people living in Vancouver, namely, that they were taking potential jobs away from Caucasian people like him, jobs rightfully belonging to him and others like him so that they might enjoy a higher standard of living.

As it turned out, many White, working-class youth were feeling threatened by the proximity of so many Asian people. Indeed, many were worried about their futures, both economically and socially. The common response was to accept the values and political ideology of a populist right-wing social and political movement, one that has since gained power in both the United States and Canada. Witness the rapid growth of the so-called Tea Party movement in the United States in 2010. To a very large extent, this conservative movement is being fueled by an attitude of *White defensiveness*.

For several months after this disconcerting event at the high school, I pondered how to address this growing phenomenon of White defensiveness, both in my teaching and in my thesis question. (I was about to embark on the research for the thesis as the last requirement for a Master's of Arts degree at the University of British Columbia.) A couple of months later, while I was walking along Commercial Drive in Vancouver's east end, I came across some unique graffiti on the side of a brick wall that read: *Class War, Not Race War!* – the proverbial light bulb immediately went on in my mind. It did not take long for me to formulate a question that would lead to some understanding of the intersections between issues of race and social class. This question was: How do working-class youth perceive racist attitudes and economic inequality?

The subsequent research resulted in a critical ethnographic study examining the ways 25 working-class youth from five different racial groups perceived racism and economic inequality (Orlowski, 2001). The most interesting finding from this research, and one that has profoundly shaped the way I teach all of my courses, is that *all of the racist attitudes that surfaced during the study were rooted in economic concerns*. Although the Aboriginal participants exhibited a more sophisticated understanding of the forms of racism, and the adolescents of East Indian ancestry could speak to the unfair labor practices inherent in capitalism, there was clearly a lack of class awareness among almost all of them.[1] To a large degree, it appears that the salience of social class issues is a factor in working-class racism.

What is often not understood in the general public is that there are many forms of racism, and that over time racism often evolves from one form into another. This is especially the case if the social conditions change. The example of the older student calling the younger students a derogatory term based on their Asian ancestry to their faces is an example of *overt* racism. This form is a highly personal, deliberate attack on members of groups perceived as culturally or biologically inferior. I have found that this form often disappears once the perpetrator becomes an adult, but it often does not mean that the person no longer holds racist attitudes.

It is clear to most people living in the United States and Canada that racism is no longer acceptable. Consequently, the ubiquitous overt racism of the past is much less frequent today, replaced by a much more *covert* form, which is either a deliberate or unconscious attempt to hide one's racist attitudes. For example, a parent who is unhappy that their child's new teacher is of Asian ancestry may request that their child be moved into another class without being upfront about the reason. A landlord in need of tenants may tell prospective tenants that the suite has been filled when it is still available – but it is unacceptable to tell the tenants that the reason for not renting to them is their race. While I was a teacher in an east Vancouver high school, a grade 12 student of Chinese descent who had lived in California and British Columbia told me that, in general, White Canadians are more inclined to hide their racist attitudes when compared to White Americans. It is noteworthy that she preferred having to contend with overt racism because she at least knew where she stood with the perpetrators.

Another form of racism that has been almost completely expunged from American and Canadian society is called *institutional* – this refers to racist laws passed by the state. Aboriginal children forced to attend residential boarding schools throughout much of the twentieth century was an obvious example, as were the laws around the slavery and segregation of Black people. Shortly after World War II, Western nations tried to eradicate racist laws, although the Jim Crow laws of the American South remained in effect until 1965. As well, a case can be made that the state-sanctioned social studies curriculum that emanates from a Eurocentric perspective is an example of subtle institutional racism. Over the years, I have been privy to many comments made by non-White students that the curriculum ignores the history and cultures of any people who do not have European ancestry. By the same token, most White teachers I have spoken with emphasize the importance of a one-size-fits-all curriculum.[2]

The fourth form of racism, *systemic* racism, often influences social relations long after racist legislation has been abolished. Systemic racism refers to attitudes that work to discriminate against a person because of their race. For example, there is little doubt that once the segregation laws were repealed, very few White parents in Alabama would want their daughter or son to marry a Black person. It is one thing for a society to abolish racist laws; it is another thing altogether to rid a person of racist attitudes. I have been in countless discussions over the years with White students who maintain that there are no more excuses for people of Aboriginal or African ancestry who complain about unfair situations. Most of these students can understand how racist laws were unfair. The problem is that they cannot see how the legacies of longstanding racist laws still influence social relations today; nor can they comprehend the power of systemic racism.

During the data collection for one of my studies, I heard many comments from the working-class adolescent participants that made me aware of just how pervasive systemic racism is today. Aboriginal students who had lived in rural British Columbia were unanimous in their claims that they had encountered White teachers who held anti-Aboriginal sentiments. The effects of systemic racism have even turned some Aboriginal people's attitudes against their own people, resulting in a form of *internalized colonialism* (see Fanon, 1952, 1967). For example, I recall one Aboriginal student who said his mother had taught him that it is a person's own fault if they get caught up in substance abuse and end up on the streets. This student had inherited this conservative attitude from his mother: he spoke in a condescending manner toward all Aboriginal people who have drug- and alcohol-related problems.

Sometimes systemic racism can be part of a seemingly benign situation. For example, the color-blind discourse that positions *whiteness* as the hegemonic norm is one example of how a non-White person's social circumstances, such as living in extreme poverty, can work against them going to a post-secondary institution for more education. As well, poverty can structure social relations away from the school. An Aboriginal female adolescent shared this with me during an interview about race and class concerns:

> Aboriginal Student #1: It's not that I choose my friends because they are Native. It just happens to work out that way. I meet a lot of people, but when it comes right down to it, I can't relate to so many of them. You know, sometimes I'm scared cuz I don't know how they're gonna react. I mean, I'm Native ... It's not like I'm ashamed but ... (hesitates) ... when it comes right down to it, we all know what we've gone through, what our families have gone through ... I can't even remember the last time I had somebody other than a Native come over to my house. I wouldn't know what to talk about. I don't know where they're coming from. I don't know how they feel.

> Paul: You don't know how they feel about what?

> Aboriginal Student #1: About a lot of things! When I go to work there are some people who say, "Your people are this and that." And I'll have to defend them, you know. I can't always explain why there are so many Natives living down on skid row. I don't want to explain it! So why should I invite them into my home?

This heart-felt reflection indicates the pain experienced by many Aboriginal people because of systemic racism and an ignorance of our colonial past. It is the responsibility of educators to help develop counterhegemonic discourses to alleviate the pain. After all, ever since Europeans settled the Americas Aboriginal people have suffered immensely because of racism.

At times, however, discriminatory actions can occur from the seemingly benign intentions of teachers. Consider the following description that a female Aboriginal grade-12 student gave of the time that a possibly well-meaning math teacher moved her from regular Math 8 into the modified Math 8 class.

> Aboriginal Student #2: I had a lot of teachers at [my former high school] who felt sorry for me because they thought I was poor. And I didn't like it. I didn't like the way . . . well, they didn't treat me badly, but they treated me differently from everybody else . . . In my math class, in grade 8, I kept to myself and I didn't get my work done all the time. That's why they put me into modified math. They didn't really give me a chance. They didn't want to get to know me. They just felt sorry for me. They thought I was stupid and slow. They didn't want to deal with me. The math teacher, actually he was pretty nice, but he told me it was going to be better for me in modified, and the next thing I knew that's where I was.

This excerpt helps to explain how well-intentioned teachers can still play into the dynamics of systemic racism and inadvertently work toward maintaining White hegemony and Aboriginal oppression. The student was removed from the regular math course and placed into a "modified math" course, which is less demanding, and therefore less likely to get her into any university program. This is an example of *tracking* or *streaming*. There is much research that suggests teachers' expectations is a crucial factor in determining the academic performances of students (Dunne & Gazeley, 2008; Orlowski, 2008; Leroy & Symes, 2001).

A Few Words About Race and Racism in the Context of North America

The United States and Canada are clearly among the world's most culturally diverse countries. Yet, both are historically rooted in colonial projects that resulted in vastly different life experiences for people. The degree to which a person was granted a life of privilege or one of oppression depended on which side of the colonial divide one was born into. For example, Aboriginal people in both countries experienced institutional racism that kept them from striving for a better standard of living. Laws that forbade them from owning businesses and private property, as well as the residential school policies that resulted in young children being taken from their parents by force, destabilize the notion of universal progress that took place during the nation-building phases of both countries. Despite the protestations of conservative critics, the legacies of these divisions live on today.

The notion of *race* is fraught with complications and challenges, including blurred racial boundaries and persuasive arguments that race is but a social construction. Yet, no one can deny the existence of racism. A significant number of people, however, articulate overt racism as the only form they are aware of. This is especially the case with people of European ancestry. There is a tendency for many people to personalize racism – they fail to see is as systemic or institutional (Orlowski, 2001). This interpretation of a few bad racist apples has the effect of leaving these other forms of racism unchallenged, thus maintaining current hegemony around race relations.

Growing up in Toronto, I was completely unaware that my status as a White person, albeit one from a less than desirable ethnic background, gave me many privileges not granted to my fellow non-White Canadians. This is the hegemonic function of situating whiteness as the invisible norm. In both Canada and the United States, most teachers are White (Orlowski, 2008; Juarez, Smith, & Hayes, 2008). Therefore, a few words about whiteness will be helpful for teachers to ponder how it has shaped their own lives.

Ruth Frankenberg (1993) postulated three dimensions of whiteness: first, whiteness is a social location of "structural advantage" and "race privilege"; second, it is a "standpoint" from which White people view themselves and the Other in society; third, whiteness is a "set of cultural practices" in the dominant culture that is unmarked and, therefore, is the invisible norm. Indeed, my conception of the dominant culture is influenced by Raymond Williams (1980), who contends that in "any society, in any period, there is a central system of practices, meanings, and values, which we can properly call dominant and effective" (p. 38). These meanings and values, then, become part of everyday social relations. Social studies teachers, as members of the dominant society, are also likely recipients of the practices, meanings, and values of the dominant culture.

The concept of whiteness structures so much of sociocultural relations in Canada, from the way minorities are portrayed in the media to the ways that educators view non-White students and teach history.[3] This understanding has certainly influenced my own teaching and research, including what I required for the writing of this book. An awareness of how whiteness is embedded in our dominant culture will help teachers convey the associated privileges to students. Of course, the powers that control what goes into the curriculum may not want students to learn about the unequal playing field. The legislation passed by the state of Arizona in 2010 attests to this. In May of that year, the governor of Arizona, Jan Brewer, signed a bill that further entrenched whiteness into the K-12 school curriculum (Santa Cruz, 2010).

Let's assume, however, that there are many educational jurisdictions that are more progressive than what the legislators in Arizona in 2010 appear to be. As well, we know that there are many autonomous progressive teachers who may disrupt the hegemony of whiteness. It is in this spirit that this discussion will continue to describe the various discourses about race in the history of both the United States and Canada. An awareness of the history of hegemonic racial discourses will lead to an understanding of why so many people overlook the more insidious forms of racism. Moreover, an awareness of these discourses offers powerful pedagogy for the teacher to help students understand present-day sociocultural relations in both the United States and Canada.

An Introduction to Racial Discourses

In *White Women, Race Matters: The Social Construction of Whiteness* (1993), Frankenberg describes the three competing discourses on issues of race and ethnicity in North America since the late 1700s. When utilized en masse, each of these discourses works to either further entrench or destabilize the dominant view toward people of other races or ethnicities. Frankenberg calls these three discourses essentialist, color-blind, and race-cognizance.

The following sections describing these various discourses will include analyses of the formal state-sanctioned social studies curriculum with excerpts of interview transcripts with veteran social studies teachers and brief anecdotes from my teaching experience. Both the curriculum and the teachers are situated in British Columbia. It is my assumption that the evolving representation of minorities and the discourses used in the social studies curriculum to justify the status quo underwent a similar timeline in most provinces and states across the continent. Moreover, the ways in which the B.C. teachers think about issues of race and social class are unlikely to be significantly different from how teachers in other places view these important issues.

The Essentialist Discourse in Social Studies

The first discourse in Frankenberg's taxonomy, which she refers to as essentialist, ascribes an overall superiority to a race because of a supposed biological birthright. Ever since the European imperialist agenda formed, essentialist racial hierarchies developed that positioned Europeans on top of all other racial groups. This was clearly the mainstream hegemonic discourse in North America as it underwent a process that transformed it from the land of the Aboriginal peoples into British colonies and then into the newly formed nations of the United States and Canada. As well, White ethnic groups were also positioned in relation to each other – in Canada, the British were almost always atop the others. This discourse influenced European attitudes toward each other and the racially marginalized Other, eventually forming a system of social relations that privileged White people at the expense of everyone else (see Fig. 5.1). The essentialist discourse dominated public debates in Canada throughout the colonial period and its nation-building phase.

The essentialist discourse, steeped in the entrenched social hierarchies of conservatism, justified the theft of Aboriginal peoples' lands and the enslavement of African people, destroying much of these indigenous cultures in the process. According to Frankenberg, there was no reason for a White person to hide racist attitudes during this period because it was in keeping with the norm. In other words, the essentialist discourse had a normalizing and regulating effect that enabled White supremacy to go, for the most part, unchallenged. The effects of this discourse were present everywhere Europeans set out to conquer other people during the empire-building period of European expansionism (Young, 1995; Stoler, 1997).

Europeans with a thirst for empire-building were not the only ones possessing a sense of racial superiority, of course. East Asians also have a racial hierarchy that is used to maintain power relations. A Vietnamese-Canadian female student shared an event that had taken place in Vancouver between her mother, who works as a waitress in a Chinese restaurant, and her Chinese boss.

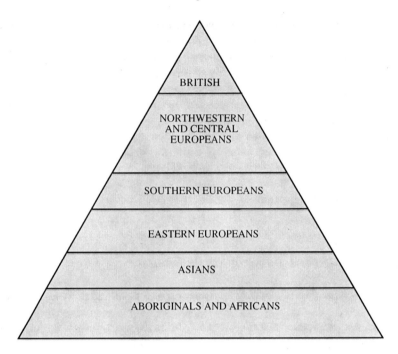

Fig. 5.1   Racial hierarchy during British empire

Vietnamese-Canadian Student: My mother complained to this man about, you know, things
to do with the restaurant, how it could be run in a better way. And do you know what he
said to her? He said, "You are at least five levels below me. You have no right to question
me about these things."

Further discussions with her, and with other students from various east Asian
countries, have made me aware that the racial hierarchy structuring their ethnic relations has to do with material well-being. The people from Hong Kong are positioned
at the top of this hierarchy, followed by people from Taiwan and Singapore, then
people from mainland China, who are followed by the Vietnamese, and lastly, the
Cambodians. However, because this book is focused on social relations in the United
States and Canada, much of the discussions will explore deconstructing the notion
of a racial hierarchy in general, especially one that posits whiteness as the hegemonic norm, as is the case in North America. The school subject that best enables
this deconstruction is, of course, social studies.

In terms of the contemporary social studies curriculum, the vestiges of the
essentialist discourse have all but disappeared. Yet, historically, examples abound.
In British Columbia, the first social studies curriculum was published in 1941.
White supremacy, or more specifically, British supremacy, was an influential discourse throughout this document. Moreover, there are no positive references about
Aboriginal, Asian, or African histories. Once again, the essentialist racial discourse
of traditional European conservatism dominates. This is clearly evident in a unit

devoted entirely to imperialism that includes the following statement: "To show how the more backward peoples of the earth became subject to the more advanced nations" (p. 165). The intention underlying this statement is most likely for students to take in the perspective that imperialism actually brings the Other to a more advanced way of living than what they would have without British or European intervention. It is noteworthy that British colonizers were using the same rationale as southern White slave owners in this regard (see Hale, 1998). Europeans are associated with the notion of progress, while all other cultures are considered to be, at best reified, and at worst, "backward." In other words, the essentialist aspect of the inferior Other was now focused on culture rather than physiology.

The essentialist discourse was related to the racist cultural ranking system developed by Herbert Spencer in the nineteenth century. According to Spencer, every society can be categorized as civilized (e.g., Western Europe), barbaric (e.g., India, China, and Japan), or savage (e.g., Aboriginal and African peoples). This system can still be seen in effect today with the preponderance of the cultural-deficit discourse. Moreover, a case can be made that Social Darwinist attitudes in the United States and Canada are part of the legacy of this cultural ranking system.

The 1956 B.C. Social Studies 10 curriculum includes other examples of the essentialist discourse, albeit from different angles. There is a unit on the British Empire entitled *Great Britain: How and Why She Became Great*, and a unit on Asia is called *Nations of the Far East* (p. 50). The suggested time allotment for students to learn about the British Empire is "7 to 9 weeks" while the unit on Asia is to take only "2 to 3 weeks." The discourse of Christianity appears in a unit entitled Imperialism and New Empires. In a section named the "White man's burden," there is a suggestion for the teacher to refer to the "work of missionaries and the desire of westerners to introduce their civilization to other peoples" (p. 65). Clearly, there is a conservative cultural hierarchy at work here.

In a study in which I was the principal investigator, I explored how veteran social studies teachers thought about issues of race and social class. One may think that the essentialist discourse would not be found in this day and age, but excerpts from the interview transcripts show otherwise. One social studies department head of a middle-class school located in Vancouver's west side answered the question about lower graduation rates among First Nations students by invoking ideas about physiology.

Teacher #1: Maybe [it's] their physiological make-up, the business of alcohol, alcohol abuse, substance abuse. That's another vicious circle and maybe it's something that through their race as it were, physiologically they can't handle alcohol as the others can and this is another ongoing problem. I mean, it's endemic!

This notion that the marginalization of First Nations people has been caused by their own physiology and actions is a classic example of the traditional essentialist racial discourse. By stating that First Nations people do not have the physiology to handle alcohol properly, yet many of them drink in abundance, serves to take the blame away from Canada's White colonizers. This exchange also demonstrates how discourses commonly heard throughout the general public are also used by some teachers.

Another veteran social studies teacher employed at a working-class school in Vancouver's east end made no apologies for his usage of the essentialist discourse, even though it had been expunged from the curriculum a half century earlier. He described the differences in teaching at the east side working-class school, primarily composed of East Asian immigrant students, and a west side upper middle-class school.

Teacher #2: One of the things that happened between my two schools, when it came government exam time with my Geography 12 classes, when I first came here my kids would bail out. "It's too tough. I can't do it. I'm giving up!"

Paul: They'd drop the course just before the exam?

Teacher #2: They wouldn't drop the course. They just wouldn't study . . . So I clued in on that and now it's a constant theme throughout the year. "Listen, don't sell yourself short." That being said, I think, in terms of the gene pool, I've dummied down the courses here.

Paul: You've dummied down the courses from how you taught it at your old (west side) school?

Teacher #2: Yep. I can give the same exam, teach the course the same way. Well, I don't quite teach it the same way because I do more visuals here because so many of the students are ESL. And still, the students here get 10 to 15% less than the students at Greenway. So, is that genetic? Or is that socioeconomic? You can't be politically correct and say it's the gene pool. But I think it is. There's a little bit of that, at least. And also socioeconomic.

Paul: So in terms of the old nature-versus-nurture debate, how exactly would you position yourself?

Teacher #2: I'm saying that I can buy the logistics that it's mainly socioeconomic. But I also think there's a genetic component.

Paul: Do you think this is why someone ends up being a laborer rather than, say, a professional?

Teacher #2: I think, although I know it's not popular to say, that there's something to that.

In this study of 10 veteran teachers of social studies, these two teachers were the only ones to use the traditional essentialist discourse, emphasizing biological or genetic explanations to explain why some racial groups are less successful in school and in life. I doubt that either of them would come across as a racist. Both would most likely be shocked to learn that I have found them to be using a related discourse to the one that Europeans used to justify the theft of indigenous peoples' land and exploitation of laborers throughout the world during their empire-building era (and, some would contend, today, as well). The main point to be taken from this is that teachers, as members of the general public, are influenced by the same discourses that affect the public at large. In other words, the essentialist discourse is still in effect in certain pockets of society.[4]

The Color-Blind Discourse in Social Studies

The second racial discourse in Frankenberg's taxonomy is referred to as color-blind. Its major tenet is that beneath the skin, everyone is equal. This core assumption was born out of the Enlightenment; yet, it wasn't until around 1948 that it rose to prominence, primarily with the Universal Declaration of Human Rights developed by the newly formed United Nations. The color-blind discourse works in concert with a belief in the notion of meritocracy to form the underpinnings of the overall assessment of students in public schools today. In other words, an individual's academic failure in school or low standard of living as an adult can be explained by a lack of skill or work ethic, or both. In North America, the color-blind discourse is still the most dominant one in the mainstream media, although it is currently being challenged by an angry White backlash on the right as well as a more race-sensitive discourse coming from the left.

The United Nations released its *Universal Declaration of Human Rights* in 1948, an important political document intended to promote racial and religious tolerance. At the same time, the Cold War was moving into high gear, as the competing political and economic systems of capitalism and communism brought social concerns to the surface. The Cold War would make it too difficult to completely expunge conservatism from the 1956 social studies curriculum. Hence, there is evidence of both conservatism and liberalism in its content. Yet, despite myriad struggles for recognition and power, both in Canada and in international arenas, the whole notion of conflict between racial and cultural groups is absent from the entire document. As many scholars have pointed out, it is this absence of struggle that helps to conceal power (Apple, 2004; Frankenberg, 1993; Graf, 1994). More importantly, this particular hegemonic strategy works to keep from view social movements that arise out of resistance to power.

By the time the next social studies curriculum was published by the B.C. government in 1968, the color-blind discourse had become more prominent, a reflection of the wave of liberalism that was spreading across Western nation states during this period. A clear example of the color-blind discourse can be found in B.C.'s 1968 social studies curriculum with the following Generalization Statement:

> Canadians, both past and present, have interacted and co-operated in the development of the Canadian nation. (p. 89)

In this statement, usage of the term "Canadians" effectively hides the fact that *White* Canadians were given much more opportunity than others to influence the development of the "Canadian nation." This is an example of positioning White as the norm for a universal Canadian. Moreover, the use of the terms "interaction" and "cooperation" are clear attempts to conceal the more sordid parts of Canada's early history. For example, students being taught this curriculum may assume that interaction and cooperation were at the root of race relations leading up to Confederation in 1867 and the subsequent nation-building project. Moreover, using derivatives of *interaction* and *cooperation* would in no way lead students to understand the theft of Aboriginal peoples' lands and the subjugation and oppression of the indigenous peoples through the various amendments to the Canadian Indian Act[5] from 1876 until at least the 1940s. Moreover, students are unlikely to become aware of White Canadian exploitation of people of Aboriginal, Asian and African backgrounds if teachers were to present race relations in Canadian history as acts of interaction and cooperation. This example suggests why Frankenberg and other scholars consider the color-blind discourse to be "power-blind."

The 1980 curriculum uses the concept of *imperialism* as a similar hegemonic device. This is the case even though the actual term is not used. For example, the following statement is taken from the preliminary text to the teacher of grade 9 social studies:

> Grade nine focuses initially on the understanding that societies do not have sufficient human and natural resources to meet all of their desires. (p. 98)

A statement like this subtly reinforces the notion that it is understandable, perhaps even laudable, that some societies possess the drive and determination to meet all of their desires, even if this requires using the resources and the labor of other societies. In terms of hegemony, it suggests that imperialism is a natural and necessary process. The empire-building nations of Europe, specifically Britain, France, and Spain, used the land and resources of the Aboriginal peoples of the Americas to build vast amounts of wealth. Furthermore, they used the labor, that is, the human resources, of African peoples and, to a lesser extent, Asian and Aboriginal peoples, to add to their already massive advantage in the distribution of wealth. This exploitation was often institutionalized as law, either in economic systems based on slavery or with indentured agreements. Yet, none of this is mentioned in the curriculum.

The curricular statement above also has the effect of concealing what was caused by the imperial project, namely, the human degradation and suffering experienced by millions of colonized peoples. This is a typical curriculum statement within a liberal paradigm, rationalizing the achievements of the powerful and neglecting to mention the ways that power itself was used to exploit the already marginalized. In this respect, the Western concept of progress continued to be firmly entrenched in the state-sanctioned knowledge of schools in 1980. This was the case in British Columbia. Other scholars can determine if it similar in other regions of Canada and the United States.

Yet, it is not only scholars of curriculum who are aware of the Eurocentrism inherent in a color-blind social studies curriculum. I can still recall having a conversation with a group of Indian adolescents, composed of both Sikh and Hindu students, about the relevancy of school to their lives. All six students were intensely proud of their Indian heritage; yet, each one of them claimed to have never heard a teacher speak about Indian cultures or even an Indian person, Gandhi notwithstanding. They all claimed to want the social studies curriculum to be less Eurocentric. Consider the following statement that an Indo-Canadian student said to me in an interview:

> Indo-Canadian student: "I think one day the curriculum is going to have to change. And soon! Because one day soon Asians are going to outnumber White people in Vancouver. Asian people are going to want to have some of their histories taught in the schools, too. We are just not as interested in always learning about what the Europeans have done. Maybe the

White students won't be interested in our histories and our cultures, but hey, what comes around, goes around!"

From this young woman's perspective, it is time that educators understood what living in a multicultural society means, especially in terms of culturally relevant pedagogy. Although she did not say this, it is likely that a more culturally relevant curriculum will eschew the color-blind discourse.

The Race-Cognizance Discourse in Social Studies

The third discourse, according to Frankenberg, emerged out of feminist debates by socialist feminists and scholars of color during the 1980s. Called race-cognizance, it is a reaction to both of the other more dominant discourses, acknowledging that the amount of privilege or oppression people receive is dependent on their skin color as well as other factors such as their social class and gender. People who adhere to this perspective consider the color-blind discourse based within the liberal individualist paradigm to be power-blind because it overlooks the effects of historical factors and societal structures and institutions. It has been unable to displace the color-blind discourse as the dominant discourse in public debates today, however. The main reason for this is that this discourse illuminates society's structural and institutional inequities as being major root causes of racism, sexism, and poverty. In other words, some privileged Whites feel the most threatened by the ideas within the race-cognizance discourse.

In North America, one of the first sociopolitical movements to address the injustice inherent in racial hierarchies was the labor organization called the International Workers of the World (IWW). The IWW first appeared in the beginning of the twentieth century in the American Midwest and quickly spread elsewhere, including to parts of western Canada. Although the IWW, also known as the Wobblies, did not bring with it the race-cognizance discourse per se, their belief that all members of the working class regardless of race should receive equal treatment in one big union represented a massive threat to those positioned in the upper echelons of White privilege. Wobbly radicals wanted to change normal race relations across North America. They understood that racism was an obstacle that needed to be overcome in order to realize a society in which working families would enjoy job and social security, as well as a better standard of living. They also understood that the alternatives allowed the capitalist class to exploit White working-class racism to further their own interests at the expense of all workers in much the same way that Robert Dunsmuir had done with Vancouver Island coal miners. (Dunsmuir's successful exploitation of White working-class racism toward Chinese miners was discussed in the examples of race–class intersections in Chapter 4.) The race cognizance discourse, which calls for institutional and social change, is most closely related to the critical left ideology.

As an educational researcher I explored racist attitudes with a group of seven Aboriginal youth in which it became apparent that each one of them was very aware of institutional racism against their people in Canada's history. They knew a lot about the difficulties settling land treaties, the banning of the potlatch and the powwow, the Indian Act and the residential school system. One student described listening to her parents' complex usage of two racial discourses – color-bind and race-cognizance. Here she attempts to explain why her father, who lives in Bella Coola, a small town on B.C.'s central coast, has difficulty accepting White people into his life.

Aboriginal Student: I think he blames White people for what he lived through in the residential schools. He says he hates White people for what they did to him there. We try to explain it to him that it was those people who did it, not the White people he meets today. He just gets mad and says we don't know anything about it... My mother says that he should get over it because everyone is equal.

The assertion made by the student's mother that "everyone is equal" is clearly coming from the color-blind discourse, a discourse that is seen as power-blind from the perspective of the critical left. The student's father, on the other hand, seems to be aware of the power-blindness in the phrase "everyone is equal." His anger most likely indicates that he would agree with the tenets of the race-cognizant discourse, namely, that people experience varying amounts of privilege or oppression based on their race and perhaps their particular social location. It would appear that this former student of the racist residential school system has an awareness of the White privilege and systemic racism that continues to this day.

This taxonomy, as with all social taxonomies, is an approximation of the discourses describing racial and ethnic relations in North America today. Yet, it serves to illuminate the power within these hegemonic and counterhegemonic discourses, especially around issues of race relations in both the past and the present. Up until the end of the Second World War, White Christian supremacy remained unchallenged because of the essentialist discourse based on European race "science." Not surprisingly, conservatism was the dominant ideology. Since then, hegemony around White privilege in North America has been strengthened by the liberal color-blind discourse and the belief in meritocracy.

Throughout most Western nations, the liberal ideology is dominant, although there is clear evidence that since the 1980s conservatism has made a strong comeback in the United States and in Canada. Within this dynamic, for the past few decades conservative ideologues have been calling for a return to a Eurocentric curriculum for the schools, rather than what they consider to be a multicultural curriculum promoted by liberals (Ravitch, 2000; Granatstein, 1999; Cheney, 1994; Hirsch, 1987, 1996). The Arizona's school legislation in 2010 is the most overt attempt to block multicultural education in recent decades. The next section of this chapter looks at multiculturalism and its association to the various political ideologies.

Political Ideology and Multiculturalism

Hardly a day passes without some type of opinion or debate in the media around multiculturalism. Indeed, academics publish on this topic almost as frequently as journalists do. Multiculturalism is attacked by the conservative right as political correctness run amok, while those on the critical left contend that current versions of multiculturalism found in the classroom do not go far enough. Clearly, representation of the Other and of the image of the ideal individual, especially in terms of race and social class, are important to most people, regardless of their political ideologies. As with so many other terms within the field of cultural studies, multiculturalism is contested and has multiple meanings. Ideology is at the root of these various interpretations of what multiculturalism means.

In *Changing Multiculturalism* (1997), Joe Kincheloe and Shirley Steinberg have identified five different forms of multiculturalism from the enormous amount of scholarly research in the field. Their taxonomy is extremely useful in helping to understand the debates around multiculturalism, and illuminate the reasons why both conservatives and people in the critical left see liberal pluralist multiculturalism as problematic. It has been my experience that most teachers, let alone people in the general public, are not aware of the various forms of multicultural education. In terms of social justice, it would be helpful if more teachers were made aware.

Monoculturalism is within the ideology of conservatism, promoting a "return" to a mythic period in our past in which there was a "common culture." The work of many conservative education reformers emanate from this perspective (Granatstein, 1999; Hirsch, 1987, 1996). Assimilation into the dominant culture and its social arrangements, under the guise of a common Eurocentric curriculum, are the cornerstones of monoculturalism. Yet, for the majority within oppressed groups, assimilation is only for the lower rungs of the dominant Western culture. Monoculturalism promotes the notion that North American society is based upon a Judeo-Christian-Hellenic heritage. It enables conservative ideologues to blame non-European individuals and groups for their academic, economic, and social difficulties. Family values and excellence, concepts often heard from today's conservative pundits, are nothing more than codes for race and social class, reasons to continue the oppression of marginalized groups. Progressive people consider conservative rhetoric, such as from popular conservative talk radio hosts like Rush Limbaugh, to be all about blaming the victim, such as poor immigrants, for their plight. Critics of the 2010 Arizona legislation about both illegal immigration and the school curriculum consider this to be an attack on poor Latin Americans (Santa Cruz, 2010).

Rather than emphasizing the false consensus of monoculturalism, liberal multiculturalism, by contrast, "glorifies neutrality." Its basic premise is that individuals from all cultures, taking into account different racial, class, and gender backgrounds, share a common humanity that includes, among other things, festive rituals and religious holidays. There is nothing inherently wrong with this except that liberal multiculturalists also stress that everybody has the same opportunities for schooling and employment within a Western capitalist framework. Past struggles are not part of the liberal multicultural discourse, a trait that enables it to work as an effective hegemonic device. In a similar fashion, although it is supportive of participatory democracy, it never focuses on forces such as the corporate-owned media that work to undermine rather than strengthen democracy. In fact, power is effectively hidden in the color-blind, class-blind, and gender-blind discourses within liberal multiculturalism.[6]

Although the third multicultural paradigm in Kincheloe and Steinberg's taxonomy stresses difference rather than sameness, pluralist multiculturalism has major similarities with its liberal counterpart. Both versions ignore history and the workings of social, political, and economic power, enabling them to claim that in Canada and the United States, it is possible for anyone to make it on their own initiative, supporting the liberal notion of meritocracy. Moreover, both liberal and pluralist multiculturalism encourage tolerance between the various racial and ethnic groups. The major difference between the two is the actual focus: while liberal multiculturalism emphasizes commonalities across the human spectrum, its pluralist cousin highlights difference between the various groups. As Kincheloe and Steinberg (1997) point out, pluralist multiculturalism has become the dominant form of multiculturalism in schools and in popular culture in recent years. From my experience as a high school teacher, I agree with this contention made by Kincheloe and Steinberg. Many White teacher colleagues of mine consider that having posters of non-White celebrities, such as tennis stars Venus and Serena Williams, on their classroom walls is evidence of their commitment to multiculturalism.

The popularity of pluralist multiculturalism may be the result of the struggles of identity politics within the recent culture wars in the United States and Canada, a compromise of the calls for recognition of minorities on the one hand, and for more attempts at assimilation on the other hand. It may also in part be related to the notion that pluralist multiculturalism has a vital role in furthering capitalism's global interests. Capitalism can benefit from pluralism by commodifying difference, making it exotic, a latter-day offshoot of what Edward Said described in *Orientalism* (1978). Furthermore, pluralist multiculturalism subtly supports the liberal notion of individualism because it works to build group pride by celebrating the achievements of the few, a strategy employed by many teaching colleagues of mine over the years. In Chapter 7, I address the notion that the Canadian government, with its emphasis on the cultural mosaic rather than the American focus on the cultural melting pot, has developed a pluralist multiculturalism that aids in its control and management of minorities, especially Aboriginal peoples.

Kincheloe and Steinberg's descriptions of liberal and pluralist multiculturalism suggest how the unified subject of liberalism and the differentiated subject of pluralism can work toward the same ends, namely, effectively hiding power in a decontextualized, ahistorical public discourse or, for our purposes, the school curriculum. Moreover, both versions completely ignore working-class issues, except perhaps to celebrate the exceptional individual who can succeed despite humble origins. In this way, both liberal and pluralist multiculturalism clearly support meritocracy, which, as was discussed in Chapter 4, is one of the cornerstones of the liberal ideology.

Left-essentialist multiculturalism, however, focuses on the strengths of marginalized groups almost to a fault. According to Kincheloe and Steinberg, this version fails to acknowledge the historical aspect of cultural difference, thereby ignoring the social construction of knowledge. Left-essentialists believe that the moral high ground position is always with the oppressed group and that their perspective is closer to the truth than the mainstream perspective. This radical version of multiculturalism has the capacity to acknowledge social class as a significant marker of difference. Yet, as it does with aspects of race, left-essentialist multiculturalism also has a tendency to hyperbolize attributes of working-class culture.

The final form of multiculturalism identified by Kincheloe and Steinberg, critical multiculturalism, is also part of a critical left political ideology. Critical multiculturalists want each individual to understand the influence the dominant discourses have on their thoughts and feelings, including their political opinions, their racial self-images, and their class and gendered positions. In short, they demand that people comprehend how "power shapes consciousness" (p. 25). Within this paradigm, social class is a central organizing principle, especially with how "it interacts with race, gender and other axes of power" (p. 26). By emphasizing the importance of class, this form clearly differs from the others. Moreover, critical multiculturalism, like critical theory in general, is grounded in the belief that everything about teaching is political, a belief firmly rooted in the critical left ideology.

Some may see my use of a taxonomy of forms of multiculturalism developed by two White scholars as problematic – after all, I am also a White researcher. There is one major reason why I was drawn to the work by Kincheloe and Steinberg. The concept of social class was ever present throughout their taxonomy; even the absence of class was highlighted in some of the forms they describe. Moreover, their description of critical multiculturalism in particular, with its emphasis on class concerns, is what I perceive to be the most effective multicultural approach to teaching for social justice.

I want to briefly mention one more contribution to the contemporary field of multiculturalism, however, because although it overlaps with critical multiculturalism, it is clearly connected to critical left American educators such as George Counts (1932) and Harold Rugg (1921). Education that is multicultural and social reconstructionist, according to Christine Sleeter and Carl Grant (1994), "deals . . . with oppression and social structural inequality based on race, social class, gender, and disability" (pp. 209–210). Both Sleeter and Grant's and Kincheloe and Steinberg's paradigms stress the need for societal, structural and institutional change, clearly positioning themselves within the critical left political ideology.

A Few Words on Contemporary Racial Discourses

Educators must always be vigilant for the reemergence of the discredited essentialist discourse. Conservative *sociobiological* theories, originating in the work of E.O. Wilson (1975), combine aspects of culture and physiology to support Social Darwinian policies and attempt to explain social inequities in American society from a blame-the-victim perspective. The publication of *The Bell Curve* (1994) by Richard Herrnstein and Charles Murray, and myriad publications by psychologist J. P. Rushton indicate that there is still an appetite for the essentialist discourse among some White academics. In a study by Rushton and fellow psychologist A. R. Jensen (2005a, 2005b), the authors contend that it is a mistake for society to ascribe the underachievement of Black people to discrimination by White people rather than to genetic disadvantages. Educators must work to deconstruct these racist theories. In my opinion, the best defense against the appearance of genetics-based racial hierarchies is through an acute understanding of the race cognizance discourse. It is imperative that teachers be taught to utilize this discourse in their pedagogy.

Another version of the essentialist discourse ignores biology altogether as it ranks the various cultures according to how well they are suited to modern (or postmodern) culture. In this way, it reminds us of the racist cultural ranking system developed by Herbert Spencer in the nineteenth century that led to the implementation of ideas based on Social Darwinism. Because of the resultant social hierarchy, both in Spencer's time and now, this discourse can also be considered part of the conservative political ideology. Yet, liberals also tend to explain academic and socioeconomic disparities by pointing out the cultural backgrounds of those at the bottom (Lewis, 2001, pp. 800–801). Its most frequent contemporary usage is in invoking the *cultural deficit discourse* to explain why certain cultural groups find themselves marginalized in contemporary societies. As we shall see in Chapter 7, the cultural deficit discourse, especially when invoked by educators, poses serious obstacles to helping students from disadvantaged backgrounds succeed academically. This becomes even more evident when the cultural deficit discourse works in tandem with other liberal discourses, such as color-blindness.

Questions to Ponder

1. Of the three racial discourses described in this chapter – essentialist, color-blind, and race cognizance – which one best describes how you were taught in your high school social studies courses?
2. How does the concept of meritocracy work to keep racial hierarchies mostly intact in the United States and Canada?
3. Try to recall examples of the various forms of racism that you have come across in your life. These examples may be from the standpoint of the victim, the perpetrator, or a bystander.
4. Which type of multiculturalism best describes how you were taught in your high school? How would you say it affected your own attitudes toward issues of race?
5. How might teachers best deconstruct contemporary versions of the essentialist discourse?
6. The American Civil War divided the United States into those who wanted slavery to remain, those who wanted slavery abolished, and a few neutral states. Excluding Alaska and Hawaii, which joined the United States after the Civil War,

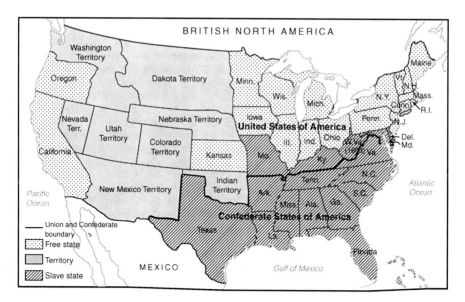

Fig. 5.2 Map of the United States during the American civil war

almost all of the states in favor of abolishing slavery voted for the Democrats in the 2004 election, while almost all of the other states voted for the Republicans. (Please refer to Figs. 5.2 and 5.3 below.) The 2004 election was focused on the American-led invasion of Iraq in 2003. What might this say about the type of multicultural education used in most American high schools? How might this be addressed in the future?

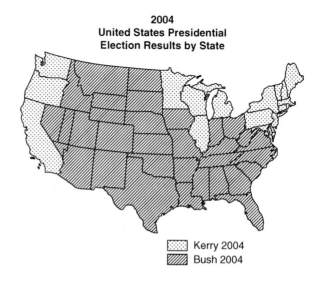

Fig. 5.3 2004 U.S. presidential election results by State

Notes

1. Although I understand that the term "Indian" is often used to denote the original inhabitants of the Americas, especially in the U.S., I use the term to describe people who have ancestry from India. I use the term "Aboriginal" to describe people whose ancestry include the original inhabitants of the Americas. The term "Aboriginal" includes people of Metis, Inuit, and First Nations ancestry.
2. Chapter 7 examines liberal discourses about Aboriginal issues in education. Part of the chapter will focus on the resistance of White teachers to employ culturally relevant pedagogy.
3. For more on the privileges of whiteness, see David Roediger (1999) and Peggy McIntosh (1988).
4. In recent years there have been "scientific" studies published that support the main tenets of the essentialist discourse, namely, that some races are intellectually superior to other races based on genetics. See Herrnstein and Murray (1994) and Rushton and Jensen (2005a, 2005b).
5. The Canadian government passed the Indian Act in 1876, effectively taking control of many aspects of Aboriginal peoples' lives and communities. This racist legislation restricted status Aboriginal people to small fragments of their former territories by the establishment of Indian reserves. Until 1951, they were banned from continuing important cultural practices. Many of their children were taken away to residential schools in which the continuity of family life and language learning were disrupted.
6. One of my former colleagues at the University of the Fraser Valley, an educator of South Asian ancestry, pointed out that the "dinner, dance, and dress" focus of liberal multiculturalism may be considered a good first step. Yet, she stressed the need for multicultural education to move past this to include issues of power and economic concerns.

References

Apple, M. W. (2004). *Ideology and curriculum* (3rd ed.). New York: Routledge-Falmer.

B.C. Department of Education, Division of Curriculum. (1956). *Junior and senior high schools of British Columbia*. Victoria: Queen's Printer of British Columbia.

Cheney, L. V. (1994, October 20). The end of history. *Wall Street Journal*, A11.

Counts, G. (1932). Dare progressive education be progressive? *Progressive Education, 9*, 257–263. Reprinted (1982) as *Dare the school build a new social order?* by New York: John Day.

Dunne, M., & Gazeley, L. (2008, September). Teachers, social class and underachievement. *British Journal of Sociology of Education, 29*, 451–463.

Fanon, F. (1952). *Black skin, white masks* (C. L. Markmann, Trans.). Paris: Éditions du Seuil.

Fanon, F. (1967). *The wretched of the Earth*. London: Penguin.

Frankenberg, R. (1993). *White women, race matters: The social construction of Whiteness*. Minneapolis: University of Minnesota Press.

Graf, G. (1994). Beyond the culture wars: How teaching the conflicts can revitalize American education. In W. E. Cain (Ed.), *Teaching the conflicts: Gerald Graf, curricular reform, and the culture wars* (pp. 3–16). New York: Taylor & Francis.

Granatstein, J. L. (1999, August 28). A politically correct history leads to a distorted past and a bleak future. *The National Post*, p. A13.

Hale, G. E. (1998). *Making whiteness: The culture of segregation in the south, 1890–1940*. New York: Pantheon Books.

Herrnstein, R. J., & Murray, C. (1994). *The bell curve: Intelligence and class structure in American life*. New York: Free Press.

Hirsch, E. D. (1987). *Cultural literacy: What every American needs to know*. New York: Doubleday.

Hirsch, E. D. (1996). *The schools we need and why we don't have them*. New York: Doubleday.

Juarez, B., Smith, D., & Hayes, C. (2008). Social justice means just us white people: The diversity paradox in teacher education. *Democracy & Education, 17*(3), 20–25.

Kincheloe, J., & Steinberg, S. (1997). *Changing multiculturalism*. Buckingham, UK: Open University Press.

Leroy, C., & Symes, B. (2001). Teachers' perspectives on the family backgrounds of children at risk. *McGill Journal of Education, 36*(1), 45–61.

Lewis, A. (2001). There is no "race" in the schoolyard: Color-blind ideology in an (almost) all-White school. *American Educational Research Journal, 38*, 781–811.

McIntosh, P. (1988). *White privilege and male privilege: A personal account of coming to see correspondences through work in women's studies*. Wellesley, MA: Centre for Research on Women.

Orlowski, P. (2001). Ties that bind and ties that blind: Race and class intersections in the classroom. In C. E. James & A. Shadd (Eds.), *Talking about identity: Encounters in race, ethnicity, and language* (pp. 250–266). Toronto: Between the Lines.

Orlowski, P. (2008). "That would certainly be spoiling them": Liberal discourses of social studies teachers and concerns about Aboriginal students. *Canadian Journal of Native Education, 31*(2), 110–129.

Ravitch, D. (2000). *Left back: A century of failed school reform*. New York: Simon & Schuster.

Roediger, D. R. (1999). *The wages of whiteness: Race and the making of the American working class* (rev. ed.). New York: Verso.

Rugg, H. O. (1921). Reconstructing the curriculum: An open letter to Professor Henry Johnson commenting on Committee Procedure as illustrated by the Report of the Joint Committee on History and Education for Citizenship. *Historical Outlook, 12*, 184–189. Reprinted in W. C. Parker (Ed.), (1996). *Educating the democratic mind*. Albany, NY: State University of New York Press.

Rushton, J. P., & Jensen, A. R. (2005a). Thirty years of research on race differences in cognitive ability. *Psychology, Public Policy, and Law, 11*, 235–294.

Rushton, J. P., & Jensen, A. R. (2005b). Wanted: More race-realism, less moralistic fallacy. *Psychology, Public Policy, and Law, 11*, 328–336.

Santa Cruz, N. (2010, May 12). Arizona bill targeting ethnic studies signed into law. *The Los Angeles Times*. Retrieved from http://articles.latimes.com/2010/may/12/nation/la-na-ethnic-studies-20100512

Sleeter, C. E., & Grant, C. A. (1994). *Making choices for multicultural education: Approaches to race, class, and gender* (2nd ed.). New York: MacMillan.

Stoler, A. L. (1997). *Race and the education of desire: Foucault's "History of sexuality" and the colonial order of things* (3rd ed.). Durham, NC: Duke University Press.

Williams, R. (1980). *Problems in materialism and culture: Selected essays*. London: Verso.

Wilson, E. O. (1975). *Sociobiology: The new synthesis*. Cambridge, MA: Belknap Press.

Young, R. J. C. (1995). *Colonial desire: Hybridity in theory, culture and race*. London: Routledge.

Chapter 6
Social Class: The Forgotten Identity Marker in Social Studies Education

In North America, discussions of social class are considered to be in questionable taste, indeed are surrounded by formidable taboos. It is less outre to converse graphically about kinky sex than to suggest that social classes exist, or that their existence has important consequences.
(Laxer, 1998, p. 32)

The above quote reminds me of something that happened during a presentation I gave at an educational research conference in Quebec City in 2002. I had just finished presenting my research that determined economic links underlie racist attitudes among working-class adolescents from various racial backgrounds (Orlowski, 2001a). As usually occurs at these conferences, I readied myself to engage in a discussion about the research. The first person to speak was a professor who offered the following comment: "That's all well and good, but we don't live in India or some place where there may be castes or social classes. Canada is a classless society." Before I could respond, the room erupted into a rather loud and lengthy argument as many of the scholars present took exception to the audience member's initial comment. Although I was somewhat surprised to hear an academic say that Canada is a classless society, I knew that her view was not uncommon among the general public.

Indeed, in recent decades many Americans and Canadians appear to have accepted the hegemonic assumption that we live in a classless society. This discourse goes further in that it supports the vilification of anyone who talks about working-class consciousness as engaging in class warfare or blaming the system as a cover for their own ineptitude and low station in life. The classless society myth supports a second myth, meritocracy, which states that people will rise to their proper stations in life based on their own effort, talents, and intelligence. The American and Canadian emphasis on the individual is also a factor in waning class consciousness. Taken together, they become a powerful discursive formation that acts as a hegemonic obstacle for progressive economic movements to gain traction. Many still believe these myths even as the wealth gaps between the economic elites and everyone else are greatly increasing. According to a recent thought-provoking study (Wilkinson & Pickett, 2010), these increasing wealth gaps are making life more difficult for everyone, regardless of their own level of income. Can the working classes,

P. Orlowski, *Teaching About Hegemony*, Explorations of Educational Purpose 17, DOI 10.1007/978-94-007-1418-2_6, © Springer Science+Business Media B.V. 2011

and even the middle classes, come together to protest this system that fosters great economic inequality?

In order to explore this question, this chapter is going to be similar as Chapter 5 in that it relies upon an examination of the social studies curriculum itself, in addition to a sociological study I undertook with veteran social studies teachers. Some of the excerpts from the interview transcripts are rather long. I have chosen to do this to illuminate the challenges that arise when a teacher is pushed to think about issues of social class and how best to teach about them.

A Waning Class Consciousness – Can Ideology Critique Help?

I am writing this chapter about social class and education at a time when almost every economist and media pundit concerned with global and national economies has acknowledged that we have entered a period of economic shrinkage that could possibly rival the Great Depression of the 1930s. During the two decades prior to this economic crisis, governments in both countries, especially the United States, engaged in an attack on unions that began with the Reagan administration's successful battle with the air traffic controllers (Klein, 2007; Zinn, 2003). In 1987 President Reagan replaced Paul Volcker as Federal Reserve Chair with Alan Greenspan, a libertarian economist who believed that the financial industry did not need government regulation (Greenspan, 2007). Volcker was first hired to be the Federal Reserve Chair by the former U.S. President Jimmy Carter. Volcker believed that the financial industry required regulatory legislation (Treaster, 2004). The Reagan administration wanted a Federal Reserve Chair who shared their philosophy of deregulating the financial industry. Consequently, Alan Greenspan was chosen to be Volcker's successor. Hence, once the Wall Street financial problems became public during the first half of 2008, there is little wonder why Americans, especially the working classes in the United States and elsewhere, became more than a little concerned for the economic well-being of their families.

Alan Greenspan served as the Chair of the Federal Reserve from 1987 until 2006. He espoused a similar economic philosophy as Milton Friedman, an economics professor at the University of Chicago. Both economists have been especially influential in American economic policy in the domestic and foreign realms for most of the past 30 years. This philosophy is often referred to as *neoliberalism*, an economic philosophy that has gained much corporate support with its emphasis on globalization and minimum government intervention in financial matters. Neoliberalism can be seen as a more contemporary version of laissez-faire economics, which discouraged government intervention in the eighteenth and nineteenth centuries in the economies of industrialized nations. In this way, neoliberalism is the antithesis of the economic philosophy developed by John Maynard Keynes, an economist who supported government involvement in the economy if it helped the general public (Davidson, 2007). From the Great Depression until the 1970s, laissez-faire economic policies were completely discredited in Western nations as there was strong support for Keynesian economics and the development of the social welfare state.

From the 1980s until 2008, however, neoliberalism has been the dominant economic paradigm in both the United States and Canada. The economic crisis of 2008–09 could eventually dislodge neoliberalism's dominance, especially if common citizens are open to this.

Yet, the lack of public outrage toward massive amounts of tax dollars going to the de-regulated financial industry in 2008–09 is an indication that forcing massive policy change toward a more Keynesian approach is going to be difficult. The populace in the United States, for instance, seems sedate, especially given the fact that hundreds of billions of tax dollars was handed over to the financial industry without any financial reforms or regulations imposed upon it. The so-called Tea Party movement, organized by the ultra-conservative Fox News Network shortly after President Obama replaced President George W. Bush, often expresses outrage at the current situation in the United States. But this almost entirely White populist protest movement does not put forth a class analysis, failing to see the connections between corporate power and the Republican Party.

Most Americans, however, are not being organized into a serious and sophisticated protest movement. There are several factors involved with this relative passivity. First, since the 1950s there has been a significant identity shift away from a working-class consciousness to a consumer consciousness as more and more people attempt to enjoy the pleasures and material goods offered within a capitalist society (Walker, 2002). Second, and related to the first factor, is that the media does all it can to render working-class consciousness as obsolete through its use of language. Hence, rather than speak of class concerns as any Marxist would, most North American journalists prefer to use terms such as white collar, blue collar or even pink collar. Since the economic crisis of 2008, the preferred phrase to use in the United States is Wall Street and Main Street. Labeling differentiated employment status in these ways goes against massive amounts of academic literature using terms such as social class and class consciousness. Indeed, any study of a major university library would illuminate the richly detailed histories of the working classes and working-class consciousness.

Since the Reagan presidency, which corresponded with the first majority Conservative Canadian government in over two decades, the gap between the rich and poor has widened significantly in both countries (OECD, 2008). Free trade deals such as NAFTA add to the lowering of wages, job security, and working conditions for vast numbers of the working classes in both Canada and the United States (Laxer, 1998, pp. 17–18). The United States is the only Western nation in the world not to have a universal public healthcare system for its citizens. The difficulties to create one is clear since the vociferous and orchestrated reaction to President Obama's plans for healthcare reform during the summer of 2009. The eventual healthcare reform policy passed by Congress was still completely a private venture.

In Canada, there is increasing corporate pressure, supported by their media outlets, to develop a two-tiered system which would enable people who can afford it to jump queue and experience different doctors than those who do not have enough money to do so. These are only a few examples of how government policy has moved away from universal principles of social equity and toward more competitive models that allow for increased private profit. Just as ideology was instrumental in helping to build the post-Second World War social welfare state, it is also involved in its current dismantling.

Ideology and Economic Issues

How well understood is the role of ideology in our day-to-day economic lives? If one were to examine the ways in which the mainstream media portray the current economic crisis, they would discover that the notion of ideology is rarely mentioned. Occasionally there is some mention of the different approaches to the crisis between the Democrats and Republicans, but because both parties are beholden to large corporations, the options open to them that do *not* support maintaining the current economic system are rarely mentioned in any serious way. An example of this is the reluctance of American and Canadian political leaders to move toward the nationalization of banks, something that has recently been done in several countries in Europe. There is also reluctance in Canada and the United States to implement a bank tax (Carmichael, 2010). Such moves likely seem to be too close to socialism, an ideology much discredited in Canadian and American media, especially since the collapse of the Soviet Bloc.

Yet, an understanding of political ideology and the role of government in economic matters would be beneficial to the citizens of both the United States and Canada. Chapter 2 included a large discussion about the major political ideologies that arose in Western nations out of the Enlightenment. For our purposes here, a brief discussion highlighting the main economic differences of each of the main ideologies will be helpful.

Classic liberalism focused on the rights of the individual, including the right to make as much money as possible, as necessary for the freedom of the masses. This support for unbridled capitalism disturbed conservatives in the Post-Enlightenment era because traditional social class hierarchies were rapidly changing. In other words, many people were able to jump class by capitalizing on economic opportunities, thereby destabilizing existing class relations.

The discussion in Chapter 2 highlighted the differences between liberalism and conservatism on social issues. Indeed, myriad media reports in recent years, especially in the United States, focus on these differences in social policy. The same cannot be said for economic policy. In the early twenty-first century, both liberalism and conservatism accept the basic tenets of corporate capitalism, although liberals have a tendency to accept the role of government on economic matters a little more than conservatives. Since the 1980s, however, Republican and Democratic federal governments in the United States and Conservative and Liberal federal governments in Canada have supported the corporate agenda of deregulation, privatization, and the dismantling of the social welfare state (Laxer, 1998).

At the other end of the economic spectrum, communism does not allow any space for private enterprise, a position that often results in the creation of a black market economy that is unregulated by any level of government. Socialism is for the most part opposed to profit-oriented economic policies for large corporations, although it does allow for small businesses to exist. The original socialist ideology articulated a vision for a socially just world in a similar vein as its liberal predecessor. There was a major difference, however. The liberal conception of freedom fit in perfectly with the economics of capitalism, and on these terms appears to be coherent. Yet, as Marx pointed out in the first volume of *Capital* (1961), the liberal idea of freedom is unattainable for most people within capitalism. This is because of the basic contradiction that workers cannot be free while they are vulnerable to the capitalist tendency to exploit them and sell prices at exorbitant prices. Many historians and economic theorists interpret the fall of the Soviet Union in 1989 to mean that both communism and socialism are untenable economic systems (Fukuyama, 1992).

A popular ideology that has often guided European governments in recent decades, as well as many Canadian provincial governments, is called *social democracy*.[1] Social democrats accept capitalism, but see a need to protect those groups having difficulty living in it. Social democratic governments are likely to support legislation that helps parents (subsidized daycare), families (not-for-profit seniors housing), and workers (banning replacement workers during labor strikes). Social democracy also distinguishes itself from liberalism and conservatism in that it is opposed to corporate monopolies or privatization in aspects of life that are deemed necessary for the public good. Examples of this are public ownership of electricity, transportation (including highways and ferries), healthcare, and the K-12 school system. The question for progressive educators is how well is the K-12 school system doing to inform future citizens about the different economic philosophies behind each ideology? The next section will address this very question.

Public Education and Class Consciousness

It has been my experience that almost all adolescents enter high school without any conception of a class consciousness, and five or so years later they graduate without one either. For the two decades I taught in the high school classroom, the dominant ideology underlying the social studies curriculum was class-blind liberalism. (Orlowski, 2001a, 2001b). Indeed, my research into this void indicates that most high school students believe that there are only three social classes: rich, middle, and poor. The data collection for the research of my MA thesis involved interviewing 25 working-class adolescents from five different racial groups–almost all of them considered themselves to be middle class.[2] Because there was such a strong identification with the middle class, many bought into the middle-class argument favoring tax cuts and a belief that society can no longer look after the poor. I remember my surprise when one of my grade 11 students, who came from a single-parent family on welfare, expressed strong support for tax cuts and disdain for politicians who did not agree with the policy of cutting back on social spending. Clearly, the school system had failed to properly educate this student. My experience as a teacher tells me that this is far from uncommon.

Social studies is the high school subject best suited to explain how economics influences one's day-to-day experience and the relations between the various social classes. An examination of how the representation of working-class issues in the formal social studies curriculum of British Columbia may illuminate some of the reasons why so many students leave high school without a class consciousness. At the least, it will demonstrate how economic power is located in the curriculum, and that the notion of political neutrality in curricular documents is a fabrication.

Ideology in the Social Studies Curriculum

[A]n understanding of how the control of cultural institutions enhances the power of particular classes to control others can provide needed insight into the way the distribution of culture is related to the presence or absence of power in social groups. (Apple, 2004, p. 14)

In my quest to better teach for social justice, I came across the above quote. The book that it came from, *Ideology & Curriculum*, motivated me to examine the evolution of the British Columbia Social Studies Curriculum so that I would have a better understanding of the ways in which state-sanctioned official knowledge works to economically privilege some groups and oppress others. It is my assumption that the social studies curriculum in other provinces and states underwent a similar evolution. I may be incorrect in this assumption, but I will leave that to other educational researchers to determine. Here, the focus will be on the British Columbia Social Studies Curriculum with the intention of demonstrating how changing conditions, both on the domestic and global fronts, can affect its content.

The first published social studies curriculum in British Columbia came out during the Second World War in 1941. Not surprisingly, much of the curriculum is centered on issues concerning aspects of war and nationalism. Yet, there is no mention that the hellish trenches were filled by legions of *working-class* young men. The curriculum does include a section in a unit on "troubles arising from the [first] world war," however, entitled The Disruption of the Economic Structure (1941, p. 168). Two of the Specific Objectives that teachers were expected to cover are clearly in support of business interests. The first objective contains the phrase "increased tariffs and the strangulation of world trade" which is clearly in support of free trade. The second objective refers to "unemployment and heavy taxation" in a way that clearly links the two as problematic. It is clear that the discourse of capitalism is supported by this document. The rights of workers were very much in the background in the 1941 curriculum.

With the publication of the next curriculum in 1949, the rights of workers had completely disappeared. This may be a consequence of the growing negative attitudes toward Bolshevism and the communist movements within North America at the time. American anti-communist crusader Joseph McCarthy was beginning his rise to fame. In Canada, Cold War hostilities were evident but not at the same level as in the United States. This is reflected in the rise of the Canadian Commonwealth Federation (CCF), a socialist-based populist movement that rose to power in Saskatchewan during this era, and subsequently won five straight provincial elections in a row. Almost immediately after forming government in 1940, the CCF's leader, Saskatchewan Premier Tommy Douglas, opened a public debate on the merits of a public-funded healthcare system versus the private system that was the only option at the time (McLeod & McLeod, 1987). Yet, there is no mention of this very important debate in the 1949 curriculum. This is another example of omission as a hegemonic strategy.

By the time the next version of the British Columbia Social Studies Curriculum was published in 1956, it was generally acknowledged that the economy was robust, healthy, and growing across the continent (Laxer, 1998). Significantly, and consistent with the liberal ideology, the *conflict* between labor and capital does not appear at all. The learning objectives are worded in such a way that a student might be inclined to believe that the legalization of trade unions, for instance, came about out of the benevolence of capitalists and right-wing provincial governments. But this was hardly the case.

By the early 1950s the American trade union movement was winning the fight for many progressive contracts for its members. In particular, the United Auto Workers (UAW), led by Walter Reuther, had secured a number of innovative contract items such as cost-of-living adjustments that set a pattern for American industry to follow (Meyerson, 2008). In fact, "[d]uring the Reuther years, the UAW also used its resources to incubate every up-and-coming liberal movement in America" (p. 1). This support included providing funds for the great March on Washington led by Martin Luther King in 1963.

During the economic crisis of 2008–09, however, the UAW and the Canadian Auto Workers (CAW) have been under severe government and media pressure to roll back their wages and their pension plans if they want the government to provide public funding to help the auto manufacturers survive. The media claim that the troubles of the Big Three auto manufacturers are because of the high cost of labor. This is the case even though their cars are significantly cheaper than Japanese-made cars.[3] A case can be made that the absence of the contributions of the labor movement to the overall well-being of Americans in the school curriculum could be a factor in the lack of public outrage over the political attacks on the UAW and CAW. In other words, omission as a hegemonic strategy is an effective way to maintain the status quo or even to further entrench the corporate agenda.

Labor historians have often pointed to the role of trade unions that led to the prosperity many Americans and Canadians enjoyed in the three decades after the Second World War (Palmer, 1992; Zinn, 2003). The trade union movement also led to the 8-hour work day and the 40-hour work week. With the publication of the 1968 curriculum, however, all of the learning objectives about trade unions and labor legislation were completely removed. There was some coverage of the life of the common laborer before and during the Industrial Revolution in the grade 9 social studies course (p. 28). Yet, the representation of conflict so long ago is a safe way to maintain power and privilege for the capitalist classes (Apple, 2004; Graf, 1994). This approach is hegemonic in insidious ways. It appears to acknowledge some strife between workers and owners, but because the events described are in the distant past, it tacitly implies that life has improved for current laborers and their families. This may very likely be the case, at least for those living in Western nations. Yet, problems of representation remain – labor contributions to society during the 1950s and 1960s are completely absent.

The 1968 curriculum is noteworthy in another respect. In Canada, the CCF evolved from a socialist party to a social democratic one, renaming itself the New Democratic Party (NDP) in 1961. One of the greatest achievements of the CCF-NDP occurred in 1962 in Saskatchewan when the provincial NDP government implemented the first public universal healthcare system in North America (Whitehorn, 1992). Even though the federal Liberals championed the same service across the country a few years later, this pillar of the Canadian social welfare state is not mentioned at all in the 1968 document. This was also the case with its successor, published in 1980, although corporations and unions make their way back into the curriculum.

With the 1980 curriculum, a grade-9 unit entitled *People and Resources* states that students were expected to come to an understanding of "citizens as consumers, producers, taxpayers" (p. 100). Furthermore, two institutions were described as major "components of the Canadian economy": corporations and labor unions. One of the unit's "Generalizations" states that "students should come to recognize that all peoples and societies are faced with the same economic problem: conflict between unlimited wants and limited resources" (p. 100). By overstating the case for material consumption, the curriculum performs as a hegemonic device in that it normalizes a major aspect of capitalism, namely, the purchasing of *wants* and not just *needs*. In this way, the curriculum is serving the pro-capitalist process that transformed workers into consumers, thereby leading to a waning class consciousness (Hobsbawm, 1995; Walker, 2002). In this way, it also supports an imperialist discursive formation.

The 1988 curriculum had a similar approach as its 1968 and 1980 forerunners in its representation of economic issues. Borrowing from the 1968 document, Social Studies 9 addresses the lives of working families during the Industrial Revolution (1988, p. 46). As mentioned above, this is a very effective hegemonic strategy because it implies that workers today have it much better and, therefore, should not be complaining about wages, benefits or working conditions. Moreover, by focusing on working conditions and "worker organizations" in Britain over two centuries ago, *current* power arrangements remain hidden. Yet, it is noteworthy that in both Canada and the United States, relations between the capitalist class and labor became hostile during the 1980s, bringing to an end the relatively long truce that had more or less prevailed since the end of the Second World War (Laxer, 1998; Palmer, 1992). Yet, *these* conflicts are omitted from the liberal-influenced curriculum. Legislation around replacement workers, picketing and collective bargaining, to name but a few, are of paramount importance to working-class families. Yet, the 1988 curriculum failed to address any of them. Its successor, published in 1997, was remarkably even less forthcoming about working-class issues.

A Prescribed Learning Outcome in the 1997 social studies curriculum is worded in the following way:

It is expected that students will assess how identity is shaped by a variety of factors, including family, gender, belief systems, ethnicity and nationality. (1997a, p. A-4)

Despite the massive body of scholarly work that supports the notion that an individual's social class position significantly shapes and limits their experience throughout life, it is not included in the list of factors that the curriculum developers consider to be important in the construction of identity. Moreover, there is very little in the way of suggested learning resources that include social class issues, such as labor struggles, trade unionism, collective bargaining, tax reform, and free trade. Is this an oversight or is it an intended hegemonic strategy? Hegemony is involved either way. Even well-intentioned curriculum developers may be influenced by the dominant discourses in a corporate capitalist society that includes the meritocratic anyone-can-make-it ethos. This might blind the curriculum developers and possibly result in the omission of working-class issues in the official knowledge of the formal curriculum.

The answer to this question about intention is not as important as the omission itself. It is clear that working-class students are at a disadvantage when compared to their middle-class counterparts, especially in terms of curricular representation. Their experiences, situations, and concerns are not addressed at all, while the middle class is entrenched as the hegemonic norm in the 1997 curriculum. Although there is a Suggested Instructional Strategy about the Great Depression in Social Studies 11, the root causes of the Depression and who suffered the most are not included. A critical left interpretation of this omission is that the curriculum is based on liberal power-blindness. A critical left-influenced curriculum would have pointed out the huge discrepancies in suffering based on social class, as well as the role of the banks in creating a culture of living on credit and the role of industrialists in creating a policy of overproduction.

The authors of the 1997 British Columbia Social Studies Curriculum did not consider social class to be a factor in the identity construction of an individual. Nor did they bother to mention Keynesian economics and represent the role of the public sector as "an alternative source of capital and creative energy in both the economic and cultural spheres" to help strengthen the social welfare state as was the case in the post-war years up until the 1980s (Laxer, 1998, p. 41). This is particularly poignant considering that in 2008 and 2009 major corporations have been demanding exorbitant amounts of public monies to help them survive the economic crisis.

During this same decade, Canadians are experiencing attacks in both the economic and cultural spheres, led by Conservative and Liberal governments at both the federal and provincial levels that support the neoliberal and neoconservative agendas. The social studies curriculum on its own cannot be blamed for the lack of resistance to this dismantling, of course. Yet, it certainly is not helping Canadians to become informed around class issues. It is clear that the theories of American philosopher of education John Dewey and his dream of an informed citizenry have had very little success in the United States and, by extension, Canada. Middle-class normativity is a key hegemonic component in the liberal ideology. In this way, the curriculum helps maintain the status quo in ways that are difficult for most students, as well as teachers, to detect and resist. The most recent British Columbia Social Studies Curriculum, published in 2005–06, employs the same hegemonic strategy of omission as its predecessor toward issues of social class.

The Curriculum and the Individual

> The concept of the individual has been one of the essential misconceptions of political liberalism. Every human being is unique, but he does not exist alone. He is dependent on others; his existence is inseparable from his relations with other human beings. (Lukacs, 2009, p. 21)

There is another aspect of a liberal-influenced social studies curriculum that is worth noting for its effective influence of hiding power. The concept of the *individual,* one of the most important cornerstones of twentieth-century liberalism, made its first significant appearance in the British Columbia Social Studies Curriculum in 1949, just as this ideology was replacing conservatism as the dominant ideology in the United States and Canada. A learning objective for students in a sample unit in the 1949 document is stated as follows:

> A realization of the importance of the *individual* in the advancement of civilization. (p. 70, my emphasis)

There is no doubt that liberalism's focus on an individual's human rights has been a very important development in the quest for a socially just society. Yet, by ignoring any reference to economic rights, the curriculum once again can be seen to be in support of the interests of big business. On the other hand, the 1949 curriculum also has several references to community, an important concept in traditional conservatism. References to any collective ideals, however, have completely disappeared with the recent 1997 and 2005–06 curricula. These documents do not encourage students to recognize the benefits of the collective or of community; nor do they help students come to an understanding that the individual really exists as a social being who has responsibilities to help others, especially those who are having difficult times. This is yet another way that the school curriculum has failed to help students comprehend what is in their best interests. It is also a failure of the state to develop educated citizens aware of what is in their best collective interests. Politicians in both countries have been loudly touting the mantra of tax cuts since the 1980s. There has been very little resistance to the tax cutting legislation passed by the George W. Bush administration in 2002 even though these tax cuts clearly benefited the wealthy elites and further plunged the American government's finances into extreme debt.

The liberal focus on the individual all but obliterates social connections, supporting business interests and regressive tax reform in the process. Apple (2004) furthers this line of reasoning:

> [The curriculum] does not situate the life of an individual … as an economic and social being, back into the unequal structural relations that produced the comfort the individual enjoys. (p. 10)

Not able to see who is producing what we consume, we live in a society in which most people will wear clothes and buy stereos produced by sweatshop labor. Of course, I do not intend to imply that schools work in a vacuum, able to be a panacea for all of our social ills. They must contend with myriad social forces, especially in the corporate media, that are continually working to shape societal values.

In sum, except for a brief period of minor representation during the middle decades of the past century, working-class issues were not represented in the *formal* social studies curriculum of British Columbia. As discussed in Chapter 5, a similar curricular analysis about race showed that a liberal focus on multiculturalism appeared in the 1968 curriculum. As well, as we shall see in Chapter 7, later versions of the curriculum include space for critical left educators to address the experience and issues of Aboriginal peoples. Social class, however, seems to be a forgotten identity marker for these same curriculum developers.

Do similar attitudes toward issues of social class occur in the minds of social studies teachers? In a study I did with veteran high school social studies teachers, the discussions around social class issues revealed some very interesting findings. The study examined how the teachers think about social class, and presumably, how they teach about it. First, however, I will briefly discuss a taxonomy of social class discourses that will help discern how political ideology influences these teachers on social class issues. This taxonomy may shed light on the ways in which students of these veteran teachers engage in the *enacted* curriculum, which was discussed in some detail in Chapter 4.

Ideology and Discourses of Working-Class Academic Performance

In my research, I have studied the ways in which political ideology has influenced the teachers' attitudes around issues of social class. In order to accomplish this, I use the taxonomy developed by Curtis, Livingstone, and Smaller (1992). In "Stacking the Deck: The Streaming of Working-Class Kids in Ontario Schools," the authors refer to Bourdieu and Passeron (1977), Bernstein (1977), and Lareau (1989) among others, to support their claim that "every study of schools that has paid attention to class differences has found that working-class kids have always fared much worse than middle- and upper-class kids" (p. 7). More recent research from Britain indicates that "working-class pupils continue to leave education with fewer and poorer qualifications than pupils from middle-class backgrounds" (Dunne & Gazeley, 2008, p. 452).

An argument can be made that working-class students leave school for poorer paying jobs with little or no security because they have not been served very well by the public education system. According to Curtis et al., "working-class kids still receive less schooling, and a different kind of schooling" than kids from more privileged economic backgrounds (p. 8). They have developed a taxonomy based on the explanations people offer as to why working-class students fare less well in school.

This helped me determine the political ideologies underlying the teachers' attitudes and beliefs.

"Socially powerful people tend to encourage the less powerful to blame themselves for their own misfortunes" (Curtis et al., 1992, p. 14). This discourse, based in nineteenth-century Social Darwinism, promotes the meritocratic notion that people who are bright, talented, and hard-working will rise to the top. By corollary, lazy and dull people will fill the lower ranks of society. This version of meritocracy differs from the liberal version in that it is applied to whole groups of people rather than individuals. In this way, it is imbued with a similar component as the essentialist racial discourse discussed in Chapter 5. Many conservatives, therefore, still claim there is a genetic component to explain the conditions of poverty many social groups experience (Herrnstein & Murray, 1994; Rushton, 2000; Rushton & Jensen, 2005a, 2005b), a position still held by a couple of the teachers in my study.

Rather than using the genetic-deficit theories of traditional conservatism, people who see the world through an ideological lens of either contemporary conservatism or liberalism often explain the stratified nature of our society using various versions of the cultural-deficit discourse. Curtis et al. specify three different types of the cultural-deficit discourse. First, the value deficiency discourse claims that working-class people hold the same values as their more privileged peers, but it is their traditions or circumstances that keep them from being as successful as middle and upper middle-class people. In particular, it is the failure on the part of the working class to "defer gratification of baser subsistence needs for nobler ones like formal education" (p. 16). This translates into the idea that all people within a capitalist society, regardless of class background, want to become rich. This is hegemonic because it leads to the conclusion that if fortunes were reversed and the poor were indeed the wealthy, they would have the same attitudes toward the poor themselves. Consequently, the notion within this dominant discourse is that the less fortunate should figure out how to help themselves. This pull-yourself-up-by-the-bootstraps idea is part of the conservative and right liberal ideologies.

Sociologist Oscar Lewis (1961) developed a variation of this discourse, which he called the culture of poverty. This variant cites a lack of role models in the life of working-class youth as the main reason for their lack of academic success, as poor skills and attitudes are handed down through the generations. The focus of this discourse, the way conservatives see it, is to blame entire groups for the oppressive situations in which they find themselves. Liberals, on the other hand, focus on an individual's shortcomings. The results of these variations are the same for those at the receiving end, of course (Gorski, 2008). Cultural capital discourses, the third variant within these conservative/liberal discourses, emphasize that students from middle-class families have an advantage over their working-class peers by learning from their families the "general culture knowledge, elaborated language codes, and information about how schools work" (Curtis et al., 1992, p. 16), all things that tend to increase academic proficiency, and more likely economic security later on.

A traditional solution, according to some cultural-deficit theorists, is for the schools to provide more programs geared toward helping the working classes learn skills so they can find gainful employment. This reasoning results in a call for streaming. As with almost all aspects of cultural deficit discourses, this position "tend[s] to ignore or discount the material conditions, such as inadequate food, housing and clothing, that can limit poor people's learning potential" (Curtis et al., 1992, p. 17). Indeed, Rothstein (2008) contends that in order to close the academic achievement gap, it is vital that we "acknowledge the effects of socioeconomic disparities on student learning" (p. 8). Moreover, according to Osborne (1991), support for streaming conceals a middle-class bias. All of this supports the observations made by Oakes (2005) that the lower academic classes are filled with students from marginalized racial and White working-class backgrounds. Gorski (2008) suggests that progressive teachers should "fight to keep low-income students from being assigned unjustly to special education or low academic tracks" (p. 35). This is an intense struggle in many schools. Teacher support for streaming or tracking is not solely based on making it easier to teach. It also seems to be the case that some adolescents are not ready to be responsible and put in the effort required to be academically successful. Critical left educators explain this by pointing to the lack of relevancy in the curriculum.

The critical left-influenced class-power discourse described by Curtis et al. (1992) critiques the connections "between the forms of schooling and the structures of capitalist society" (p. 19). It also critiques a curriculum that favors the middle and upper classes. Any teacher who explains the lack of academic success of working-class students as a failure of the system to serve them properly, rather than as a failure by the students or their families, has been influenced by this discourse, whether they are aware of this or not.

The class-power discourse is related to critical multiculturalism as described by Kincheloe and Steinberg (1997), a rarely seen form of multicultural education discussed in Chapter 5. An important component of this form of multiculturalism is the demand that people comprehend how "power shapes consciousness" (p. 25). This is also a crucial feature of the class-power approach, and is similar to what Sleeter and Grant (1994) call for in "Education that is Multicultural and Social Reconstructionist." They call for students to be taught to understand the social construction of knowledge and that they become politically literate. Illuminating the hegemonic veils that conceal the ways power works to maintain the privilege of certain social groups while oppressing others is common to these discourses and theories. The variation is on the degree of emphasis they place on social class as a marker of a person's identity. The question is to determine to what degree veteran social studies teachers consider social class to be an important marker of a person's identity.

Ideology and How Veteran Teachers View Issues of Social Class and Working-Class Students

A study I once conducted consisted of 10 in-depth, semi-structured interviews with high school social studies department head teachers. Department heads are veteran teachers who often act as mentors to their more junior colleagues and are well positioned to understand how curriculum is shaped by context. Reflecting the demographic profile of social studies department heads in Vancouver overall, I interviewed 10 White men.[4] (See Table 6.1 for participant information.) I have divided the data analysis into two groups: the ways that teachers *think* about social class,

Table 6.1 Participating head teachers of social studies departments

Name	School	Years in teaching	Years in dept. head	Student demographics	Other
East side schools					
Craig Evans	Victoria Park	23	16	90% working class, 80% East Asian	Christian, working-class upbringing
Steve Graham	Turner	9	3	95% working class, most racial groups	Middle-class upbringing
Hal Nagel	Hedley	19	12	80% working class, most racial groups	Taught on a reserve
Larry Nelson	Larson	31	3	70% working class, 80% East Asian	Working-class upbringing
Carl Tragas	Wilson Heights	34	8	85% working class, over 50% ESL	Working-class upbringing
West Side Schools					
Dave Carson	Hudson	15	7	Equal groups of working, middle, and upper-middle classes	Middle-class upbringing
Ed Hitchcock	Kipling	23	6	Mostly upper-middle class, 70% Asian	Music/history major, working-class upbringing
Barry Kelvin	Chamberlain	19	12	Mostly upper-middle class, 50% Asian, 50% European	MA in curriculum, working-class upbringing
Tim Patterson	Greenway	13	3	Mostly upper-middle class, 60% East Asian, 40% European	Middle-class upbringing
Eric Quinn	Warner	18	6	Upper-middle class	Christian, middle-class upbringing

Note: Pseudonyms were used for the names of all teachers and schools and the ways that they think about *teaching* class issues. I include parts of this study so that readers can ask similar questions of teachers where they live.

How Teachers Think About Social Class

One of the questions I asked the teachers during the interviews was whether they considered social class to be an important factor in a student's identity construction. Only one of the teachers, Steve Graham, an east side teacher who ironically grew up in a middle-class family, considered social class to be very important.

> SG: I see their class as a big factor because it has a lot to do with their opportunities. And they know this from a young age. Kids at west side schools just assume they're going to end up at university. It's assumed by mom and dad. It's assumed by them, too. And guess what? The money's there for them and they'll go. Here, it's the opposite. Here the kids won't even be thinking of university but maybe some particular kids should be thinking of university. So I see it as pretty important, personally.

Graham focuses on the varying degrees of opportunities afforded to students based on their social class. He rightly points to higher education as a crucial factor in a person's future.

Most of the teachers I interviewed did *not* consider social class to be very important in a student's identity construction. In fact, six of the remaining nine expressed this very perspective. Three of these six expressed the same reason for holding this view, namely, that compared to countries in the Third World, no one in Canada is very poor. Yet, there were significant differences in their reasoning, as well as significant differences in their background. Here are quotes by two of these teachers, Eric Quinn and Barry Kelvin, responding to either my query about the importance of social class in a student's identity construction or to my follow up probe that the wealth gap in Canada is growing:

> EQ: I think we've got to have a global focus. One of the things I do with my students here is, like, point out that poverty is relative. In a way, wealth is relative. So let's have a Canadian focus but also let's remember that, for instance, poverty here is actually contextually defined. And that's not to say that it's not a problem. But let's also remember to look at this globally and realize the privileged base of all of Canadian society.

> BK: ... When I traveled, poverty is just so obvious. You know, when I was in Egypt, there were thousands of men in the streets, unemployed, smoking those tobacco things, just sitting there all day. And I'm thinking, "This is a crappy life." And I guess I just don't pay enough attention, you know, when I go downtown here, which I don't do very often, but then you see [poverty]. I'll do like probably most people do, try to give some money to the fella, depending on – but I'm also a little more severe than some people because I have a handicapped brother and he doesn't beg. He's got cerebral palsy and he tries to work. Then I get caught up in thinking, "You're only 18. What are you doing with a squeegee? You can't possibly be that run down."

Eric Quinn is clearly a liberal thinker. He grew up in a middle-class conservative Christian home and taught in what is ostensibly the wealthiest neighborhood in Vancouver. His experience is perhaps why he does not consider poverty in Canada to be significant. At the least, he has not taught very many poor students and, therefore, may have a legitimate reason for being unaware that poverty is a serious problem in Canada. Moreover, this notion is nowhere to be found in the formal curriculum. In terms of political ideology, Quinn exhibited a strong power-blind liberalism when it came to issues pertaining to social class.

The response given by Barry Kelvin, however, is very significant for a number of reasons. By pointing out what he observed on his travels to Egypt, he agrees with Quinn in looking at poverty in a global context. Yet, he knows that poverty also exists in Vancouver. In fact, more than any of the other teachers, Kelvin's philosophy around class issues is commonly referred to as pull-yourself-up-by-the-bootstraps conservatism. This explains his comments about a hypothetical "squeegee" kid. Yet, there is a reason why he feels so strongly about this.

> BK: My mom was quite sick so we were a welfare family. So in school, I had extremely low self-esteem . . . I am proud of where I am today.

Kelvin's upbringing shaped the way he perceives poverty today. Regarding issues of social class, however, Kelvin is a conservative. The influence of the conservative ideology was apparent later in the interview when the conversation digressed to the topic of unions.

> BK: I think unions were created rightly for industry. And now they've incorporated them-selves in other areas and I'm not sure that's the way it should have turned out . . . And that's not to say I'm White collar because I like playing hockey. I like to have a beer. I like to get down to earth. But I just see a difference. Arrogant or not, I like to think of myself as educated, as in a position where I've worked hard to get here. And it's a position that's fairly powerful in society, powerful in a good way . . . Self-respect is something that comes along with teaching.

Kelvin exhibits an elitist view toward unions in that he considers his high level of education to put him above membership in a union. Regarding poverty, it is the last sentence in particular that reveals the reasoning behind Kelvin's seemingly unsym-pathetic view toward poor people. "Self-respect" is particularly important to him because of his upbringing, which was laced with "extremely low self-esteem." For Kelvin, self-respect must be earned. It is not that he is unsympathetic toward the poor. In fact, Kelvin claims to protect students from ridicule who he thinks have family and financial problems. All of this would at least partially explain why he has developed a *tough love* perspective toward underprivileged students and why he disdains unions, which he claims are much too "overly protecting." It is clear that for Barry Kelvin, his own upbringing has had a large influence on the way he views social relations today, especially around issues of social class. This may be fine for him, but does it benefit his students?

In general, class-blind liberalism is the dominant ideology among this group of teachers, as it is with the current formal curriculum. It is, therefore, difficult to imag-ine the enacted curriculum dealing with social class in a critical manner, if at all. Yet, conservative teachers are even less likely to do so.

Carl Tragas described the differences in teaching at an east side working-class school, primarily composed of East Asian immigrant students, and a west side upper middle-class school.[5]

CT: I can give the same exam, teach the course the same way. Well, I don't quite teach it the same way because I do more visuals here because so many of the students are ESL. And still, the students here get 10 to 15% less than the students at Greenway. So, is that genetic? Or is that socioeconomic? You can't be politically correct and say it's the gene pool. But I think it is. There's a little bit of that, at least. And also socioeconomic.

Paul: So in terms of the old nature-versus-nurture debate, how exactly would you position yourself?

CT: I'm saying that I can buy the logistics that it's mainly socioeconomic. But I also think there's a genetic component.

Paul: Do you think this is why someone ends up being a laborer rather than, say, a professional?

CT: I think, although I know it's not popular to say, that there's something to that.

Tragas' reasoning is what Curtis et al. (1992) call the genetic-deficiency theory. Recent controversial studies associating intelligence with race support what this teacher is saying (Rushton & Jensen, 2005a, 2005b; Herrnstein & Murray, 1994). Curtis et al. dismiss the premise of any essentialist explanations of a stratified socioeconomic society as false.

> The variations are much greater within than between such groups of people. These criticisms do not necessarily deny that there is some genetic basis to intelligence. But they definitely refute the long-standing claim that there is a primary biological basis for either class differences in schooling, or the intergenerational reproduction of social classes. (pp. 15–16)

These educators believe that the problem lies in the environment, and in using the structural deficit discourse, emphasize the role of the school system in a similar way as reproduction theorists do (Bowles & Gintis, 1976). There are clear implications here about the life chances for working-class students: teachers in primarily working-class schools who accept the essentialist discourse will be less likely to develop critical thinking skills in their students. Clearly, ideology matters.

Usage of the essentialist discourse demonstrates that the conservative ideology has influenced these teachers. Moreover, it is not very difficult to see how this conservative view can negatively impact on the learning and subsequent future options of students from marginalized groups. On the other hand, the pull-yourself-up-by-the-bootstraps philosophy of Barry Kelvin also stems from conservatism; yet, his perspective may lead to increased motivation for both teacher and student. Kelvin's approach is associated with meritocracy.

In terms of political ideology, it was also interesting to note the teachers' thoughts around why children who come from poor families graduate from B.C. high schools at much lower rates. Two teachers mentioned curriculum relevance but spoke of it in conservative terms, indicating that vocational courses need to be increased for working-class students who show a lack of ambition.[6] Most teachers used versions of the cultural-deficiency discourses to explain the low graduation rates. In particular, all of these teachers utilized elements of the culture of poverty discourse to make their points. These teachers pointed to a lack of positive role models in the home. The quote that sums this position best was offered by teacher Barry Kelvin who posited "it could be low self-esteem of the parents, who didn't succeed in school either . . . family problems . . . money problems . . . split parents . . . a feeling of failure." Other teachers cited parental consumption of alcohol and a lack of reading materials in the home as factors.

Two of the teachers cited financial problems as a key reason for academic problems. Dave Carson said it best: "I think that there is a whole cocktail of social reasons that lead to people dropping out of school . . . I work under the assumption that poor kids have harder lives. For example, they might have a desire to work, to help their families out." Three other teachers pointed to the latch-key phenomenon as the main reason, which can obviously be linked to familial financial concerns, as well. This view tends to be more liberal than conservative.

In short, the majority view of this group of teachers is that it is the home life of poor students that causes them to leave school before graduating. The discourse most frequently used by the teachers was the culture of poverty discourse, which locates the central problem within the lives of the victims themselves. Yet, Kelly (1996) suggests that such reasoning ignores the role of the school system itself in "pushing out" these students from the regular mainstream schools. Schools are exonerated from any blame. Teacher attitudes, however, are one of the forces that can result in lower academic achievement and ultimately, students leaving school before graduating (Dunne & Gazeley, 2008; Ornstein & Levine, 1989).

All versions of the cultural deficit discourse used by the teachers seem to be used to justify what those on the critical left would describe as a blame the victim mentality. Most teachers used these discourses to explain the academic shortcomings of poor students. What is most curious, then, is the reluctance on their part to teach about disparities in wealth and the current dismantling of the social welfare state in social studies. Is this because of hegemony and the power of the capitalist discourse? Is it because of a hegemonic influence around meritocracy and social hierarchies? The next section explores this concern.

How Teachers Think About Teaching Social Class Issues

One of the questions I asked each of the teachers pertained to their thoughts on how labor issues are represented in the latest social studies curriculum. Four of five east side teachers, who are much more likely to teach mostly working-class students, claimed that the problem with teaching about labor issues, working-class issues, or the dismantling of the social welfare state resided with the students themselves. Hal Nagel stated that it has nothing at all to do with either the formal curriculum or the teacher's role in the enacted curriculum.

> HN: Well, when you look at the content, you try to cram knowledge into them and that's it . . . Hopefully in grade 11 you can draw on it, *if* they remember it. That's a big if! I think it's a natural maturity that the kids, when they get to grade 11, have different issues. They're getting a part-time job. They may have to support themselves in their own living space, or support the family. Whatever the case is, they're more involved in society from a tax payer's point of view. So I think it's partly the socialization that naturally occurs that they're dealing with.

Nagel points out that the working-class students have more important things to do at that time in their lives than learn about working-class issues. He described a right-wing populism developing in the students as they get to grade 11 in which they resent having to pay taxes. As a veteran teacher of working-class students myself, I have come across these same right-wing populist sentiments (Orlowski, 2001a). The mention of taxes and any notion of the social-welfare state have long disappeared from the formal curriculum. Yet, the enacted curriculum in the social studies courses that I teach has units on these very topics. Nagel, on the other hand, is opposed to these adaptations because of an already over-crowded curriculum.

East side teacher Carl Tragas, who also taught for over 20 years at a west side school, made the following comparison:

CT: The east side students are less aware than the west side students.

Paul: Do you mean that the east side students are less aware politically? Or that they don't know what's in their own best interests compared to west side students?

CT: I think the first. The knowledge isn't there because of, I don't know, I don't even think it's so much a language barrier. I think it's a socioeconomic generalization you can make that that they're less attuned to be interested in [politics]. Whereas a west side kid has the home life where there's expectations, academic expectations, where there's news, newspapers, *Time, Macleans, The Economist*, those kinds of things . . . I could start a current events class in grade 11 socials, and be quiet for the rest of the hour. And they, generally, in a civil manner, would have a pretty intelligent conversation.

Tragas' position around teaching working-class students about working-class issues is the same as Hal Nagel's, namely, they do not teach about labor issues because the students are not interested. He claimed that all students, regardless of social class, have a "lack of sympathy for unions," which he said he doesn't understand. Yet, he uses the culture of poverty discourse by pointing out part of the blame resides with the homes the students come from, homes that he believes do not have high academic expectations for their own children, nor reading materials that may help them better understand the world they live in.

There was one teacher, however, who experienced teaching working-class students about working-class issues quite differently. Like Carl Tragas, Steve Graham also taught for several years on the west side before becoming the head teacher at an east side school. In fact, the two were colleagues at the same west side school for two years.

SG: At [the west side school], I found myself being the devil's advocate for what could be broadly called socialist perspectives, because the kids, like kids in every school, they bring what they bring from home. There'd be a handful of kids who, perhaps, would bring the minority point of view. And there'd be the overwhelming majority that would have what we might call the Vancouver Sun's right wing view . . . At that school, you feel kind of like a person who's been in a war zone, providing an alternative perspective, and you'd get a barrage of kids coming at you going, "Wow, those people on welfare!" Here [at the east side school], it's a lot less. It's not to say that every kid here comes from a family that is, you know, more left wing. That's not true.

The different descriptions offered by Graham and Tragas about teaching working-class students versus upper middle-class students could not differ more.

This is especially interesting considering that both of them are describing classroom discussions that occurred in the *same* west side school. What is the crucial factor for these different perspectives? It has to be the political ideology of the teachers themselves. For the most part, Tragas has been influenced by conservatism. On the other hand, Graham is progressive in his thinking around class issues.

Ornstein and Levine (1989) consider teacher attitudes to be of paramount importance. Although their work is not recent, I have found a similar dynamic at work today. They contend that one of the major reasons for low achievement among many working-class and non-White students is teacher perceptions of student inadequacy.

> [M]any teachers in working-class schools reach the conclusion that large numbers of their students are incapable of learning. This view becomes a self-fulfilling prophecy because teachers who question their students' learning potential are less likely to work hard to improve academic performance, particularly since improvement requires intense effort that quickly consumes virtually all of a teacher's energy. Because students are influenced by their teachers' perceptions and behaviors, low teacher expectations generate further declines in students' motivation and performance. (pp. 153–154)

Ornstein and Levine believe that the perspectives of conservative teachers have most likely negatively affected the motivation and performance of their working-class students. There are differing discourses within the conservative ideology, of course. The tough love approach of Barry Kelvin's bootstraps conservatism is *not* what Ornstein and Levine are referring to. Kelvin believes that students from under-privileged backgrounds *can* succeed, provided they get the support they need, whether from peers or the teacher, *and* they put in the effort. The genetic-deficiency discourse espoused by Tragas, however, *is* what Ornstein and Levine are referring to about negative effects on teachers motivating students and, by corollary, student performance.

As we have also seen in Chapter 5 and will see again in Chapter 7, the prevalent use of cultural deficit discourses among the teachers indicates that they have lower expectations about what their students are capable of achieving. This, in turn, lowers the inspiration to learn that the students would likely feel had there been higher teacher expectations.

All ten teachers I interviewed stated that the current social studies curriculum was *not* fair in its depiction or lack of depiction of labor or working-class issues. Despite this uniform perspective, there was very little agreement on what should be done about this. Three teachers gave responses that are progressive in nature, or somewhere in the overlap region of left-liberal and the critical left. For example, east side teacher Steve Graham stated emphatically that teachers of working-class students *should* teach about working-class issues even if they are not covered in the curriculum. According to Graham, "I think it's important for them in their development as citizens." He admittedly found it difficult in "bringing to life the Winnipeg General Strike" of 1919 for his students. Yet, he found it "easy" to teach them about current examples of working-class exploitation, such as the recent lowering of the minimum wage in British Columbia.

Cornbleth (1990) would approve of Graham choosing relevant topics for his working-class students to discuss, such as lowering the minimum wage in British Columbia.

> Sociocultural context includes demographic, social, political, and economic conditions, traditions and ideologies, and events that actually or potentially influence curriculum. (p. 6)

As discussed in Chapter 4, Cornbleth calls for contemporary and historical conflicts to be brought to the fore in the enacted social studies curriculum (p. 34). She theorizes that "curriculum is contextually shaped" and "always mediated by students" (p. 53). Part of what Cornbleth means by contextually shaped is the sociocultural characteristics of the local population. Working-class students *should* learn about working-class issues.

Two teachers claimed that the reason that they do not cover working-class issues in the classroom is because they "don't have the information needed to cover" them. Indeed, *all* of the teachers were aware that the gap between the wealthy and the poor has reached unprecedented rates in British Columbia and in Canada, but not one of them discusses this in their classroom. Carson wished that we taught in a system that sent teachers back to university "with pay" in order to learn about these topics. This is highly unlikely, but teacher education programs should consider filling the knowledge gaps that many teachers have, especially in social studies.

A variety of reasons among the remaining six teachers were stated for not teaching about poverty and labor issues. Two of them, Carl Tragas and Hal Nagel, put the blame on textbooks and the lack of coverage there. (Although it is beyond the scope of this paper to address the textbooks used in B.C. social studies courses, there are more references to labor struggles in some of the prescribed texts than in the formal curriculum itself.) The two remaining teachers, Tim Patterson and Barry Kelvin, were able to articulate a few examples of labor issues they covered in the classroom. Patterson emphasized twice in the interview that he "signed a piece of paper" to cover the curriculum and "not to push a particular personal agenda." Consequently, the only topics he named were "the Industrial Revolution in Socials 9" and "the 1919 Winnipeg General Strike in Socials 11," both of which are included in the formal curriculum.

Summary and Conclusions

The most important conclusion of this study is that there is a clear mirroring between the political ideology underlying the formal curriculum with the attitudes of the teachers and, by corollary, the enacted curriculum. Simply put, *issues of social class were absent from both data sources*. This is not surprising when one considers that neither the formal curriculum nor the vast majority of the teachers claim social class to be an important factor in a person's identity construction. In fact, the curriculum currently used in B.C. social studies classrooms emphasizes that each student should understand that a person's identity construction is affected by a list of factors that sociologists have proven, *except for social class*.

The evolution of the British Columbia Social Studies Curriculum has undergone an ideological shift in terms of social class representation from conservatism to liberalism. What began as a stridently conservative document in 1941 underwent changes such that it is now almost completely liberal and, therefore, class-blind, in its ideological orientation. The 1997 and 2005–06 documents presently used in B.C. social studies classrooms make only two references to working-class matters: the Winnipeg General Strike of 1919 and the Great Depression of the 1930s. It is no wonder that the social historian Howard Zinn did not learn about the Ludlow Massacre until he heard Woody Guthrie singing about it.

Mirroring the formal curriculum, only one teacher considered social class to be a central factor in a student's identity construction. Teacher education programs should address this glaring omission in their program admission requirements. Of course, professional development for practicing teachers should also address this, but funding for this may raise red flags among the economic elites and common citizens duped by hegemonic discourses about tax cuts and public education funding.

The *class-power discourse* was almost completely absent from the thoughts of the teachers. This indicates a paucity of critical left thinking among the entire group. Three of the teachers turned any mention of poverty in Vancouver or Canada to worse conditions for poor people elsewhere in the world. The hegemonic strategy of displacing a local and present concern for social class to economic conditions perceived to be worse in distant places or long ago was also reflected in their teaching: almost all of them taught about class issues either outside of Canada or in a historical context. The gains made through the construction of the social welfare state and its current dismantling were also omitted from the enacted curriculum that each of them described. This is another near perfect match with the formal curriculum.

In terms of explaining the lack of academic success by poor students, the most common discourse used by the teachers was the *culture of poverty*. Almost all of the teachers considered the *home* of unsuccessful students to be the root cause rather than the curriculum, their teaching, or the school system itself. Half of the teachers also cited familial financial concerns for the main reason poor students often fare poorly in academic terms. These teachers are using the traditional culture of poverty discourse that straddles conservative and right-liberal perspectives. Two teachers used the conservative essentialist discourse to explain low graduation rates of poor students. One of these educators spoke of a genetic deficiency as a major reason why people become laborers. In the contemporary context, this is simply an unacceptable view for teachers to hold.

Despite the awareness of class issues, teachers were, by and large, extremely reluctant to address a critique of material inequality in our society. Part of the reason for this was that some consider the Canadian poor to be much better off than the poor elsewhere. This reluctance may also be a result of the normalizing effect of certain hegemonic discourses in support of capitalism in both the curriculum and in mainstream media (Ross, 2000). Fear of rebuke from authority figures may also be a factor.

All ten of the teachers considered the curriculum to be unfair in its depiction of labor and working-class issues. Yet, there was a lot of disagreement over what to do about it. Several of the teachers who grew up in working-class families claimed that working-class students are simply "not interested" in working-class issues. Ironically, a middle-class teacher was the only one who described his working-class students as enthusiastic learners, especially if they felt "the heat of the issue." The ways in which the teachers perceived working-class students and their abilities appeared to be very influential in the academic expectations they held for their students and, subsequently, student efforts. Political ideology was involved in the ways teachers described their students' learning interests and in the topics they chose to cover.

In sum, most discourses used by teachers to describe issues of social class were traditional ones that incorporated ideas from both conservatism and liberalism. In this way, they are a clear reflection of the formal social studies curriculum itself. Although the latest versions are mostly liberal, their predecessors had a conservative perspective. The teachers also demonstrate this combination. Occasionally, a few demonstrated a critical left influence on their thinking and, presumably, their teaching.

The analysis about *social class* indicates that there has been an ideological struggle between conservatism and liberalism during the twentieth century in British Columbia social studies education. In my research, the critical left ideology that critiques capitalism made only fleeting appearances. In fact, despite the overwhelming evidence pointing to the importance of social class in identity construction and determining one's life chances, there is very little directly referring to this in the curriculum or in the thoughts of the teachers. The curriculum matches the low comfort level of most people when the topic of social class enters the conversation. The curriculum both reflects and entrenches this reluctance.

Implications: Can Social Studies Help Bring Social Class to the Public Consciousness?

American and Canadian teachers today have a responsibility to consider whether their teaching practices are discriminatory in the education of racial minorities and students with disabilities. As the discussion in Chapter 5 indicates, this type of deep reflection is difficult for many teachers to do, most often because they do not possess the knowledge required to understand the obstacles themselves. Yet, it is quite telling that teachers are not asked to consider how what they do in the classroom may be discriminatory toward students from working-class backgrounds.

It is clear that if social studies education is to be used for the purposes of social and economic justice, changes must be made to both the formal curriculum, ongoing professional development for teachers, and teacher education. A number of teachers in the study mentioned they do not cover poverty and working-class issues because they have not been taught about them themselves. Requiring some labor history in teacher education would clearly go a long way toward rectifying this situation. In other words, a more radical approach to social studies teacher education is required. Moreover, the current liberal-influenced British Columbia Social Studies Curriculum highlights the individual to such an extent that it virtually ignores all aspects of social class. At the same time, there has been a concerted movement to dismantle the social welfare state, including public education, in both Canada and the United States. Are the two related? I will let the reader decide.

The populist movements that swept Western nations beginning in the 1920s and culminating in the Post-Second World War construction of the social welfare state should also be taught in the social studies curriculum. The struggles that first took place in Saskatchewan resulting in the first public funded healthcare system in North America should be the focus of social studies lessons for *every* student in Canada. Today's concerted attacks to dismantle the egalitarian and universal Canadian healthcare system would undoubtedly meet a higher level of public resistance if this were the case. In both countries, examples of the positive contributions of labor should be a mandatory part of every student's education. All students should be given the opportunity to grapple with economic issues such as private versus public ownership, the effects of corporate political campaign donations, and the average income of CEOs versus laborers.

A critical left-influenced enacted curriculum should include labor struggles, union contributions to civil society and the construction of the social-welfare state, and subsequent threats to their survival. Moreover, an emphasis on race–class intersections in our past would undoubtedly go far in helping citizens understand contemporary struggles for economic justice. A class consciousness among members of the working class would result in fewer racist attitudes because they would understand that they have more in common with each other across racial and ethnic lines than they do with the economic elites in the United States and Canada.

Progressive educators who teach in a state or a province with a regressive social studies curriculum should still attempt to make the curriculum more relevant for students by supplementing the curriculum with historical and current examples of social conflict. This is part of the enacted curriculum. From my own teaching experience, I can attest that this does work. Yes, state and provincial testing is an impediment to supplementing an already packed curriculum, but with some careful planning, some of the mandatory units can include a class analysis. War, for example, can be deconstructed along class lines by simply focusing on what social classes most soldiers are from.

Such a curriculum would better enable students to become informed citizens who are aware of past struggles, as well as aware of *what is in their best future interests*. This would engender a stronger democracy supported by participatory citizens, rather than the current one in which so many people are passive and unaware. After all, progressive changes have always come about as a result of the agency of dominated groups, rather than out of the kindness of dominant ones. I contend that not only working-class students would benefit from this; rather, most Canadians would.

Questions to Ponder

1. Reflect back upon your own high school experience. What did you learn that has helped you become aware of differing social class concerns among the public today?
2. Do you agree with the contention that if the working classes had more of a class consciousness that racist attitudes would decrease? Why or why not?
3. Why do you think that the United States is the only Western nation that does not have a viable social democratic political party?
4. What obstacles, if any, might a progressive teacher expect if part of the enacted curriculum included a class analysis about free trade with Mexico? Around privatizing prisons? Around implementing and maintaining a strong publicly funded universal healthcare system?
5. What obstacles, if any, might a progressive teacher expect if part of the enacted curriculum included past and current labor struggles?
6. Do you think a social studies teacher should teach a class analysis around war? This might entail noting which social class(es) make up the bulk of the soldiers and which one(s) reap any economic benefits from these military endeavors.
7. What do you think would be the effect on students if a teacher were to teach about past capitalist transgressions such as the Ludlow Massacre (see Chapter 4) and more recent fiascos such as what occurred at Enron and A.I.G.?

Notes

1. In Canada, the social democratic party is called the New Democratic Party, or the NDP. The NDP has formed provincial governments in Ontario, Manitoba, Saskatchewan, British Columbia, and Nova Scotia. There are also significant social democratic elements in the federal Bloc Quebecois, and their provincial counterparts, the Parti Quebecois.
2. Of the 25 adolescent participants in my study, only three described their families as working class. It is noteworthy that all three had parents belonging to a union.
3. During the crisis of 2008–2009, governments around the world quickly moved to save their auto industries. By contrast, in the United States and Canada the restructuring has been delayed by a "phony confrontation over auto worker wages" (Stanford, 2009). It is noteworthy that autoworkers in Germany and Japan make more than they do in North America, yet these union contracts were not considered when car manufacturers in Germany and Japan received public monies to help the companies survive.
4. The one (White) female department head in a Vancouver public high school declined an invitation to participate.
5. The following interview excerpt is also included in the discussion about the essentialist discourse in Chapter 5. I include it in both chapters because of its relevance to educational issues of race and of social class.
6. Throughout much of the twentieth century there have been advocates for the streaming of working-class youth into vocational programs. See Kliebard (1986). Some of these advocates are members of the working class who are concerned that their children gain skills to that they will be regularly employed. See Barman (1988).

References

Apple, M. W. (2004). *Ideology and curriculum* (3rd ed.). New York: Routledge-Falmer.

Barman, J. (1988, Fall). "Knowledge is essential for universal progress but fatal to class privilege": Working people and the schools in Vancouver during the 1920s. *Labour/Le Travail, 22,* 9–66.

B.C. Department of Education. (1941). *Programme of studies for the senior high schools of British Columbia.* Victoria: Queen's Printer of British Columbia.

B.C. Department of Education. (1949). *Experimental outline of the programme of studies for the junior and senior high schools of British Columbia.* Victoria: Queen's Printer of British Columbia.

B.C. Department of Education, Division of Curriculum. (1968). *Secondary school curriculum guide: Social studies.* Victoria: Queen's Printer of British Columbia.

B.C. Department of Education, Division of Public Instruction, Curriculum Development Branch. (1980). *Curriculum guide: Social studies, K – 11.* Victoria: Queen's Printer of British Columbia.

B.C. Department of Education, Division of Public Instruction, Curriculum Development Branch. (1988). *Curriculum guide: Social studies, K – 11.* Victoria: Queen's Printer of British Columbia.

B.C. Ministry of Education, Skills and Training. (1997a). *Social studies 8 to 10: Integrated resource package 1997.* Victoria: Queen's Printer for British Columbia.

B.C. Ministry of Education, Skills and Training. (1997b). *Social studies 11: Integrated resource package 1997.* Victoria: Queen's Printer for British Columbia.

Bernstein, B. (1977). *Class, codes and control* (Vol. 3). London: Routledge & Kegan Paul.

Bourdieu, P., & Passeron, J. C. (1977) *Reproduction in education, society and culture.* London: Sage.

Bowles, S., & Gintis, H. (1976) *Schooling in capitalist America: Educational reform and the contradictions of economic life.* New York: Basic Books.

Carmichael, K. (2010, May 20). Merkel leads pro-bank-tax forces against Harper. *The Globe & Mail.* Retrieved from http://www.theglobeandmail.com/news/world/g8-g20/blog-global-view/merkel-leading-pro-bank-tax-forces-as-g20-looms/article1575631/

Cornbleth, C. (1990). *Curriculum in context.* London: The Falmer Press.

Curtis, B., Livingstone, D. W., & Smaller, H. (1992). So many people: Ways of seeing class differences in schooling. In B. Curtis, D. W. Livingstone & H. Smaller (Eds.), *Stacking the deck: The streaming of working-class kids in Ontario schools* (pp. 6–25). Toronto: Our Schools Our Selves Educational Foundation.

Davidson, P. (2007). *John Maynard Keynes* (Great Thinkers in Economics series), New York: Palgrave MacMillan.

Dunne, M., & Gazeley, L. (2008, September). Teachers, social class and underachievement. *British Journal of Sociology of Education, 29,* 451–463.

Fukuyama, F. (1992). *The end of history and the last man.* London: Macmillan.

Gorski, P. (2008). The myth of the culture of poverty. *Educational Leadership, 65*(7), 32–36.

Graf, G. (1994). Beyond the culture wars: How teaching the conflicts can revitalize American education. In W. E. Cain (Ed.), *Teaching the conflicts: Gerald Graf, curricular reform, and the culture wars* (pp. 3–16). New York: Taylor & Francis.

Greenspan, A. (2007). *The age of turbulence.* New York: Penguin Press.

Herrnstein, R. J., & Murray, C. (1994). *The bell curve: Intelligence and class structure in American life.* New York: Free Press.

Hobsbawm, E. (1995). *The age of extremes: A history of the world, 1914–1991.* New York: Pantheon Books.

Kelly, D. M. (1996). Choosing' the alternative: Conflicting missions and constrained choice in a dropout prevention program. In D. M. Kelly & J. Gaskell (Eds.), *Debating dropouts: Critical policy and research perspectives on school leaving* (pp. 101–122). New York: Teachers College Press.

Kincheloe, J., & Steinberg, S. (1997). *Changing multiculturalism*. Buckingham, UK: Open University Press.

Klein, N. (2007). *The shock doctrine: The rise of disaster capitalism*. Toronto: Alfred A. Knopf Canada.

Kliebard, H. (1986). *The struggle for the American curriculum: 1893–1958*. New York: Routledge & Kegan Paul.

Lareau, A. (1989). *Home advantage: Social class and parental intervention in elementary education*. London: Falmer Press.

Laxer, J. (1998). *The undeclared war: Class conflict in the age of cyber capitalism*. Toronto: Penguin Books Canada, Ltd.

Lewis, O. (1961). *The children of Sanchez: Autobiography of a Mexican family*. New York: Random House.

Lukacs, J. (2009, Winter). Putting man before Descartes. *The American Scholar, 78*(1), 18–29.

Marx, K. (1961). *Capital, Volume I*. Moscow: Foreign Languages Publishing House.

McLeod, T., & McLeod, I. (1987). *Tommy Douglas: The road to Jerusalem*. Edmonton: Hurtig.

Meyerson, H. (2008, December 17). Opinion: Destroying what the UAW built. *The Washington Post*. Retrieved on 9 June 2011, from http://washingtonpost.com

Oakes, J. (2005). *Keeping track: How schools structure inequality* (2nd ed.). New Haven, CT: Yale University Press.

OECD. (2008). Retrieved on 9 June 2011, from http://stats.oecd.org/Index.aspx

Orlowski, P. (2001a). Ties that bind and ties that blind: Race and class intersections in the classroom. In C. E. James & A. Shadd (Eds.), *Talking about identity: Encounters in race, ethnicity, and language* (pp. 250–266). Toronto: Between the Lines.

Orlowski, P. (2001b). The revised social studies curriculum in British Columbia: Problems and oversights. *Our Schools/Our Selves, 10*(4), 85–102.

Ornstein, A. C., & Levine, D. U. (1989, September/October). Social class, race, and school achievement: Problems and prospects. *Journal of Teacher Education, 21*(5), 17–23.

Osborne, K. (1991). *Teaching for democratic citizenship*. Montreal: Our Schools/Our Selves Education Foundation.

Palmer, B. (1992). *Working-class experience: Rethinking the history of Canadian labour, 1800–1991*. Toronto: McClelland & Stewart.

Ross, E. W. (2000). Redrawing the lines: The case against traditional social studies instruction. In D. W. Hursh & E. W. Ross (Eds.), *Democratic social education: Social studies for social change* (pp. 43–64). New York: Falmer Press.

Rothstein, R. (2008). Whose problem is poverty? *Educational Leadership, 65*(7), 8–13.

Rushton, J. P. (2000). *Race, evolution, and behavior: A life-history perspective* (2nd special abridged edition). Port Huron, MI: Charles Darwin Research Institute.

Rushton, J. P., & Jensen, A. R. (2005a). Thirty years of research on race differences in cognitive ability. *Psychology, Public Policy, and Law, 11*, 235–294.

Rushton, J. P., & Jensen, A. R. (2005b). Wanted: More race-realism, less moralistic fallacy. *Psychology, Public Policy, and Law, 11*, 328–336.

Sleeter, C. E., & Grant, C. A. (1994). *Making choices for multicultural education: Approaches to race, class, and gender* (2nd ed.). New York: MacMillan.

Stanford, J. (2009, April 20). The economics, and politics, of auto workers' wages: Only in North America has the industry's future been linked to a frontal attack on unions. *The Globe & Mail*. Retrieved on 9 February 2011, from http://www.theglobeandmail.com

Treaster, J. B. (2004). *Paul Volcker: The making of a financial legend*. New York: Wiley.

Walker, T. J. E. (Ed.). (2002). *Illusive identity: The blurring of working-class consciousness in modern western culture*. Lanham, MD: Lexington Books.

Whitehorn, A. (1992). *Canadian socialism: Essays on the CCF-NDP*. Toronto: Oxford University Press.

Wilkinson, R. & Pickett, K. (2010). *The spirit level: Why equality is better for everyone*. London: Penguin Books.

Zinn, H. (2003). *The twentieth century*. New York: HarperCollins Publishers.

Chapter 7
Liberal Discourses About Aboriginal Students – A Case Study of Power Blindness

> *If one does not uncover the influence such hegemonic ideologies have on teachers' thinking, then teachers often "normalize" these racist and classist ideological orientations and treat them as "natural."*
> *(Bartolome, 2008, p. xiii)*

In this chapter, the focus will be on examining how certain liberal discourses – in particular, the color-blind discourse and the cultural-deficit discourse – are to this day entrenched within the minds of veteran social studies teachers. The attitudes of these teachers are an obstacle to increasing the number of Aboriginal students graduating from high school.[1] In other words, it is a critique of liberal discourses from a critical left standpoint. In terms of countering hegemony, these discourses must be challenged. As we shall see, in terms of Aboriginal representation, the British Columbia Social Studies Curriculum seems to have progressed further than the teachers themselves have. I do not know whether this is the case with the social studies curriculum in other parts of North America toward minority representation. Chapters 5 and 6 analyzed discourses on race and class respectively in the formal curriculum and in the interview transcripts of the teachers. This chapter will utilize the same data sources, yet the analysis will be somewhat different.

This case study is situated in Vancouver, British Columbia. Teacher educators and educational researchers can decide whether the discourses affecting the veteran social studies teachers in the study are prominent in other regions of North America. As well, one important question to ponder is whether the attitudes these discourses are associated with would also affect the ways teachers think about other racial and cultural groups such as African Americans and Latinos. These discourses are discriminatory in a subtle way, yet are very powerful obstacles for many Aboriginal students to overcome. Before we examine this case study, some information to set the context will be helpful.

Ours is a modern nationalism: liberal, decent, tolerant and color blind. (*Globe & Mail* editorial November 4, 1995)

[I]t is necessary to challenge the assumption that Canada has always been a fair nation. (St. Denis & Schick, 2003, p. 59)

P. Orlowski, *Teaching About Hegemony*, Explorations of Educational Purpose 17, DOI 10.1007/978-94-007-1418-2_7, © Springer Science+Business Media B.V. 2011

Schooling for Aboriginal youth has come a long way from the residential school policy that was institutionalized in Canada in the 1870s until the last school closed over a century later (Barman, 1995). Indeed, even the representation of Aboriginal peoples in the social studies curriculum has greatly improved from its overt racist beginnings in the 1940s (Orlowski, 2001). Yet, the situation for Aboriginal youth in Canada's westernmost province is still anything but equitable: 42% of them graduate from high school, while the rate for their non-Aboriginal peers is almost double that at 78% (B.C. Ministry of Education, 2008).

In this chapter I explore a dynamic that Aboriginal people have known for a long time, namely, that despite the lofty rhetoric of liberalism around tolerance and equality, Aboriginal students are still at an academic disadvantage at succeeding in high school. In particular, I examine the role that social studies, the course that ostensibly explores social relations in Canada's past and present, might have in exacerbating the situation for Aboriginal high school students. There have been other studies, some done by Aboriginal researchers that have determined causes for this discrepancy and ways to improve the situation (Battiste & Barman, 1995). There have also been many Black scholars who have examined a similar dynamic around Black youth in high schools (James, 1990; Ladson-Billings, 1995; Ogbu, 2002). Yet, this chapter differs in perspective because it is about the work of a White researcher (me) discussing Aboriginal issues in education with ten veteran White social studies teachers. It is an example of what Aboriginal scholar Jeanette Armstrong describes as a member "from the dominant society [turning] over some of the rocks in [his] own garden for examination" (cited in Mackey, 2002, p. 1). This paper implicitly asks the question: What can teachers do to help more Aboriginal students graduate from high school?

Aboriginal youth comprise 10.3% of the overall student population in British Columbia, and their numbers are growing (B.C. Ministry of Education, 2008). In other regions of Canada, the percentage of Aboriginal students is much higher. I taught in B.C. high schools for 19 years in a variety of settings: a small northern town, a small city close to Vancouver, as well as mainstream and alternative schools in Vancouver. In each one of those settings, Aboriginal students were present in all of the courses I have taught, sometimes small in number, while at other times they were a significant minority. Most teachers, on the other hand, are White. Although the teaching population in British Columbia includes a sizeable minority of educators from non-European backgrounds, there are very few Aboriginal teachers.

This chapter describes a segment of qualitative research I undertook in 2004. I describe the results of segments of interviews with the head teachers of social studies departments in ten Vancouver high schools that pertain to Aboriginal issues. Although the interview transcripts are the main source of data, for the purposes of context I include a brief discussion of representations of Aboriginal peoples in certain versions of the formal social studies curriculum used in B.C. high schools. Canada presents itself to the world as a nation that prides itself on its tolerance and fair treatment of minorities, an idea that became institutionalized with Canada's Multicultural Act of 1971. Multiculturalism is often attacked from the right of the political spectrum. Much of this discontent emanates from White Canadians who feel that they are the disadvantaged ones in the "new" Canada (Mackey, 2002). The alarming situation of a growing white defensiveness is also occurring in the United States (Hursh & Ross, 2000, pp. 7–10), as the 2010 rise of the almost all-white Tea Party movement demonstrates.

There is no doubt that Aboriginal peoples have many different issues from other minorities in Canada. Yet, liberal-pluralist multiculturalism provides the framework that enabled me to examine the discourses used in the formal curriculum itself and in the thoughts of White social studies teachers about Aboriginal peoples. This form of multiculturalism paradoxically stresses both similarities and differences between Eurocentric mainstream culture and all other cultures. Yet, it does not include past conflicts or power imbalance in the social, political, and economic realms.

It is clear that the school itself is a filter for how Aboriginal people are seen in social and political terms. Eva Mackey (2002) has analyzed the ways in which the dominant culture in Canada has almost always been able to successfully manage the ways in which minorities, especially Aboriginal peoples, have been represented and, by corollary, managed. The school, of course, is part of the state apparatus, to borrow from Althusser (1971), and therefore is at least partly responsible for how Aboriginal people are seen in social and political terms. Teachers are also members of the public who are inundated with these representations in the media and, even more so, in state-sanctioned materials such as textbooks and the curriculum.

A recent Canadian study found that "preservice teachers systematically devalued the performance of students whom they were led to believe were of Aboriginal ancestry in comparison with their non-Aboriginal counterparts with identical student records" (Riley & Ungerleider, 2008, p. 378). The study simulated an exercise in which the participants were to decide and recommend student placement in remedial, regular, or advanced school programs. It is clear that teachers are in the role of hegemonic agents, or possibly counter-hegemonic agents, whether or not they are conscious of this. These are the reasons why in this study I focused on the attitudes of teachers to explore the issue of why Aboriginal youth have more difficulty finding academic success in mainstream high schools than their peers.

Settings and Methods

For this study, I contacted the social studies department head teachers in all 18 public high schools in Vancouver. All of them were White, and all but one male. (The lone woman declined to participate in the study.) Data for this article were collected through a series of one-on-one interviews with the ten teachers who were the only ones of the 18 to accept my invitation to participate. Half of the participants taught in west side middle-class schools, while the other half taught in the working-class schools of east Vancouver. (See Table 6.1 in Chapter 6, p. 169.) Although I am aware of the pitfalls of power differentials in qualitative research, this was *not* the case with these interviews; after all, I am also a White male, and at the time of the interviews, was teaching social studies in a Vancouver high school. Because of my *insider* status, I consider this research to be an example of *studying sideways* rather than studying up or down. The participants were aware that I had been a teacher for a significant length of time. In my opinion, this helped the participants feel at ease with me, as they considered me to know the demanding conditions under which they must work. As well, I assume that the fact I am White made the teachers feel more comfortable during the interviews than if I had been an Aboriginal researcher. I also assume that the data enabled me to determine how public discourses about Aboriginal people affect how teachers think and what they do in the classroom.

It is noteworthy that at the time this study took place in all but one of the Vancouver high schools White students comprised less than half of the student population. Although most of the non-White students are from various Asian cultures, Aboriginal students are present in all of the schools in varying amounts. Hence, the paper describes the ways veteran White teachers think about certain Aboriginal issues in education. In particular, it examines their responses to two questions. First, "Why do you think that Aboriginal students graduate from B.C. high schools at about half the rate of their non-Aboriginal peers?" And second, "Do you think that the social studies curriculum adequately represents the contributions and experiences of Aboriginal peoples? (If not) Do you do anything to compensate for this? What? Why?"

Framing the Study

This study describes how a researcher from the dominant culture analyzes the thoughts of teachers who are also members of the dominant culture about Aboriginal issues in education. It is important to note that although I am exploring how members of the dominant culture think about the Other, I am by no means suggesting that there is a monolithic view toward Aboriginal peoples that all White Canadians share. Yet, my conception of the perspectives within the dominant culture is influenced by Raymond Williams (1980), who contends that in "any society, in any period, there is a central system of practices, meanings and values, which we can properly call dominant and effective" (p. 38). These practices, meanings and values, then, become part of everyday social relations. As mentioned above, social studies teachers, as members of the dominant society, are also likely recipients of the practices, meanings, and values of the dominant culture.

Everyone involved in the interviews were White. Therefore, as I did in Chapter 5, it is prudent for me to say how the socially constructed variable of whiteness is involved in this research. To this end, I once again rely on the work of Frankenberg (1993) who postulated three dimensions of whiteness: first, it is assumed that whiteness is a social location of "structural advantage" and "race privilege"; second, it is a "standpoint" from which White people view themselves and the Other in society; third, and reminiscent of Williams' concept of the dominant culture, whiteness is a "set of cultural practices" that is unmarked and therefore, is the invisible norm (p. 1).[2] I assumed that these three dimensions of whiteness were at the core of what was said during the interviews.

There are three other theoretical components that provided the basis for my analysis: a taxonomy of racial discourses, Canadian pluralist multiculturalism, and an examination of the liberal discourses used by the Canadian state to represent and manage the minority populations, particularly Canada's Aboriginal peoples.[3]

Racial Discourses

Throughout the book, I use the term *discourse* in the Foucauldian sense: a social theory imbued with power. Discourse and discursive practices affect values, beliefs, and social relations. Frankenberg (1993) describes the conservative racial discourse that drove much of the early periods of the American nation-building project as *essentialist*. This discourse, sometimes referred to as the *genetic-deficit* discourse, posits that one race, in this case the European race, is biologically superior to all other races.

The racial discourse most closely associated with liberalism is the *color-blind* discourse, which has as its basic tenet that beneath our skin, we are all the same (Frankenberg, 1993). As well, the liberal perspective points to cultural deficiencies to explain social inequities rather than genetic deficiencies. It is more acceptable today to talk about the failings of certain groups of people with cultural explanations rather than genetic ones. Yet, both discourses emanate from a blame-the-victim perspective.

Frankenberg describes a third racial discourse in her taxonomy that contends the color-blind discourse is power-blind. Adherents to this *race-cognizance* discourse claim that an individual receives or experiences varying amounts of privilege or oppression based on their racial background. This discourse explains that the reason there appears to be a *glass ceiling* for certain groups is that there are structural obstacles, including systemic attitudes, in the public education system that hold more of their members back.

This chapter critiques the discourses of liberalism, especially ones that focus on egalitarianism, tolerance, fairness, and cultural deficiency, from the standpoint of the race-cognizance discourse. I will attempt to locate the nexus of power-blindness within the liberal discourses of social studies and within Canadian multiculturalism today.

Canadian Multiculturalism – A Brief Overview

Multiculturalism in Canada, including minority rights such as for Aboriginal peoples, has always emanated from the liberal ideology. Paradoxically, it emphasizes both sameness and difference. Canadian multiculturalism assumes that individuals from all cultures share a common humanity that includes, among other things, festive rituals and religious holidays.[4] Past struggles are not part of the liberal multicultural discourse, a trait that enables it to work as an effective hegemonic device. Power is effectively hidden in the color-blind, class-blind, and gender-blind discourses within liberal multiculturalism. It contains the assumption that anyone can make it on their own initiative, supporting the liberal notion of meritocracy. Yet, Canadian multiculturalism also emphasizes difference. This pluralist perspective encourages tolerance between the various racial and ethnic groups. Since the 1970s, pluralist multiculturalism has become the dominant form of multiculturalism promoted by the Canadian state, including government policy involving schools and in popular culture in recent years (Mackey, 2002).

Canadian multiculturalism emphasizes difference, but it erases the conflicts and struggles that have arisen throughout history. As Mackey points out, Canada's liberal values of tolerance, inclusion, and cultural pluralism are "an integral part of the project of building and maintaining dominant power, and reinforcing Western cultural hegemony" (p. 163). A perhaps predictable outcome of promoting these discourses is a backlash from White Canadian commoners, who begin to see themselves as the victims in the new multicultural Canada. An examination of the attitudes of the White social studies teachers toward Aboriginal issues will determine if this dynamic is in evidence. First, it is best to contextualize the study by giving a brief overview of the British Columbia Social Studies Curriculum for examples of these liberal discourses that are pertinent to Canada's Aboriginal peoples.

The British Columbia Social Studies Curriculum as Context

First published in 1941, all eight versions of the state-sanctioned British Columbia Social Studies Curriculum offer an excellent opportunity to explore from a longitudinal perspective Canada's national identity as a liberal, tolerant, and fair nation. It is beyond the scope of this paper to delve into these curricular representations in depth. Yet, a few indicative statements taken from the curriculum will serve two purposes: one, to demonstrate how the state creates certain representations of Aboriginal peoples to manage and control both the people and the discourses about them; and two, to illustrate what kind of discourses were present in the social studies classroom when most veteran teachers were high school students themselves.

The second social studies curriculum was published in 1949. It is here that we see the provincial government supporting what is one of the defining myths of Canadian national identity. In contradistinction to the militaristic jingoism of the United States., Mackey (2002) points out that Canada's national narrative has almost always focused on the tolerance of Canadians. In Social Studies VIII, Unit II, the first "Attitude" listed as one of the "Objectives" is: "*Tolerance* toward the customs of other peoples" (p. 65, emphasis mine). Moreover, the representation of Canada's dominant culture as morally superior to the U.S is further demonstrated in a subsequent objective for the same unit: Students should develop "an appreciation of the responsibilities of both private enterprise and government *in the fair treatment of native peoples*" (p. 69, emphasis mine). These learning objectives were part of almost every high school student's education when the federal government continued to make it illegal for Aboriginal people to practice any of their rituals and customs, and developed policies that made it difficult for people living on the reserves to get out of poverty (Dickason, 1992, p. 286). It demonstrates the willingness of state authorities to ignore the facts because in 1949 the only Canadian adults without the vote in federal elections were Aboriginal people. One would be hard pressed to call this "fair treatment of native peoples" with any honesty.

The fourth social studies curriculum, published in 1968, marks a turning point as the curriculum developers utilize the liberal color-blind discourse.[5] Students are to know that "Canadians, both past and present, have interacted and co-operated in the development of the Canadian nation" (p. 89). Usage of the term "Canadians" masks the fact that White Canadians were given much more opportunity than others to influence the development of the "Canadian nation." This example illuminates the positioning of *White* as the norm for a universal Canadian working for progress. Moreover, the use of the terms "interaction" and "co-operation" are clear attempts to conceal the more sordid parts of Canada's history. This example demonstrates why many consider the color-blind discourse to be power-blind.

Moreover, the 1968 document was the first to acknowledge Canada's diverse cultural composition. The Social Studies 8 curriculum includes these two Generalization Statements:

Distinctive cultures develop distinctive artistic, religious and aesthetic characteristics which reflect their distinctiveness. (p. 89)

Knowledge of Canada's cultural groups may help to resolve issues involving the future of Canada as a multi-cultural society. (p. 90)

Both of these statements are examples of pluralist multiculturalism, and fit in with the prevailing policy of celebrating cultural diversity that was part of the federal government's festivities around the centennial celebrations of 1967 (Mackey, 2002, p. 60). The first statement may have the intention of supporting people who are not from dominant British backgrounds the opportunity to celebrate aspects of their traditional cultures. The second statement suggests that increased knowledge of non-dominant cultures among the general public has some positive value. Yet, as long as it excludes negative experiences with the colonization of Aboriginal peoples, it was unlikely to "resolve *issues* involving the future of Canada as a multi-cultural society" (emphasis mine).

In 2005, the B.C. Ministry of Education published a new Social Studies 11 cur-riculum, followed by a new Social Studies 10 curriculum in 2006. Both include a small introductory section that encourages teachers to make connections to the local Aboriginal communities in order to help teachers develop different instructional and assessment strategies, as well as learn from respected local elders. There are other changes, as well. The grade 10 document has a Suggested Achievement Indicator stating that students should be able to "critique the rationale for treaties" up until 1914 (p. 25). The grade 11 curriculum includes a unit entitled *Society & Identity*, which contains a Prescribed Learning Outcome requiring students to "demonstrate knowledge of the challenges faced by Aboriginal people in Canada during the twen-tieth century and their responses to residential schools, reserves, self-government and treaty negotiations" (p. 21).

A teacher aware of the long struggles that Canada's Aboriginal peoples have experienced might have success in making the curriculum more relevant to

Aboriginal learners. Yet, are teachers aware of this history, current issues, and culturally relevant pedagogical strategies? Are they themselves willing to learn about them? The next section will attempt to answer these questions.

Teacher Attitudes

All ten participating department head teachers were not only members of the dominant society, but they were members of the most privileged group in Canadian society: White males between the ages of 38 to 58. This undoubtedly was a factor in how they perceived educational issues about Aboriginal students. All of them went to high school in British Columbia. The crucial hegemonic strategy that they were subjected to in high school was one of omission – very few students in this province have learned about Aboriginal cultures or history. Nor did they learn about institutional and systemic forms of racism Aboriginal peoples have been subjected to in the name of progress and nation-building. The following discussion explores the presence of the liberal discourses of color-blindness, tolerance, fairness, cultural deficiency within a pluralist multicultural paradigm in the thoughts and attitudes of ten veteran White social studies teachers.

All three racial discourses – essentialist (including genetic-deficiency), color-blindness (including cultural-deficiency), and race-cognizance (including structural deficiency) – were utilized by the teachers as a whole, although to varying degrees. It appears that the essentialist discourse is not confined to extreme right-wing racists. Indeed, it is within our school system, although in a modified form. This racist discourse was used by one teacher in response to the question about why Aboriginal students are less successful than their non-Aboriginal peers at graduating from B.C. high schools. Ed Hitchcock is the department head at Kipling Secondary, an upper middle-class school with few Aboriginal students. He answered the question by highlighting physiology.

> EH: Maybe [it's] their physiological make-up, the business of alcohol, alcohol abuse, substance abuse. That's another vicious circle and maybe it's something that through their race as it were, physiologically they can't handle alcohol as well as the others can and this is another ongoing problem. I mean, it's endemic!

This idea that the marginalization of Aboriginal people has been caused by their own physiology and behavior is a classic example of the traditional essentialist racial discourse. By stating that Aboriginal people do not have the physiology to handle alcohol properly, yet many of them drink in abundance, serves to take the blame away from Canada's White colonizers of the past, as well as present-day educators. To be fair to Hitchcock, once I offered a different explanation, one based on postcolonial considerations, he expanded his thinking.

> Paul: What about the theory I've heard that the abundance of drinking amongst many Aboriginal people today has everything to do with colonialism and the residential school system rather than their physiology?

EH: Well, it could be that, too. They're trying to get away from what happened in the past, to cover up the abuses of the past and the fact that they haven't got the education, they haven't got the options that others may have.

Hitchcock was open to accepting an alternative explanation for the discrepancy in graduation rates. This exchange also demonstrates how various discourses and political ideologies can simultaneously influence the thoughts of an individual. In discussing Aboriginal students, Hitchcock was the only teacher to use the traditional essentialist discourse, emphasizing genetic explanations to explain why some racial groups are less successful in school and in life.[6] I doubt that he would come across as a racist. He would most likely be shocked to learn that I have found him to be using an aspect of the discourse that Europeans used to justify the theft of indigenous peoples' land.

Based on my rather long experience as a Vancouver teacher, I did not expect to come across the essentialist discourse in the teacher interviews. Rather, I expected to find a more contemporary discourse that ranks the various cultures according to how well they are suited to modern (or postmodern) culture. Liberals today often tend to explain the academic and socioeconomic disparities by pointing out the cultural backgrounds of those at the bottom rungs of society (Brantlinger, Majd-Jabbari, & Guskin, 1996).

Six teachers used the cultural deficit discourse in responding to the question about low graduation rates among Aboriginal students. They each suggested various aspects of what they knew or thought they knew of Aboriginal cultures to explain the discrepancy. Carl Tragas was an east Vancouver teacher who grew up in a northern B.C. town and was a year away from retirement. His narrative was infused with the cultural deficit discourse.

CT: Well, I went to school in a large Native community. And socially, the social interaction was great! You know, the fit was nice. I didn't see a lot of racism there, other than the 'drunken Indians on the weekend' kind of thing. But, by and large, it was a very positive experience. But in all those years, as well as in all my years of teaching, which together is now close to 50 years, I see no success. I see no success for Natives in my whole experience. Sure, there's a few more graduates at the universities. How many of those go back to the villages to help out? Some but not many. There really hasn't been much success.

Paul: Why do you think that is?

CT: Well, you know, people would go back to the whole cultural indignity of [the] Europeanization of the New World. I don't particularly buy it, that they haven't been given the opportunities. Like, some of my good Native friends, they argue that they should just have been assimilated. They would have been better off.

Paul: Do you think the residential schools tried to assimilate the Native students?

CT: They were bad news, no doubt about that, those schools were bad news.

Paul: So do you think that the colonial experience, including taking the Native kids from their families to go to these residential schools, could be responsible for their lack of success in schools?

CT: I don't know. You know, that would be the easy answer. It's like breaking the poverty cycle. Somewhere, you have to combine a respect for education and dignity. That has to happen... And there are some heroes. But boy oh boy, it's tough to, on the weekend, go down to the reservation and the alcohol and the abuse that happens. We don't even want to hear about it, it's so bad in some instances. And for those students to have to handle that?

In this particular exchange, Tragas used a version of the cultural deficit discourse called the culture of poverty discourse, which includes a lack of respect for schooling, to describe an attitudinal flaw in Aboriginal cultures toward education and toward their own family members. He eschewed any blame on the part of the dominant culture. It is interesting that Tragas states that his Aboriginal friends wish that they had simply been assimilated into mainstream White Canadian culture. Assimilation was the stated goal of the residential school system upon its creation by the federal government in the 1870s. Yet, the intent of the residential school system was never to successfully assimilate Aboriginal people into mainstream Canadian society (Barman, 1995). Its purpose was to control them by attempting to destroy their cultures (Dickason, 1992).

At one point in the interview, I suggested to Tragas that perhaps the best way to help Aboriginal students was to offer a plethora of options such as Native alternative programs and band-run schools. His response to this was: "That's certainly spoiling them a lot." Tragas dismissed postcolonial explanations as "the easy answer." He was one of a significant number of the participants unwilling to accept more progressive alternative views that I suggested. Tragas' response seemed to imply a belief that mainstream White society has been more than fair in its dealings with Aboriginal people. As well, he seemed to be somewhat influenced by the White backlash phenomenon that Mackey (2002) points to as resulting from the liberal discourse of tolerance (p. 5).

Larry Nelson, a teacher at Larson Secondary in Vancouver's east end, did not consider the colonial experience to have anything to do with the low graduation rates. Nor did he consider the curriculum or the school system to be problematic. Rather, Nelson located the problem to lie with the unsuitability of Aboriginal cultures today with contemporary society.

LN: A [Native] kid just dropped out 3 weeks ago, out of grade 9, so he's got a grade 8 education. And his big rationale was that dad's got a grade 7 education and he's making out okay, so therefore "I'll be okay." I think what comes around, goes around. The role models that they see I think sometimes maybe just aren't in place enough. In this case, coming right out of the horse's mouth, this kid was content doing what dad had achieved 20 or 30 years ago.

I was not quick enough to probe about the father's occupation. Yet, the salient point is that Nelson used the culture of poverty discourse to point to a lack of positive role models around schooling within the typical Aboriginal family as the major reason for their low graduation rates. Moreover, he also insinuated that there is a misunderstanding with Aboriginal people about how the economy has changed over the last 30 years. Consequently, Nelson speculates that the lack of Aboriginal success in B.C. high schools has to do with Aboriginal cultures themselves: a lack of positive role models and a misunderstanding of the way the economy works today. Throughout the entire interview, Nelson gave no indication that he considers the marginalization of Aboriginal students in mainstream secondary schools to be caused by the dominant White society.

Hal Nagel began his teaching career on a northern Aboriginal reserve. Since 1985, he has taught in Vancouver, mostly at Hedley Secondary in Vancouver's east end. He used the cultural deficit discourse to explain the discrepancy in graduation rates based on his experience of teaching in the east Vancouver high school.

> HN: [The] Aboriginal kids there, they don't really care if they pass or fail. They're there. They like coming to school because it's a community thing. It's social. Like any kid, they want to come to school because their friends are here and learn about what other people are doing . . . Maybe for the Aboriginal community, hey, [if] you show up and try your best, that's great! If you learn something, great. If you get an 'A,' great. If you pass, great. If you fail? As long as you show up and do something, that's fine. It's an attitude, you know.

In Nagel's usage of the cultural-deficit discourse, the emphasis is on the *attitude* of Aboriginal people toward schooling to explain the plight in which many of these people find themselves. According to Nagel, the motivation for Aboriginal students to attend school is purely social. Any academic learning that may take place is considered to be a side benefit.

Nagel used the cultural deficit discourse several times throughout the interview. Here he suggests two other aspects of Aboriginal cultures that work to hinder their academic success.

> HN: The culture itself is more verbal than written. Story-telling is huge. So actually sitting and watching a video or writing an essay and then, you know, actually putting those stories and ideas down onto a piece of paper and constructing, well, I don't know if culturally it's in their mindset . . . Some people say it's like Indian time, you know – whenever we get around to it. There's no such thing as a clock. When I taught on the reserve it was like, "Oh, I'm late? Oh, I didn't know that." No such thing as a clock. They work on their own time . . . You know, the White-collar workman is out by 8 o'clock and gets home by 4 or 5 o'clock. That's your workday. There has got to be some structure. And maybe it's Aboriginal culture, that it's not their forte to actually pursue academic life.

Nagel explains the problem of low graduation rates by repeatedly pointing to Aboriginal cultures themselves: their traditions of "story-telling" over the written word, no precise conception of time, and especially his suggestion that "it's not their forte to pursue an academic life" clearly indicates that he does not believe the dominant society is to blame for the marginalization of Aboriginal peoples.

In case I thought that Nagel considered poverty to be part of the problem, he added:

> HN: Within the city, some people just say it's socioeconomics, their poor standard of living. But I don't know if economics has much to do with it rather than, I guess, the encouragement of the parents.

Nagel was consistent in his usage of the cultural deficit discourse in explaining that low graduation rates for Aboriginal students had everything to do with the attitudes of their parents and communities toward schooling. In fact, pointing the finger at the parents was a common finding among the group of teachers.

Tim Patterson teaches social studies at a west side school. Over the years he has taught many Aboriginal students because his school is close to a small reserve.

> TP: Some of the kids you get in a class, their parents are in varying degrees of sobriety. So I've got to think that, yeah, I think it comes from the home. I think that it is basically, like it's not about something like "I've gotta leave school to go work to pay the rent." I think it's more likely that they just don't see school as a vehicle to get ahead.

This explanation concurs with the story that Larry Nelson described above about the grade 9 student who recently quit school. These teachers suggest that Aboriginal people do not understand how increased education will help them. In other words, Aboriginal adults are misreading how the economy has changed in recent decades. Eschewing any material or postcolonial considerations, the views of Nelson, Nagel, and Patterson were indicative of most of the veteran social studies. This group seemed to think that the main reason that so few students of Aboriginal ancestry graduated from B.C. high schools was because their cultures were not suited to academic success.

Eric Quinn, who teaches at Warner Secondary in an upper-middle-class neighborhood, acknowledged that he has taught very few Aboriginal students in his 18 years as an educator. Yet, he also emphasized the role of the parents to explain their lack of academic success. The discourse used by Quinn, however, brought another element into the discussion:

> EQ: I think there is a parenting issue. And I'm not sure if the parenting issue is just differences between parenting styles. Like if Natives were living with Natives in a community and did not have to go to a school set up by others, or did not have to participate in another's economy, I don't know, maybe it would work out very well. Maybe parents are doing a good job within their own frame of reference. Or maybe there's a lot of parents, like an adult generation, that are still feeling the after-shocks and stress of the intense, cataclysmic family breakdown that comes from our colonial history.

During the first part of the quote, Quinn uses the cultural deficit discourse by focusing on the role of parenting to explain the low graduation rates. By the end, Quinn emerges from this more common explanation to suggest that perhaps White people can share some of the blame because of the suffering Aboriginal peoples have endured through colonization.

There was one teacher who questioned the notion that the B.C. school system has been fair in its representation of Aboriginal peoples and in its treatment of Aboriginal students. Dave Carson, who teaches in a west side, middle-class neighborhood, was the only teacher to provide a response in which the race-cognizance discourse appeared.

> DC: Well, to begin with, I don't think the education system suits the majority of First Nations kids at all. I think the whole phenomena of the way the school runs and operates has time after time after time been shown to be unsuccessful for most First Nations kids.
>
> Paul: Are you suggesting that aspects of schooling like the regimented, structured schedule are contrary to traditional Native values?
>
> DC: Yeah, partially, at least. I don't think the curriculum helps either. Most of the curriculum is about White culture. How can they relate? They can't relate. It's just that. School is an exercise in perpetuating imperial White culture.

Although it might seem that the first part of Carson's comments use part of the cultural-deficit discourse, his wording refrains from using a blame-the-victim rationale. Rather, he puts the onus on the school authorities to rectify the problem. Carson also clearly believes that the social studies curriculum is Eurocentric to the degree that Aboriginal students are at a disadvantage. His reasoning used the race-cognizance discourse, indicating that he implicitly questions certain liberal discourses about fairness and tolerance so often heard in the school setting and society at large.

Almost all of the participating teachers relied extensively on the cultural-deficit discourse to explain why Aboriginal students fare less well in high school. White liberals, which these teachers would classify themselves as, often rely on the discourse of meritocracy to explain academic and economic disparities rather than acknowledging white privilege. According to St. Denis and Schick (2003), "[m]eritocracy assumes that power is equally available and distributed, thereby ignoring social, economic, historical, and political conditions" (p. 64). The cultural-deficit discourse ignores all of these conditions, and its usage keeps White privilege from view. These teachers, like many White people, are either "unaware of, or choose to forget, how disadvantage has been constructed historically" (p. 67). Do they have any interest in altering the curriculum to perhaps increase Aboriginal students' chances of succeeding, at least in social studies? The next section addresses this very issue.

Teachers and the "One-Size-Fits-All" Color-Blind Curriculum

Throughout the preceding data analysis, the most significant aspect was not the discovery of the presence of the essentialist discourse or the preponderance of the liberal cultural-deficit discourse. Nor was it the fact that only one teacher used the race-cognizance discourse. Rather, what was most surprising for me, as well as the most disturbing, was the absolute refusal of most teachers to accept the race-cognizance discourse in both the ways they see social relations and in their teaching of social studies. Most were aware that some people would like to see social studies taught from other perspectives, but dismissed this as some sort of movement steeped in "political correctness," as one teacher put it.

Despite occasionally utilizing other discourses, Eric Quinn was the one teacher who utilized the clear-cut examples of the liberal color-blind discourse several times.

EQ: It took us 75 years of teaching history to actually start deconstructing history and understand a new way of teaching it in a way that is inclusive, that attempts to basically give a sense of equality of voice. Right? And now, for instance, this is what I have against doing a women's studies approach or a First Nations studies approach. Basically, now we are reconstructing a monolithic window, like a mono-story, to teach our kids. I can't agree with teaching history the way that we traditionally taught it because it just doesn't work and it's not true of our world anymore. But I can't see going to the equal opposite extreme . . . I personally couldn't teach Socials 11 through a First Nations perspective.

Quinn was very aware that history used to be taught in an extremely Eurocentric manner. He approved of attempts to deconstruct it, although he said elsewhere that there are "real dangers to this [deconstructive] way of teaching." His comment about teaching social studies "through a First Nations perspective" was in reference to the implementation of First Nations Studies 12, a relatively new course that was resisted by many social studies teachers (Steffanhagen, 2000).

Ladson-Billings (1995) strongly suggests that teachers develop culturally relevant pedagogy for students from minority backgrounds. When I asked Quinn if he would alter the curriculum at all to address the social backgrounds of students in his class, such as having a class composed of Aboriginal students, he replied in the negative.

> EQ: I'm not sure that you would present it much differently... How do we create a pluralistic view of history without creating victimization? That is the question for me. I'm not interested in teaching a victimized history of, you know, "Can you believe how awful we were to this group and that group?" Teaching social studies would become a flaying exercise in hating ourselves.

Quinn was steadfast in his position of not teaching the wrongs of the past because, in his opinion, it is tantamount to "creating victimization." Interestingly, he considered the race-cognizance discourse to be nothing more than "creating victimization," as though it is the discourse rather than past actions that has caused much suffering within socially marginalized groups. Quinn's attempt at teaching social studies in a way that he considers to be objective is one of the main reasons why Frankenberg (1993) claims that the color-blind discourse is also power-blind. It is also an example of what Mackey (2002) cites as the contradictions that often lie beneath the surface of Canadian discourses of fairness and fair treatment (p. 23). Indeed, Quinn's views mesh perfectly with the Canadian state's position to eschew any mention of intolerance and unfairness in our country's history with the original inhabitants of the land.

I asked Barry Kelvin, a west side teacher at Chamberlain Secondary, if he thought that the social studies curriculum fairly represents the contributions or experiences of Aboriginal people. I also asked him if the teacher should compensate for any shortcomings.

> BK: It's quite a debate. I'm not sure where I stand on it either. I don't like the idea of usurping the land of the people who were here long ago. But then again, when you study history throughout the world, you find that tons of people have been put in that position. Is it fair? I don't think so. But do you try and do an about-face and correct all the wrongs in history? I don't think you do.

Kelvin's answer was very much in keeping with what his peers felt about giving voice to Aboriginal peoples about their experience. He understands that the past is filled with injustices, that it has been anything but fair. Yet, his view is that because there has always been so much past suffering, it is best to wipe the educational slate clean, and carry on as if these events never occurred. Kelvin demonstrated how the color-blind discourse of liberalism ignores the historical conditions that benefited certain racial groups at the expense of others, in the process effectively demonstrating the discourse to be power-blind. It also indicates a lack of awareness of how systemic racist attitudes are continually reinforced.

Ed Hitchcock was very clear in his refusal to alter the social studies curriculum in order to better reflect the past from the point of view of Aboriginal students.

EH: That would be an apologist's approach to teaching history. I want no part of it.

Paul: But what if research showed it could help Native students improve academically?

EH: Look, it is important for Canadians to have a common curriculum, one that teaches the past to everyone in the same way. We have a lot to be proud of in this country. We need to know the facts about how this country came to be where it is today.

Paul: What facts do you suggest students learn?

EH: Facts about the structure of government, how it has changed over time, that sort of thing. Canada's role in the two world wars. These are important things that every kid should know. There are lots of them.

From Hitchcock's response, it is clear that he had no intention of eschewing a color-blind orientation to the teaching of the past for one that suggests that not all groups were treated fairly in the nation-building era, or the present era, for that matter. He was steadfast in his response, even when I suggested that utilizing the race-cognizance discourse might benefit Aboriginal students, implying that this "apologist's approach" is misguided.

If pressed further, I am almost certain that Hitchcock and most of the others would agree with the notion of the common curriculum, as described by educators such as Hirsch (1996) and historians such as Granatstein (1999) and what in 2010 became law in Arizona (Santa Cruz, 2010), rather than using culturally relevant pedagogy such as Ladson-Billings (1995) suggests. Tim Patterson made his position clear in his response to my question about adapting the curriculum so that it is more relevant to Aboriginal students.

TP: Teaching is not a vehicle to promote your own agenda. You have a job, when you sign that piece of paper, to teach the curriculum. You are not there to create an army of followers to your way of seeing the world.

Apparently, Patterson did not see the curriculum as a political document, or that the curriculum developers might have had an agenda of their own. Apple (2004) makes a strong case to show the formal curriculum is anything but apolitical. Indeed, it is laden with power. Unfortunately, especially for Aboriginal students in his classes, Patterson is one of a significant number of teachers in British Columbia who consider the formal curriculum to be "neutral" and not to be tampered with (Kelly & Brandes, 2001). All of these teachers, whether consciously or not, support what Mackey (2002) contends is the state's strategy of representing the other in ways that make it easier to manage them (p. 5). This strategy also works to promote a sense of innocence and "colonizer generosity" in students subjected to this conflict-free, mostly color-blind curriculum (p. 25).

There was one participating teacher, however, who seemed to understand the political nature of the curriculum. Dave Carson, the same teacher to invoke the race-cognizance discourse, was the only one who mentioned teaching the Canadian past using different perspectives. The following is indicative of several of his statements that showed an awareness of the complex nature of teaching.

> DC: Students in my classes are always made to question whether Columbus and James Cook are heroes. I make sure that it is not as cut and dry as they might at first think. For me, I guess, this is how I get the students to think critically about history.

Carson, who taught in a west side school with only a few Aboriginal students, was one of the younger teachers in the study. Yet, he still had graduated from a Vancouver public high school prior to the 1988 curriculum being used in social studies classrooms and, therefore, was taught from a liberal-pluralist multicultural frame. I do not know why Carson was more open to the race cognizance discourse in his teaching, and it is beyond the scope of this case study to even speculate. The point I wish to make here is that he was the lone participating department head who did not solely rely on the color-blind discourse in his teaching of the past.

When I pressed Carson further on teaching about the land and treaty negotiations currently going on in British Columbia, he gave an illuminating reply.

> DC: Hey, I wish I knew about the treaty negotiations myself! But I don't know enough to teach about them. You know what I'd like to see? Teachers be given time off to take some university courses in areas like Aboriginal history. I just don't have the time to do it on my own.

Carson brought up two crucial issues. First, most social studies teachers simply do not know enough about Aboriginal issues to feel comfortable teaching about them. Second, teachers are too busy to learn about these issues and develop unit plans about them. Both of these points partially explain why the color-blind discourse is still used so much in the classroom. This also is an example of how Mackey conjectures how the state mediates power so that it is (mostly) in the hands of members of the dominant culture (p. 89). Despite the emphasis on teacher accountability and province-wide testing in recent decades, it is the teachers who ultimately decide what details, even what topics, to teach their students about.

All of the teachers were aware of the statements in the social studies curriculum for teachers to offer multiple perspectives and to teach about past injustices. Yet, Carson was the only one who said he sometimes did this. Some teachers didn't think that "wrongs of the past" can be made right, a position that led them not to teach about them. For these teachers, the color-blind discourse is the one that they feel most comfortable with in teaching the history of Canada. It is as if these teachers do not understand how past actions affect the social relations of today.

Summary and Conclusions

The case study described in this chapter showed evidence to suggest that social studies education is at least part of the problem for the high drop-out rates of Aboriginal students from B.C. high schools. Liberal discourses frequently permeate both the social studies curriculum and the attitudes of the teachers. Yet, the preponderance of these discourses should not be surprising, given that the Canadian state has gone to great pains to promote our national identity as one that has been fair in its treatment of minorities.

The teacher interview transcripts demonstrate the use of a plethora of different liberal discourses. In answer to the question of low Aboriginal high school graduation rates, the cultural deficit discourse was most utilized. This took various forms such as the unsuitability of Aboriginal cultures for contemporary life, their misunderstanding of how today's economy operates, a lack of positive role models, a lack of respect for education itself, especially for academics, and dysfunctional parents. One teacher emphasized his point that socioeconomics had nothing to do with their plight. In all of these comments, the common theme is that the dominant culture is not to blame for the poor standard of living that many Aboriginal people find themselves in. This may not be surprising when one considers that the federal government has consistently employed liberal discourses of tolerance and fairness toward Aboriginal peoples throughout much of Canada's history. To be fair, one teacher countered the predominant view of his colleagues that there was nothing schools could do to ameliorate the situation: he rightly pointed to the Eurocentric curriculum as being problematic. There was also evidence of a conservative "essentialist-lite" discourse used by one teacher.

Overall, the teachers refused to accept the suggestion that they alter the curriculum to help make it more relevant for Aboriginal students. Instead, they were almost unanimous in their support of the color-blind curriculum. One teacher called race cognizance in social studies nothing more than "an apologist's approach to teaching history," while another said it would result in "creating victimization." In fact, the strength of their refusal to accept the race cognizance discourse or to develop culturally relevant pedagogy was quite surprising. This finding leads me to think that the White backlash phenomenon whereby White Canadians feel victimized by multiculturalism has infiltrated the thinking of the teachers, as well.

On the other hand, the teacher who pointed out the Eurocentric nature of the social studies curriculum also employed the *multiple perspectives* pedagogical strategy to teach Canadian history. Yet, this same teacher expressed an inability to teach about current land conflicts and treaty negotiations involving Aboriginal peoples and the dominant society because he felt he simply did not understand the issues, nor did he have enough time to learn about them. (As a veteran teacher myself, I can attest to the lack of time teachers have to learn so that they fully comprehend complex sociopolitical issues.) Citing a lack of time is a much different attitude toward helping Aboriginal students than what his colleagues had, an attitude that is perhaps best summed up in the words of one teacher who responded to my suggestion of changing the conditions for Aboriginal students with: "That would certainly be spoiling them a lot."

The attitudes of most of the teachers in this study are evidence that supports Eva Mackey's (2002) contention that the discourses of Canadian liberalism enable the state to manage both the Aboriginal peoples and the discourses about them. Increased representation in the curriculum, including the celebratory nature of difference, can effectively hide the power wielded by the dominant society, especially if the representation is apolitical. After all, it is members of this very same dominant group who decide what differences to highlight (e.g., customs) and what ones to ignore (e.g., prison statistics), a very clear expression of social power. As well, the teachers do not have a grasp of the knowledge needed to alter their teaching from either the one-size-fits-all color-blind curriculum or the celebratory aspects of pluralist multicultural education to a power-focused critical multicultural education. In sum, even though the social studies curriculum has evolved into a document that allows for race-cognizance discourses, the teachers are reluctant or unable to do so.

The intention of this case study is not to lay blame with the social studies teachers. Indeed, they are merely members of the dominant society and must contend with the same hegemonic discourses that are found almost everywhere in Canada. Moreover, even if they had the inclination to deconstruct these discourses, they have very little time to do so. Yet, the discrepancy in B.C. high school graduation rates for Aboriginal students remains at about half the rate of their non-Aboriginal peers. This is an ethical issue that must be addressed.

Teacher Education Programs in Canada and the United States have a responsibility to deconstruct these liberal discourses to locate the power inherent within them. As well, preservice teachers need to learn other pedagogical strategies to help increase the academic success of Aboriginal youth. Ladson-Billings' (1995) work on culturally relevant pedagogy should be applied to Aboriginal students. Although focused on elementary schooling, Goulet (2001) emphasizes the need for teachers to learn how to make connections to local Aboriginal communities and to learn their histories.

Lastly, it was very significant that the social studies department heads in all of the Vancouver public high schools were White. I have no doubt that I would encounter less support for the color-blind and cultural-deficit discourses had there been Aboriginal participants. The study demonstrates the dire need for more Aboriginal teachers in the public education system.

Despite obvious difficulties, these ideas are worth implementing because educators have a major responsibility to help all students, including Aboriginal learners. Liberal discourses have failed Aboriginal students. As Mackey (2002) points out, "[t]his celebration of Canadian tolerance, and how far Canada has come … erases the difficult question of how far the nation still needs to go to have genuine justice and equality for Aboriginal people" (p. 87). An examination of the teachers' attitudes, however, partially answers this question.

For Reflection

To test your own awareness of Aboriginal peoples, take the following quiz:

(a) What is the name of the tribe of Aboriginal People nearest to where you grew up? Where was their traditional lands?

(b) What are three geographical places near to where you grew up that use the Aboriginal peoples' name?

(c) How did these people relinquish their land rights, if they did at all? If not, where are the negotiations currently at?

(d) Name an Aboriginal person who is:
(i) a writer, (ii) an actor, (iii) a musician, (iv) a professional athlete

Questions to Ponder

1. The Canadian government outlawed the *Sun Dance* in the 1880s, and then made it legal again in 1951. The American government outlawed it in 1904, before Jimmy Carter made it legal in 1978. Why do you think these two federal governments outlawed this traditional Aboriginal ceremony (as well as many others)? If a powerful culture were to overtake your country and outlaw ceremonies such as Christmas and Easter, what do you think the long term result would be?

2. What was the *stated intention* of the Canadian and American governments to forcibly send Aboriginal children to residential (Canadian) or boarding (American) schools? Do you believe that this was the actual intention? Why or why not?

3. What long term effect do you think it would have on the ethnic or racial group you belong to if the government forcibly removed your children at age 6 to attend these residential or boarding schools for 10 months of each year for five generations?

4. Why do you think that there is so little mentioned about Aboriginal peoples and their strained relations with the dominant society in the social studies curriculum?

5. What do you think teachers can do to help improve the lives of Aboriginal peoples?

6. Do you think that there are other groups in North America that have experienced something similar to what Canada's Aboriginal peoples have gone through? Which groups? What are the similarities and differences between Aboriginal peoples' experience and the other groups'?

Notes

1. A version of this chapter appeared in *The Canadian Journal of Native Education* (2008) 31(2), 110–129.

2. For a recent example that intimates all three dimensions of whiteness, the corporate media described 2008 Vice Presidential candidate Sarah Palin's family as a *regular* American family with challenges when her 17-year old daughter announced she was pregnant. Further, the biological father was depicted as a great son-in-law to be despite his own vulgar on-line representation of himself. Would the media have behaved differently if Barack Obama's family had similar challenges?

3. These racial discourses were covered in more detail in Chapter 5. I include them here in shortened format to make it easier for the case study to stand alone.

4. For a more detailed description of liberal and pluralist multiculturalism, see Kincheloe and Steinberg (1997).

5. It is noteworthy that when most of the teachers in the study were high school students they had *this* version of the curriculum in their social studies classroom.
6. Chapter 5 includes an excerpt from an interview with a veteran White teacher using the essentialist discourse to explain the low test scores of immigrant working-class students.

References

Althusser, L. (1971). Ideology and ideological state apparatuses. In P. Bourdieu & J. P. Passeron (Eds.), *Lenin and philosophy and other essays* (pp. 127–186). New York: Monthly Review Press.

Apple, M. W. (2004). *Ideology and curriculum* (3rd ed.). New York: Routledge-Falmer.

Barman, J. (1995). Schooled for inequality: The education of British Columbia Aboriginal children. In J. Barman, N. Sutherland, & J. D. Wilson (Eds.), *Children, teachers and schools in the history of British Columbia* (pp. 57–80). Calgary: Detselig.

Bartolome, L. I. (Ed.). (2008). *Ideologies in education: Unmasking the trap of teacher neutrality.* New York: Peter Lang Publishing.

Battiste, M., & Barman, J. (Eds.). (1995). *First Nations education in Canada: The circle unfolds.* Vancouver: UBC Press.

B.C. Ministry of Education. (2008). *How are we doing? Performance data.* Retrieved on 2 April 2011, from http://www.bced.gov.bc.ca/abed/performance.htm.

Brantlinger, E., Majd-Jabbari, M., & Guskin, S. L. (1996, Fall). Self-interest and liberal educational discourse: How ideology works for middle-class mothers. *American Educational Research Journal, 33*, 571–597.

Dickason, O. P. (1992). *Canada's first nations: A history of founding peoples from earliest times.* Norman, OK: University of Oklahoma Press.

Frankenberg, R. (1993). *White women, race matters: The social construction of Whiteness.* Minneapolis: University of Minnesota Press.

Goulet, L. (2001). Two teachers of aboriginal students: Effective practice in sociohistorical realities. *Canadian Journal of Native Education, 25*(1), 68–82.

Granatstein, J. L. (1999, August 28). A politically correct history leads to a distorted past and a bleak future. *The National Post*, p. A13.

Hirsch, E. D. (1996). *The schools we need and why we don't have them.* New York: Doubleday.

Hursh, D. W., & Ross, E. W. (Eds.). (2000). *Democratic social education: Social studies for social change.* New York: Falmer Press.

James, C. E. (1990). *Making it: Black youth, racism and career aspirations in a big city.* Oakville, ON: Mosaic Press.

Kelly, D. M., & Brandes, G. M. (2001). Shifting out of "neutral": Beginning teachers' struggles with teaching for social justice. *Canadian Journal of Education, 26*, 347–454.

Kincheloe, J., & Steinberg, S. (1997). *Changing multiculturalism.* Buckingham, UK: Open University Press.

Ladson-Billings, G. (1995). Toward a culturally relevant pedagogy. *American Education Research Journal, 32*, 465–491.

Mackey, E. (2002). *The house of difference: Cultural politics and national identity in Canada.* Toronto: University of Toronto Press.

Ogbu, J. (2002). Black-American students and the academic achievement gap: What else you need to know. *Journal of Thought, 37*(4), 9–33.

Orlowski, P. (2001). The revised social studies curriculum in British Columbia: Problems and oversights. *Our Schools/Our Selves, 10*(4), 85–102.

Orlowski, P. (2008). "That would certainly be spoiling them": Liberal discourses of social studies teachers and concerns about Aboriginal students. *Canadian Journal of Native Education, 31*(2), 110–129.

Riley, T., & Ungerleider, C. (2008). Preservice teachers' discriminatory judgments. *The Alberta Journal of Educational Research, 54*, 378–387.

Santa Cruz, N. (2010, May 12). Arizona bill targeting ethnic studies signed into law. *The Los Angeles Times*. Retrieved on 15 February 2011, from http://articles.latimes.com/2010/may/12/nation/la-na-ethnic-studies-20100512

St. Denis, V., & Schick, C. (2003). What makes anti-racist pedagogy in teacher education difficult? Three popular ideological assumptions. *The Alberta Journal of Educational Research, 49*, 55–69.

Steffanhagen, J. (2000, March 3). Natives vetting grade 12 course. *Vancouver Sun*, p. A1.

Williams, R. (1980). *Problems in materialism and culture: Selected essays*. London: Verso.

Chapter 8
Ideology, Democracy, and the "Good" Citizen

Despite its flaws, democracy is the best system for the distribution of social, political, and economic power that humans have ever devised in industrial state society. Only people at the extreme ends of the political ideological spectrum, such as fascists and Stalin-influenced communists, would disagree with this statement. Even corporate conservatives such as George W. Bush spoke of the desire to spread democracy to other parts of the world.[1] Certainly peasant people living under feudal arrangements would prefer to live in a society where they have a venue to express their concerns. Women and other minorities would certainly agree that being full citizens with the right to vote is better than having to live under the control of wealthy White men. Yet, democracy is waning across the globe. In western nations in Europe and North America, voter turnout rates are, for the most part, decreasing during election time. Voting is only a small fraction of what it means to participate in a democracy – yet, democratic participation *between* elections is also off the radar for most Americans and Canadians.

This chapter is mainly about how social studies can help to reverse this trend. After all, the state-sanctioned social studies curriculum includes a proviso that one of the main goals of social studies is to teach for a stronger democracy. My experience suggests that this is one area where social studies teacher education should focus more attention. The social costs of not doing so are much too great. The second half of this chapter will focus on the three aspects of how I teach for and about democracy. My approach has three main components: first, students must understand political ideology; second, they must be made to realize that corporate media have corporate interests; and third, they should comprehend the inherent benefits for citizens in a strong democracy, and be aware of the flaws in our democratic traditions.

A Brief Discussion About Modern Democratic Concerns

Modern democratic principles arose out of the Enlightenment and have been debated every step of the way by conservative, liberal, and socialist ideologues. Each ideology holds strong positions on *who* should be allowed to participate in democratic decision making and in certain institutional arrangements. The notion of *citizenship*

P. Orlowski, *Teaching About Hegemony*, Explorations of Educational Purpose 17, DOI 10.1007/978-94-007-1418-2_8, © Springer Science+Business Media B.V. 2011

also arose out of conflicts that originated during the Enlightenment, struggles around inclusion and exclusion, and in the process of developing citizenship rights it displaced the related concept of *subject*. In the Canadian context, this displacement lagged behind other western nations. It wasn't until the Citizenship Act of 1947 that people became Canadian citizens instead of solely British subjects (Sears, Clarke, & Hughes, 1999, p. 114). At the center of these struggles were issues of race, ethnicity, and class, as well as gender and sexuality. It has been a difficult process to extend full citizenship rights to more groups, as current struggles over gay rights indicate, especially in the United States.

Citizenship is clearly related to democratic principles. It is also clearly a concern of this chapter. In Western nations, the past few decades have seen an increase in social movements of groups calling for increased recognition and increased access to the power nexus. This is part of the democratic process, of course, and it is important that social studies teachers adapt their teaching to include an analysis of identity politics and democracy.

Indeed, discourses about race and social class in Western nations have been influential in the struggles around citizenship. It is the unifying conception of citizenship, namely, who is included and who is excluded in our society that is particularly pertinent to the development of a progressive society. Moreover, the liberal notion of meritocracy, now also favored by most conservatives, is "fully consistent with democracy" (Laxer, 1998, p. 36) because in theory no one gains power through inheritance. Yet, as I have mentioned in earlier chapters, the assumption that Canada is a meritocracy in which all people are given an equal chance at power and a higher standard of living is simply a falsehood.

Democracy has long been a hotly contested term. Ever since its appearance during the Enlightenment, it has been a source of vociferous debate over its overall viability, which groups should have a voice, and over the kind of democracy. I will not endeavor to enter this debate over the true meaning of democracy, other than allowing voice to as many groups and individuals as possible. I will also refrain from distinguishing between the various conceptions of democracy.[2] Nor do I wish to go back to the roots of democracy in ancient Greece and discuss the writings of Plato and Aristotle. In this introduction, however, I will make a brief case as to why the related concepts of democracy and citizenship are important considerations for contemporary social studies education, particularly in the context of ideological representations of race and social class.

The conceptual framework of democracy among academics and activists includes ideas of representative government, political and social justice, equality, liberty, and human rights. Yet, the layperson's view of what democracy means is not much more than simplified notions of elections and representative government. Whether the reason is our consumer culture bombarding us with advertising, a feeling of unease over the lack of political response over various issues, or a general lack of education to think critically about complex social issues, the end result is that we live in an era of acute political apathy. As Deirdre Kelly (2003) succinctly puts it, "[o]ur existing democracy engenders widespread passivity and disconnection" (p. 124). Yet, can we afford to sit back and let certain powerful forces have their way? For example, in the present context, many citizens are concerned about making society safe from corporate control in areas as diverse as water quality, air quality, food quality, healthcare, education, and, under the George W. Bush administration, even social welfare. Yet, ever since the Enlightenment, many have been concerned about making society safe from all sorts of evils, including tyrannies, oligarchies, plutocracies, and anarchy. The question that always follows is: What is the best way to accomplish this?

As one response, political philosophers Nancy Fraser (1997) and Iris Marion Young (1997) suggest that democracy must embrace the idea of a politics of inclusion through vigorous debate and public dialogue. But how do regular people enter into the debate? This is the starting point for this brief discussion on why it is imperative to look at the ways democracy and citizenship should be taught in social studies classrooms today. In fact, the second half of this chapter will describe my own experiences as an educator teaching for and about democracy, including its flaws. First, in order to provide context for current concerns, there will be a brief overview of historical concerns about *American* democracy.

American Democracy: Achieving Dignity for the Masses?

One of the leading nineteenth-century liberal thinkers, Alexis de Tocqueville, believed in the inevitability of democracy. Yet, one of his major concerns was its potential to fall into a kind of despotism in which a head of state presides over a congregation of isolated individuals who may be equal but who also may be powerless. In the classic *Democracy in America*, Tocqueville reasons that his worry was not so much that the masses would become active ideological followers of the leader (Heffner, 1956). Rather, he saw the potential for the masses to be dumbed down to the point where they would not even be interested in large-scale political action. The current political apathy in most Western nations attests to the validity of Tocqueville's concerns.

Tocqueville influenced another great liberal thinker of the nineteenth century, John Stuart Mill. In *Considerations on Representative Government* (1861/1991), Mill thought it a good idea for every adult to have the vote. He was an outspoken supporter of the Pankhurst sisters' agenda before British women were enfranchised. But Mill put a condition on this universal enfranchisement: compulsory secondary education must be instituted for all. Mill considered *education* to be most important in order to safeguard democratic society from degenerating into the despotism Tocqueville feared.

In early twentieth-century America, John Dewey, the founder of American pragmatism who made a massive contribution to the philosophy of education, wrote extensively on the potential of public education to strengthen democracy. In *Democracy and Education* (1916), Dewey argues that public education offers the best hope against the possibility of despotic regimes. The public school, according to Dewey, must have a major mandate of developing in each student critical thinking skills so that they will become citizens capable of solving complex social problems. "The essential need," according to Dewey, "is the improvement of the methods and conditions of debate, discussion and persuasion" (1927/1954, p. 207). In this way, democratic American society emphasized the importance of liberty, and would attempt to reconcile the inevitable tensions between individual rights and freedoms with the good of the overall community.

Liberal thinkers such as Tocqueville and Dewey made major contributions to theorizing about American democracy. Yet, one aspect of democracy was not a major focus of their theories, namely the notion of equality. After Dewey, thinkers from the critical left began making contributions to this dilemma in North America. Almost at once, the debates shifted from concerns around liberty to those concerned with equality (Foner, 1998; Lindbloom, 1977).

In the 1920s and 1930s, early American Social Reconstructionists such as Harold Rugg (1921) and George Counts (1932) went a few steps further than Dewey in imagining a role for public education, especially its teachers. These theorists considered the biggest threat to democracy to be the concentration of economic, social, and political power. Their solution was for teachers to become leaders of social change (Stevens & Wood, 1995). The values teachers were to impart to students were to run "counter to the meritocratic ideology" by stressing the discourse of an egalitarian society (p. 127). Counts in particular argued that teachers should "seek power and then strive to use that power fully and wisely and in the interests of the great masses of the people" (cited in Stevens &Wood, 1995). In 1932, he posed the underlying question for this study: "Dare the schools build a new social order?"

Contemporary Social Reconstructionists have continued the call for teachers to employ agency in order to make it a better world. In "Education that is Multicultural and Social Reconstructionist" (1994), Christine Sleeter and Carl Grant stress similar issues, focusing on the need for teachers to help students understand two vital points: first, that knowledge is socially constructed; second, that by gaining political literacy, people are in a better position to fight for what is in their best overall interests. This is particularly poignant given the current situation in the United States in which significant numbers of working-class people vote against their own best interests (Frank, 2004).

Both eras of Social Reconstructionist theorizing stress the need for structural and institutional change across society, which is clearly positioned within the critical left political ideology. Teacher agency of the magnitude called for by Sleeter and Grant requires a significant number of progressive teachers aware of pedagogical strategies who would do two things in particular: first, help students understand the insidious ways in which power operates to shape individual consciousness and ways of seeing; second, not run into difficulty with people threatened by such activism. Despite the difficulties in recruiting large numbers of critical left teachers, not to mention the systemic adaptations required, the possibility of educators willing to engage in a politicized *enacted* curriculum exists, and with it, so does hope. This kind of pedagogy will be described in the second half of this chapter.

It seems to be a commonly held view that the goal of democratic societies is to reach a popular consensual agreement on values. But it might be that democracies are better suited for managing existing and continuing social tensions and conflicts over values and interests. These struggles over values and interests must allow the discussion to include in depth debate about political ideology. The debacle that took place around President Obama's plan for health care reform in 2009 demonstrates that corporate media outlets such as Fox News are not going to be the sites where these much needed debates take place. I contend that the classroom can fill this void. The stakes are simply too high to let Fox News pundits block rational debate.

In Canada and in the United States, debates continue to rage unabated over values on myriad social and economic issues. Yet, every significant progressive change in the social relations of our two countries has occurred through the efforts of liberals and social democrats over the vociferous opposition of conservatives. Healthcare, old-age pensions, collective bargaining, welfare, the establishment of a minimum wage, affirmative action, voting rights for women, and – especially in the United States – civil rights are only some of the positive gains initiated and supported by progressives that were opposed by traditional conservatives. Not only did every one of these initiatives increase the dignity of a large segment of our societies, but they also strengthened our democracies, as well. Some liberals, such as former Democratic presidential candidate George McGovern (2002), consider conservatives to play a vital role in American society by challenging progressive ideas, and forcing proponents to examine their viability. According to McGovern, serious problems arise, however, when conservatives come to power. The Republican Party has twice passed legislation taking away the rights of American citizens: the Prohibition Law after the First World War, and the Patriot Act passed by the Bush administration after September 11, 2001.

As philosopher Richard Rorty (1998) points out, the hard-fought-for gains made for the benefit of common people are always vulnerable to dismantling by conservative governments. In the present historical moment, Americans might become acutely aware of this. The George W. Bush-led Republicans took measures to dismantle social programs and individual rights and freedoms at the same time that they have spent lavishly on the military and cut taxes, especially for the wealthy. Even his successor, Barack Obama, has continued with the bailout of major financial institutions through the use of tax dollars. Neither the United States nor Canada has done what many other Western nations have done, namely, nationalize banks. Yet, there is hope before despair! Because we live in democracies the pendulum can swing back and regressive conservative legislation repealed. Teachers have an important role in reversing the swing of the pendulum. The time has come to tackle Tocqueville's greatest fear head-on by countering the tendency toward creating a society mainly composed of uninformed individuals.

Political philosopher Nancy Fraser may have provided at least part of the answer on how best to rectify the situation. In *Justice Interruptus* (1997), Fraser postulates around what she calls the "subaltern counterpublic." She describes this as a space in which "members of subordinated social groups . . . invent and circulate" counterhegemonic discourses (p. 81). These newly formed "discourses of possibility," in turn, can lead to new representations and identities that conceivably lead to an understanding of where their interests lie. For our purposes, the creation of subaltern counterpublics requires teachers who are skilled in encouraging the enacted curriculum to move in this direction.

In *Critical Democracy and Education* (1999), Joe Kincheloe suggests an outline based on critical pedagogy that would encourage the enacted curriculum to lead to something resembling Fraser's notion of the subaltern counterpublics: "the curriculum becomes a dynamic of negotiation where students and teachers examine the forces that have shaped them and the society in which they live" (p. 73). In other words, Kincheloe calls for teachers to develop an enacted curriculum that encourages self-reflection and lifts the hegemonic veil away from the hidden power structures. In fact, the ideas of Kincheloe, Fraser, and Young suggest using education to deconstruct hegemonic forms of meaning making. Their focus on critical pedagogy is in the spirit of John Dewey and his desire to use the classroom to develop critically thinking citizens.

Very few people would argue *against* the discourse of strengthening democracy. As mentioned earlier, even the Republicans call for the need to spread democracy across the world. In fact, during the 2003 invasion of Iraq, once it became clear that there were no weapons of mass destruction, President George W. Bush explained to the American people that there was a need to bring democracy to Iraq. There has been much debate about the true intentions of the Bush administration's reasons for attacking Iraq (Huffington, 2007), but the point I want to make here is that politicians know that democracy is a motherhood term and is, therefore, considered to be very important to almost all Americans. This is the case even though involvement in the political process appears to be waning for the past several decades.

Education clearly has to be part of the solution. Political ideology defines what the role of the teacher should be in teaching for and about democracy. Yet, before the discussion moves toward pedagogical ideas I have tried in the classroom, it is prudent to briefly examine the discourses around democracy and citizenship used in conservatism, liberalism, and socialism.

Ideology and Competing Visions of Democracy and Citizenship

> Virtually everyone believes democracy is desirable . . .The nature of their underlying beliefs, however, differ. For some, a commitment to democracy is associated with liberal notions of freedom [and] equality of opportunity. . . For some, good citizens in a democracy volunteer, while for others they take active parts in political processes by voting, forming committees, protesting, and working on campaigns. (Westheimer & Kahne, 2004, p. 237)

In an article entitled "What Kind of Citizen? The Politics of Educating for Democracy" (2004), Joel Westheimer and Joseph Kahne describe a study they conducted in which they explored different ideological conceptions of what it means to teach for democracy. They posit that although John Dewey has perhaps had the most influence on the connection between democracy and education, educators have "interpreted his ideas in multiple ways, so no single conception emerges" (p. 238). Political ideology is once again at the root of these differing interpretations.

According to Westheimer and Kahne, political ideology affects the various ways of teaching for democracy that leads to these three different kinds of citizens. Differing discourses of the good citizen are somewhat analogous to what each of the three political ideologies desire. The personally responsible citizen is the ideal vision of conservatives. The participatory citizen, one who engages in much more than voting, is what liberals want. The justice oriented citizen is the ideal result of what the critical left hopes to develop. How each ideology views the role of the teacher is a crucial aspect of the development of their version of the ideal citizen. The role of the teacher is also related to epistemological concerns: each ideology regards knowledge itself differently.

The taxonomy developed by Westheimer and Kahne differentiates between three conceptions of citizenship that map onto the three major political ideologies in Canada and the United States in a fairly coherent and logical manner. Westheimer and Kahne consider a strong sense of personal responsibility to be the main characteristic of the conservative discourse of the good citizen. Citizens should be law-abiding and act responsibly in the community. Conservative educators emphasize "honesty, integrity, self-discipline, and hard work" (p. 240). Kelly and Brandes (2001) add that conservatives want teachers to see themselves as "public servants carrying out decisions made elsewhere." In Chapter 7, I mentioned a veteran social studies teacher who spoke against supplementing the curriculum to make it more culturally relevant: "Teaching is not a vehicle to promote your own agenda. You have a job, when you sign that piece of paper, to teach the curriculum. You are not there to create an army of followers to your way of seeing the world." This is a classic example of a conservative perspective toward teaching. On the other hand, critical left educators contend that "efforts by teachers to remain neutral are impossible and likely to end in indoctrination for the status quo" (Hursh & Ross, 2000, p. 11).

The role of the conservative teacher in teaching for democracy is to help students "understand the rule of law and respect traditional authority" (Kelly & Brandes, 2001, p. 437). In other words, "the purpose of preparing democratic citizens is [either] downplayed or equated with building patriotism and national unity" (p. 438). According to conservatives, teachers are not to engage in what they see as political activity in any aspect of schooling. Kincheloe (1999) points out that a conservative notion of teaching about "democratic citizenship involves the uncritical acquisition of a neutral body of traditional knowledge" (p. 79). In other words, conservatives are more likely to support the positivist notion of school knowledge being produced in a value-free, objective manner. Some conservatives may also acknowledge certain biases in their preferred curricular knowledge, but consider their version to be the best to maintain social cohesion. Others, such as Edward Wynne (1985–86), are more overt. Wynne contends that "on the whole, school is and must be indoctrinate" (p. 9). Wynne wants teachers to teach all students, regardless of cultural background, the importance of Western values. If students fail, Wynne places the blame entirely on the students and their cultural backgrounds.

In contrast to the personally responsible citizen of conservatism, a liberal discourse of the good citizen is one who is an active member of community groups and participates in community efforts to help those in need or to perhaps clean up the neighborhood. Liberals believe that the good citizen participates and perhaps leads "within established systems and community structures" (Westheimer & Kahne, 2004, p. 242). Educators within this paradigm "want to teach knowledge and skills necessary for civic engagement in community affairs" (p. 243). Liberal teachers do not place much emphasis on encouraging students to critically analyze the current system of unequal social relations. According to Kelly and Brandes (2001), a liberal pluralist vision of democracy sees the teacher as a neutral facilitator of discussions who creates the space for multiple perspectives to be heard (p. 438). Although some liberals have the epistemological understanding that there can be many perspectives of the same event, they seem to hold "an implicit assumption . . . is that these perspectives compete on a level playing field," and that the best ideas rise to the top (p. 438). As with liberal views toward issues of race and class, I have found that there is a power-blind aspect to the common teacher perspective of teaching for democracy.

The third discourse of the good citizen is the one Westheimer and Kahne call the justice oriented citizen. This critical left view shares with liberalism a focus on participation in order to help the community, but there is a major difference: the justice oriented citizen works for structural and institutional change in order to eliminate human suffering. Observing or even engaging in social protests is a pedagogical strategy I have used to help foster this type of citizen. Although this type of teaching may make political issues explicit, Westheimer and Kahne make it clear it is not to be confused with political indoctrination (p. 243). This is a fine line on which to walk. Kincheloe (1999) claims that critical left educators should not adhere to a "pretense of neutrality." Rather, they should "expose their values and openly work to achieve them" (p. 72). Kincheloe describes what I have been calling the enacted curriculum by invoking elements of the Freirian notions of *conscientization* and *praxis* (1973): the classroom "becomes a dynamic of negotiation where students and teachers examine the forces that have shaped them and the society in which they live. In this context, the curriculum is ever-changing and evolving" (Kincheloe, 1999, p. 73). Kelly and Brandes (2001) agree that critical left educators emphasize collective problem solving, stating that "[s]tudents need to learn analytic, communicative, and strategic skills" (p. 438). This perspective has been very influential in the ways that I teach for and about democracy, as will be seen in the next section.

The goal of citizenship education from the perspective of the critical left is to develop justice oriented citizens who are able to critique societal structures in order to understand the root causes of social inequities. This understanding is crucial if solutions are to be developed and implemented. Critical left notions of epistemology assume the social construction of knowledge, acknowledging that power is entwined in its construction and representation. Moreover, they consider the notion that knowledge is neutral to be a false assumption of conservatism and much of liberalism.

Westheimer and Kahne (2004), however, found that the justice oriented conception of citizenship education is by far the least represented in the American high school programs that they studied. From my own experience as a veteran teacher and teacher educator in British Columbia, I would concur with their findings. Moreover, a study that took place in Saskatchewan found that a student's "social location mediates the extent to which the official social studies curriculum is able to produce students as 'good' citizens" (Tupper, Cappello, & Sevigny, 2010, p. 1). In other words, for working-class students the "discourse of universal citizenship is in sharp relief to their lived realities" (p. 32). It would be prudent for progressive teachers to keep both of these points in mind as they prepare lessons around democracy and citizenship.

Thus far in this chapter, I have briefly described the historical debates about democracy in the United States and, to a lesser extent, in Canada, and the competing ideological discourses of the good citizen. At this point, the discussion moves away from theoretical considerations and toward the practical aspects of teaching for a stronger democracy. The last section in this chapter will describe pedagogy that I have found to be somewhat successful in teaching for an informed and active citizenry.

Teaching For and About Democracy, Including Its Flaws

During the U.S. presidential election in November 2004, many people across the globe watched the television coverage with deep anticipation as the results were being posted. There is little doubt that most of these people outside of the United States were disappointed at the results. Yet, these people must have been surprised at another revelation about the results from election night: only half of the American registered voters even bothered to vote. Of course, with the election victory of Barack Obama on November 4, 2008, voter turnout increased to around the 63% mark – although many Americans declined to exercise their franchise, it was the highest turnout since 1960. The situation in Canada is no better – the recent election that took place on October 14, 2008 had a turnout of 59%, the lowest in the history of Canadian federal elections.

For both countries, there is simply no denying the obvious, namely, even the most basic action of democratic expression, to vote in an election, is suffering from citizen apathy. Even more disconcerting, in both countries there are many people who put in the effort to vote on election day, yet, they vote against their own best interests. The question all concerned citizens must ask themselves is: *Why?* The question all concerned educators must ask themselves is: *What can be done about this?* The first question is beyond the scope of this chapter. It is the second question that I seek to address here.

As a concerned citizen, I consider myself to be a very strong democrat. Despite its myriad flaws, I believe that democracy is the best system to distribute political power. Perhaps democracy cannot operate in its ideal form in tribal societies, but in advanced industrial and (mostly) secular state societies like the United States and Canada, tribal affiliations do not exist like they do in, say, countries like Iraq. Without these kinds of obstacles, there are still flaws in the American and Canadian democracies such as low voter turnout and, even more important, people voting against their own best interests.

I am a veteran educator who grew up in Toronto with immigrant working-class parents. I have spent almost all of my adult life as an educator in British Columbia, Canada's westernmost province. For 19 years I taught various courses in B.C. high schools, including social studies, civic studies, and Aboriginal studies. After completing my PhD, I became the department head of a teacher education program in a university just outside of Vancouver. Currently, I am on faculty at the College of Education at the University of Saskatchewan. Throughout my entire teaching experience, I have focused on pedagogy for a stronger democracy: teaching about ideology critique (Orlowski, 2008), critical media literacy (Orlowski, 2006), and the flaws in our democratic system (2009).[3] This chapter will focus on all three strategies so that, when taken together, they may one day result in a citizenry capable of critical thinking and engaged action. The next section, however, addresses the issue of why some people vote against their best interests.

Hegemony and Counterhegemony

As mentioned in earlier chapters, *hegemony* refers to the ideal representation of the interests of the privileged groups as universal interests, which are then accepted by the masses as the natural economic, political, and social order. This conception of hegemony explains how social hierarchies and order are maintained within capitalist societies. Force is not required to maintain these hierarchies if the public willingly give their consent to accept it.

In *What's the Matter With Kansas?* (2004), Thomas Frank contends that the backlash against progressive politics in many parts of twenty-first century America is about a conservative elite that has managed to manipulate "cultural anger . . . to achieve economic ends" (p. 5). He posits that the corporate elites obtain support from the working classes by trumpeting conservative positions on moral issues such as gay rights and abortion. Frank further extrapolates that there is a "primary contradiction of the backlash: it is a working-class movement that has done incalculable harm to working-class people" (p. 6). President George W. Bush's tax cuts for the country's most wealthy citizens attest to this, and demonstrate how hegemonic processes work to further entrench their interests.

The effects of hegemony are so difficult to combat because hegemony shapes how people view life itself through a set of social relations that enables meaning to be made. Unfortunately for those people not belonging to elite groups, this meaning often results in an unfair distribution of privilege and power, and paradoxically, by their acceptance of this arrangement. In the example of the conservative Tea Party movement in the United States, hegemonic discourses seem to be keeping many of its members from realizing that economic uncertainty in their country has much to do with the deregulation of the financial industry. The common view of Tea Party members appears to be that high taxes and big government are the causes of the unstable economy (Yakabuski, 2010).

The process through which this situation arises can be explained by the role of Gramsci's *organic intellectuals*, a group made up of educators, journalists, and experts within various fields. These organic intellectuals play a hegemonic role in the way that they can control and further entrench certain discourses that support the dominant ideology, as well as strengthen the privilege of those who benefit from the dominant ideology and its resultant social, economic, and political arrangements. In short, their role is to manufacture consent. In the case of The Tea Party, the "expert" appears to be Fox News commentator Glen Beck, a born again Christian who suggests to his followers to "question government programs aimed at helping the poor or minorities" (Yakabuski, 2010). Yet, these groups are not monolithic entities sharing the same views, thereby making it possible to destabilize these roles. In particular, the role of the autonomous educator offers hope for counterhegemonic discourses to develop.

There is one important aspect of attempting to replace hegemonic discourses with counterhegemonic ones that must be considered, namely, that of *false consciousness*. This term features prominently in critical theory, and refers to the purpose served by thought itself in the collective life of humanity. It attempts to explain why some people, for instance, the working classes, consider themselves to be politically conscious and yet vote against their best interests. Once again, working-class votes for the Bush administration in the 2004 election serve as an excellent example of a false political consciousness. Crucial considerations for educators revolve around the depth of hegemonic discourses within the consciousness of American and Canadian voters, the degree to which it is possible to vote free from the influence of these hegemonic discourses, and in complex societies such as ours, the degree to which it is even possible to vote in a manner that is consistent with one's interests. It is clear that progressive educators may get easily discouraged from coming up against such concerns, either in theory or in the classroom itself. That said, I believe that pedagogical approaches exist that can at least kick start the deconstructive process in the minds of people to minimize the effects of hegemonic discourses and false political consciousness.

In short, wherever there is power, there is resistance to that power. Organic intellectuals who trumpet the dominant discourses work to maintain the status quo, while those who attempt to create space for counterhegemony are in the business of challenging the status quo and replacing false consciousness with a more politically astute consciousness. Attempts to strengthen democracy through the development of an informed and active citizenry would include analysis of the more effective hegemonic devices in Canadian society. Corporate media is clearly on the side of corporate privilege. Teachers of Social Studies need not be. It is time to discuss what teachers can do about it.

Teaching for a Political Consciousness

Informed citizens are the basis of any democratic society. (B.C. Ministry of Education Civic Studies 11 IRP, 2005a, p. 12)

I completely agree with the statement above, which was taken from the state-sanctioned formal curriculum of 11th grade Civic Studies, a course I taught in 2005–06, the first year it was offered in British Columbia. Throughout my entire teaching career, I am always taken aback by how many students tell me that they cannot understand the news in the media when it focuses on politics. To be fair to them, I am also astounded by how many adults I meet away from the classroom who tell me the same thing. This indicates to me that therein resides a major reason for our waning democracies: when it comes to understanding politics, a significant portion of the population is unable to do so: they are politically uninformed and unaware of how social power operates.[4] Others may be able to understand politics but choose to avoid involvement. Democracy in both countries would be strengthened if somehow citizens were to become politically engaged. Being able to comprehend what is going on politically on the local level, the national level, and the international level is crucial to this political engagement. In order for schools to teach for a strong democracy, students must be given "some opportunity to examine the impact of ideology on consciousness shaping" (Hyslop-Margison & Sears, 2008, p. 32). Bearing this important point in mind, the first concept I teach in every social studies course, at both the high school and the university level, is ideology critique.

Ideology Critique

It is expected that students will describe the key features of prominent 20th and 21st century political and economic ideologies, including communism, conservatism, fascism, liberalism, and socialism. (B.C. Ministry of Education Social Studies 11 IRP, 2005b, p. 32)

Every social studies course I have taught has always had a focus on the role of political ideology in influencing important movements and events of the past and present. Each ideology has three aspects: a critique of society, a vision of the ideal society, and agency to attain that vision (Schwarzmantel, 1998). For example, the appearance of large numbers of homeless people in our cities since the 1980s will yield differing critiques from people influenced by various ideologies. A conservative might explain this situation by blaming the state welfare programs for creating a lazy population; a liberal might consider increasing charity donations; a socialist, on the other hand, might point the finger at laissez-fare government policies that promoted tax cuts and unregulated rent controls. At the least, the individual will employ agency by voting for the political party or politician that they think shares certain important values.

Indeed, I contend that the ideologies emanating out of Modernity – liberalism, conservatism, and socialism – are still extremely important concepts to help explain Western social, economic, and political issues in both the past and the present. Fortunately, in senior level social studies courses, there is always a prescribed learning outcome (PLO) like the one above that gives state-sanctioned permission to do so.[5]

In order to help lead students to an understanding of the major political ideologies, I first categorize myriad issues as either *social* or *economic*. For example, minority rights are on the left side of the social spectrum, while the conservative pro-life and pró-death penalty positions are on the right side. On the economic spectrum, tax cuts are on the right side and, by corollary, strong publicly funded social welfare programs are on the left side. In the American context, the conservative party, the Republicans, is on the right side of both spectrums, while the liberal party, the Democrats, is on the left side of the social spectrum and the right side of the economic spectrum. In other words, both major American parties serve corporate interests rather than the economic interests of the common individual. In Canada, the Conservative Party and the Liberal Party are positioned where their fellow American ideologues are; yet, the social democratic NDP is on the left side of both the social and economic spectrum.

By the end of every course I teach, either in the high school classroom or in teacher education programs, the student has at least a basic understanding of where the political parties stand on the various social and economic issues. The next step in teaching about democracy is to emphasize the role of the corporate media in influencing the way people see the world.

The Case for Critical Media Literacy

It is expected that students will demonstrate effective research skills, including accessing information, assessing information, collecting data, evaluating data, organizing information, and presenting information. (B.C. Ministry of Education Civics 11 IRP, 2005a, p. 32)

Although the PLO above does not explicitly call for media literacy, it is clear that certain interpretations could see it this way. Regardless, it is imperative that American and Canadian citizens understand the role of the corporate media to influence the political ideologies of the general public. As Edward S. Herman and Noam Chomsky (1988) point out, the major role of the corporate media is to "manufacture consent,"[6] to shape the collective consciousness in ways that further the interests of the elite. The meaningfulness of media analysis in the classroom and its relationship to an informed citizenry should be evident to all social studies teachers.

Media literacy can mean different things to different people. It can take two basic forms: one looks at the pleasures within a capitalist society and how certain groups are represented; the other looks at politics and the media's role in shaping public opinion. This second approach is the one I focus on in my goal of teaching for a stronger democracy. It enables the teacher, for example, to illuminate the effects of various hegemonic strategies used by different media sources that supported John McCain's 2008 bid for the presidency: Despite his assertions otherwise, there is ample evidence demonstrating McCain's past support for deregulation of American financial institutions (Murphy, 2009; Sherman, 2010). The economic recession that began in 2008 notwithstanding, one has to wonder at media support for McCain's campaign.

There are myriad examples of the media ignoring certain events and policies if there is a perceived threat that the public might turn against the ruling classes. For example, there was limited coverage in the major U.S. newspapers of the links between Vice President Dick Cheney and the Halliburton Corporation, or the connections between the extended families of President George W. Bush and Osama Bin Laden. These examples demonstrate the media using omission as a hegemonic strategy.

Another hegemonic strategy involves understanding the power of language. We are living in a time in which bias, or spin, in its commonly understood form, has been hyperbolized to grotesque proportions. Lakoff (2004) points out legislation that the first Bush administration passed. He contends that The Clear Skies Act, despite its name, enables polluting corporations to increase the amount of toxins they produce. Likewise, The Healthy Forests Restoration Act allows for more forests to be clear-cut, some within formerly protected parklands. As a further example of current spin, numerous educators have criticized Bush's No Child Left Behind Act for leaving behind too many marginalized, underprivileged children (Shaker & Heilman, 2008). The shift to mega spin has reached new heights (or lows) with the revelation that the Bush administration had been engaged in a political scandal in which the U.S. Department of Education paid influential journalist Armstrong Williams $240,000 to write columns in support of the controversial No Child Left Behind Act (Kirkpatrick, 2005).

A counterhegemonic strategy I employ in the high school classroom relates to the PLO at the top of this section, especially its call to have students access and assess information. Students demonstrate the degree to which they have become adept at explaining cultural struggles in ideological terms in their "current events" presentations. Each chooses an article from one of the mainstream newspapers or from an alternative news source, most of which come from the Internet. The chosen article must address a cultural issue, namely, race, class, gender, sexuality, or war. Each student provides a one-page written analysis to address issues of bias to show which groups benefit and which ones lose from the given ideological perspective. They must offer their thoughts about *who* was quoted and *why*, and which affected groups were excluded. Each student must also present his or her findings to the class with a four-to-five minute presentation.

I provide the students with the names and websites of the mainstream newspapers and of the alternative news sources. Some students choose only articles from mainstream sources, while others willingly, even enthusiastically, search the alternative sources. This has worked well, pedagogically speaking, because students often choose articles on similar topics – the 2004 American election and the Iraq war were two favorites – and the ideologies emanating from mainstream and alternative sources are not difficult to discern. These assignments offer students a framework in which to critique the media in terms of the ideological influences of journalists, and in the process, they understand how mainstream media often reflects the views of powerful interests.

Through ideology critique, students have become quite adept at understanding the Orwellian spin inherent in commonly used media terms like labor flexibility (code for union-busting and downsizing) and Bush's right-to-work legislation, which virtually allows for the elimination of the minimum wage (Winter, 2002, p. xvii). Indeed, when students challenge the language and the assumptions that many journalists use, they see how the hegemonic function of the media works in the interests of large corporations and other privileged groups. Some are able to see past the effects of a false consciousness.

The somewhat recent anti-feminism backlash has also been at the center of the way I use the media in educational settings. The lesson plans on ideology are successful in helping students understand conservative support for patriarchy, as well as the different kinds of feminism – liberal, socialist, and radical – supported by progressives. Female conservative journalists, such as Fox News' Ann Coulter, are becoming a ubiquitous entity in North American media outlets. When I asked why there were so many anti-feminist positions espoused by female journalists, one grade 11 female student answered: "It's easy – because the media is owned by conservative rich guys who hate feminists!"

Students come to understand that the oft-repeated conservative claim that the media in both countries are too liberal is a myth. The dominant discourses in the corporate media in the past 25 years – free trade, tax cuts, deregulation, debt reduction, cuts to social programs, and globalization – have been the building blocks for a resurgence in economic and political power for the elites in North America. All working-class people, as well as a significant percentage of the middle class, have had their lives significantly disrupted by this series of political policy shifts that the corporate media have supported.

The current financial crisis is further proof of this. For example, the much publicized 2009 debate over whether to give financial support to the three large American automobile manufacturers has been turned into an attack by the conservative Republicans against the United Auto Workers union. Although I have not had the opportunity to address this topic with students, it has great potential to aid in the deconstruction of false political consciousness – the Republicans are blaming poor car sales on the unionized and fairly well-paid workforce when most Americans are aware that, on the whole, Japanese cars are much more expensive than American ones. Clearly, their financial problems must lie elsewhere, such as with their management decisions, and perhaps with their engineering designs, as well.

I have been experimenting with a more sophisticated kind of media literacy, one based on reframing political discourse from different ideological perspective. Reframing techniques have come from the work of linguist George Lakoff (2004). The basic theory behind reframing is to address the observation that people who are strongly influenced by one ideology cannot hear certain facts that might shake their beliefs. The facts do not seem to matter; they seem to bounce off the intended listener. Rather than become frustrated, progressive ideologues need to use positive discourses on policy that rely on progressive values and language. In other words, rather than using the frames of the conservatives that become commonplace because of ubiquitous use in media outlets such as Fox News, progressives use ones based on progressive values.

One example from my teacher-education course may help to explain the value in reframing. For corporate conservatism to continue, it requires that significant numbers of poor and working-class people vote against their own best interests because of false political consciousness – or not vote at all. The necessary reframing efforts on the part of conservatives were successful because a commonly held belief today is that conservative ideas are *populist*, while liberal or progressive ideas are *elitist*. Part of the media literacy strategies I use with the preservice teachers is to have them reframe conservative arguments using progressive values. For example, conservatives usually attack any notion of increasing the mandated minimum wage by either calling it antithetical to business interests or, if pressed, suggesting that people unhappy with a low wage simply look for a better paying job. Instead of defending an increase in the B.C. minimum wage, one student reframed the debate and focused on the value of "prosperity for all who work hard." This is an idea that people across the ideological spectrum could support.

Another student took on the current conservative slogan of "small government is best" by distinguishing among the roles that government should have in society. Rather than promote the idea of big government, this student challenged the typical conservative role for government simply by asking, "In light of the fact that we will always have government, what is the role it should have to best help its citizens?" Conservatives do not necessarily desire small government. They want government for the military and other policing agencies. Left liberals and social democrats, on the other hand, want government to focus on nurturing aspects of people's lives such as education, healthcare, social programs for those in need, and a healthy environment. In other words, a progressive response to the matter of government's roles is to present more humane roles, rather than the tough-minded ones that conservatives assign it. An effective approach is not to debate the size of government, but to challenge people with the best role for government.

On the related issue of tax reform, one student produced a defense of taxes not by buying into the conservative frames of "tax relief" or "taxes as burden," but also by using a progressive frame – "fair tax reform" – which indicates that wealthy people should pay more tax, and that taxes are an investment for the future prosperity of everybody. Of course, media access and media compliance are important obstacles to these progressive frames becoming commonly accepted. For now, however, if teachers can comprehend what is happening with current media concerns, they should be better able to help their students deconstruct the Orwellian spin that they are being inundated with. After all, a major objective of critical media literacy is to help students *interpret* the news rather than simply absorb it without reflection. This is a crucial pedagogical strategy to develop a political consciousness so that they take an interest in participating in our democracy. An understanding of the flaws in our democracies will also help strengthen our democracies.

Teaching About the Flaws in Our Democracy

A few years ago, I designed a social studies unit entitled *Flaws in Our Democracy*. This unit began in December 2005 and ended shortly after the Canadian federal election in late January 2006. The usual factors were part of this unit: low voter turnout, voter apathy, uninformed voters, media spin, announced poll results during election campaigns, the Prime Minister's notwithstanding clause (which is similar to the President's veto), no-paper voting machines, and the first-past-the-post voting system[7] (rather than proportional representation). I also emphasize that a strong democracy has more than two parties to choose from because of corporate influence.

As the unit was winding down a couple of days after the Canadian federal election in 2006, students became acutely aware of another flaw, that of "floor crossing." David Emerson ran as a Liberal and won the east Vancouver riding (voting district), narrowly defeating his NDP rival. A few days after the election, he crossed the floor to become a member of the governing Conservatives, and was instantly rewarded by Prime Minister Stephen Harper with a cabinet position. Vancouver voters were incensed – after all, the Conservatives had garnered only 18% of the votes in the riding – and several rallies were organized to demonstrate their frustration with the democratic system. I was surprised when one of my students, a 17-year old named Zoe Miller, came to me with an unsolicited speech she wrote about her outrage. A few phone calls later allowed her some time on stage in front of over a thousand protesters (see Fig. 8.1), clearly explaining to the crowd why Emerson's move

Fig. 8.1 17-year old Zoe Miller, a high school student in Vancouver BC, speaking at a Pro-Democracy rally in 2006

was anti-democratic and encouraged voter apathy, especially to younger Canadians. The reason I mention this is to demonstrate how the classroom can ignite the passion within young people to become involved in the democratic process (Burrows, 2006). In other words, it is possible for them to become *active* citizens, and with a justice orientation.

During the final term of the school year, students in my Civics 11 classes were given a series of assignments that they had to fulfill in order to indicate that they had participated in the political process and were not merely armchair critics. Each student had to write a letter to the editor on a political issue and, after some editing on my part, submit it to a major newspaper (and some were even published!); they had to volunteer on a community-related issue (and many chose to volunteer for the World Peace Forum, which Vancouver hosted in June 2006); and the last requirement was that they had to attend a political rally or protest as a participant or an observer, whether progressive (like myriad anti-war rallies in Vancouver) or conservative (such as pro-life rallies). Students were to hand in to me a pamphlet of the rally, a one-page report that described the crowd in terms of race, gender, and age, as well as quotes they read from rally signs. Not one student complained about these assignments because, I presume, they had become politicized. Zoe's rally speech about the Emerson floor-crossing fiasco more than fulfilled this last course requirement, of course. Moreover, it became clear that her classmates who attended that particular rally were quite impressed at just how involved one of their peers had become on a political matter.

Reflections on Teaching for and About Democracy

I am not certain how many of my former students vote in elections. Yet, I am certain that the vast majority of them are much more informed on political issues important to them. Most have a somewhat sophisticated political consciousness, a more Freirian *critical* consciousness rather than a false consciousness so common in the citizenry of both countries – this is a necessary requirement if democracy is to be strengthened. In my teaching career, I have found that an approach utilizing ideology critique, critical media literacy, re-framing hegemonic discourses with counterhegemonic ones, followed by assignments oriented toward developing active citizenship has been more effective than other approaches in fostering an acute political consciousness that is less influenced by hegemonic discourses.

Every critical educator understands this one maxim: *Teaching is a political act.* The goal is to use various pedagogical strategies so that students can understand that almost everything in the social realm is a political act. Once this occurs on a large-scale basis, there will be stronger democracies in both the United States and Canada. As the saying goes, democracy is not a spectator sport.

Conclusions

Very few people would argue with the assertion that democratic traditions in the United States and in Canada are on the wane. Paradoxically, very few people would posit that a better society is possible without a democratic system. Therein lies the conundrum: the masses are becoming less engaged with the political process, both in voting and with participation between elections, as well; yet, despite supporting democracy in principle, they are not willing or perhaps not able to become more involved. These were some of the concerns of the early thinkers on American democracy.

It has been my experience that there are pedagogical approaches that can effect positive involvement in the democratic process. First of all, students must be able to understand political news, and the best way to do this is to focus on political ideology. If the students are able to understand typical positions by conservatives, liberals, and social democrats on both social and economic issues, they will be less vulnerable to the spin spewed by corporate media. Moreover, if teachers can help students become involved in various political events, the seed may be planted for further involvement on other issues. Students must understand that protesting in a nonviolent manner is simply enacting their civic right to express their position on a particular issue, and that this is only engaging in the democratic process. John Dewey would approve of such a citizen, as would the Social Reconstructionists of the past and present. If educators do not make the effort to teach for and about democracy, we will one day wake up and realize what a wonderful opportunity was missed.

Questions to Ponder

1. Read over Westheimer and Kahne's descriptions of the three versions of the "good citizen" (see pp. 223–227).

   (a) What are the pros and cons for society if schools focused on only the *socially responsible citizen* in citizenship education?

   (b) What are the pros and cons for society if schools focused on only the *participatory citizen* in citizenship education?

   (c) What are the pros and cons for society if schools focused on only *the justice-oriented citizen* in citizenship education?

   (d) Think of some influential people in your own life. With Westheimer and Kahne's taxonomy in mind, what kind of citizen would these people be? What makes you think this?

2. Much of the rhetoric around citizenship education today emphasizes the socially responsible citizen. Why do you think that this version of the "good citizen" is the one that education policy makers have directed schools to emphasize since the 1990s?

3. Chomsky and Herman make a case that one of the major roles of corporate media is to "manufacture consent." Think of some recent examples in which the vast majority of corporate media sources attempted to create consent among the majority of the public on various issues. (These issues may be based upon the economy, immigration, the environment, war, the oil industry, or myriad other topics.)
4. For the most part, voter turnout has been decreasing in recent decades, hovering not much above the 50% mark. If this trend continues, at what point might we expect the public to question the *legitimacy* of government?
5. A strong democracy is part of a society in which the citizens are informed and engaged during elections and between elections. What are some ways that you might consider having your high school students or preservice social studies teachers become active in the democratic process?

Notes

1. This is not to suggest that President Bush expressed American foreign policy with sincerity. Transforming the political systems of non-democratic countries is not an issue if the foreign government supports American interests. For example, the CIA helped General Augusto Pinochet replace the democratically elected Salvadore Allende, a move that resulted in a military dictatorship that forbade Chileans from holding elections until 1990 (Klein, 2007).
2. Much has been written about liberal democracy, deliberative democracy, communitarian democracy, and radical democracy. I am inclined to take the advice on a bumper sticker I once read in Toronto: *Eschew Obfuscation!* The descriptions and distinctions of the various models are very important, yet it is beyond the scope of this book to delve into them. If I attempted to do so with limited space, confusion would likely be the result.
3. A version of the remainder of this chapter appeared in the journal *Democracy & Education* (2009) 18(2), 54–61.
4. As I have done throughout the book, I am using the term *social power* in the Foucauldian sense of the word, as a mostly invisible hegemonic regulator of social relations.
5. The political ideology called *social democracy* is missing from the list, as is *progressivism*, a term more commonly used in the U.S. that grew out of liberal humanism. Social democracy has the same progressive social values as liberalism, but emphasizes economic issues more in favor of the common person such as public healthcare and workers' rights. All western nations except the U.S. have a major social democratic political party, most likely a legacy of McCarthyism. The Canadian social democratic party is called the New Democratic Party (NDP). The relatively new yet small American Green Party shares many positions with the NDP.
6. Chomsky and Herman borrowed the phrase "the manufacture of consent" from Walter Lippman's book called *Public Opinion* (1922).
7. In this voting system the single winner is the person with the most votes; there is no requirement that the winner gain an absolute majority of votes. The main criticism of the first-past-the-post voting system is that the elected representatives belonging to certain political parties are not a true reflection of how the people voted. For example, the Green Party of Canada received 6.8% of the vote in the 2008 federal election, yet they did not elect one member from their party because their support was not concentrated enough in each voting district (Elections Canada, 2008). In a proportional representation voting system, such as they have in Germany and many other countries, the Green Party would gain a number of elected representatives that would reflect their percentage of the popular vote.

References

B.C. Ministry of Education, Skills and Training. (2005a). *Civic studies 11: Integrated resource package 2005*. Victoria: Queen's Printer for British Columbia.

B.C. Ministry of Education, Skills and Training. (2005b). *Social studies 11: Integrated resource package 2005*. Victoria: Queen's Printer for British Columbia.

B.C. Ministry of Education, Skills and Training. (2006). *Social studies 10: Integrated resource package 2005*. Victoria: Queen's Printer for British Columbia.

Burrows, M. (2006, April 6). Teen decries party defection. *The Georgia Straight*. Retrieved on 3 February 2008, from http://www.straight.com/article/teen-decries-party-defection

Counts, G. (1932). Dare progressive education be progressive? *Progressive Education, 9*, 257–263. Reprinted (1982) as *Dare the school build a new social order?* by New York: John Day.

Dewey, J. (1916). *Democracy and education*. New York: MacMillan.

Dewey, J. (1927/1954). *The public and its problems*. New York: Holt.

Elections Canada. (2008). 40th general election, October 14th, 2008. *Elections Canada*. Retrieved on 23 May 2010, from http://www.elections.ca/content.asp?section=pas&document=index&dir=40ge&lang=e&textonly=false

Foner, E. (1998). *The story of American freedom*. New York: Norton.

Frank, T. (2004a, April). Lie down for America: How the Republican Party sows ruin on the Great Plains. *Harper's Magazine*.

Frank, T. (2004b). *What's the matter with Kansas?* New York: Henry Holt & Co.

Fraser, N. (1997). *Justice interruptus: Critical reflections on the "postsocialist" condition*. New York: Routledge.

Greenwald, R. (2008, September 30). John McCain: Economic disaster. *Huffington Post*. Retrieved on 23 May 2010, from http://www.huffingtonpost.com/robert-greenwald/john-mccain-economic-disa_b_130526.html

Heffner, R. D. (Ed.). (1956). *Democracy in America (by Alexis de Tocqueville)*. New York: The Penguin Group.

Herman, E., & Chomsky, N. (1988). *Manufacturing consent: The political economy of the mass media*. New York: Pantheon Books.

Huffington, A. (2007, May 17). McCain and Bush: Making a mockery of democracy in Iraq. *Huffington Post*. Retrieved on 25 May 2010, from http://www.huffingtonpost.com/arianna-huffington/mccain-and-bush-making-a-_b_48479.html

Hursh, D. W., & Ross, E. W. (Eds.). (2000). *Democratic social education: Social studies for social change*. New York: Falmer Press.

Hyslop-Margison, E., & Sears, A. M. (2008). The neo-liberal assault on democratic learning, *UCFV Research, 2*(1), 28–38.

Kelly, D. M. (2003). Practicing democracy in the margins of school: The teen-age parents program as feminist counterpublic. *American Educational Research Journal, 40*, 123–146.

Kelly, D. M., & Brandes, G. M. (2001). Shifting out of "neutral": Beginning teachers' struggles with teaching for social justice. *Canadian Journal of Education, 26*, 347–454.

Kincheloe, J. (1999). Critical democracy and education. In J. G. Henderson & K. R. Kesson (Eds.), *Understanding democratic curriculum leadership* (pp. 70–83). New York: Teachers College Press.

Kirkpatrick, D. (2005, January 8). TV host says U.S. paid him to back policy. *The New York Times*. Retrieved on 25 May 2010, from http://query.nytimes.com/gst/fullpage.html?res=9A02E4DD1E39F93BA35752C0A9639C8B63

Klein, N. (2007). *The shock doctrine: The rise of disaster capitalism*. Toronto: Alfred A. Knopf Canada.

Lakoff, G. (2004). *Don't think of an elephant! Know your values and frame the debate*. White River Junction, Vermont: Chelsea Green Publishing.

Laxer, J. (1998). *The undeclared war: Class conflict in the age of cyber capitalism*. Toronto: Penguin Books Canada, Ltd.

Lindbloom, C. E. (1977). *Politics and markets.* New York: Basic Books.
McGovern, G. (2002, December). The case for liberalism: A defense of the future against the past. *Harper's Magazine,* 37–42.
Mill, J. S. (1861/1991). *Considerations on representative government.* Amherst, NY: Prometheus Books.
Murphy, J. M. (2009, Summer). Political economy and rhetorical matter. *Rhetoric & Public Affairs, 12,* 303–315.
Orlowski, P. (2006). Educating in an era of Orwellian spin: Making a case for critical media literacy in the classroom. *Canadian Journal of Education.* Special issue on *Popular Media, Education, and Resistance, 29*(1), 175–198.
Orlowski, P. (2008). Social class: The forgotten identity marker in social studies education. *New Proposals: Journal of Marxism and Interdisciplinary Inquiry, 1*(2), 30–63.
Orlowski, P. (2009). Teaching for and about democracy, including its flaws. *Democracy & Education, 18*(1), 54–61.
Rorty, R. (1998). *Achieving our country: Leftist thought in twentieth-century America.* Cambridge, MA: Harvard University Press.
Rugg, H. O. (1921). Reconstructing the curriculum: An open letter to Professor Henry Johnson commenting on Committee Procedure as illustrated by the Report of the Joint Committee on History and Education for Citizenship. *Historical Outlook, 12,* 184–189. Reprinted in W. C. Parker (Ed.), (1996). *Educating the democratic mind.* Albany: State University of New York Press.
Schwarzmantel, J. (1998). *The age of ideology: Political ideologies from the American revolution to postmodern times.* New York: New York University Press.
Sears, A. M., Clarke, G. M., & Hughes, A. S. (1999). Canadian citizenship education: The pluralist ideal and citizenship education for a post-modern state. In J. Torney-Purta, J. Schwille, & J. Amadeo (Eds.), *Civic education across countries: Twenty-four national case studies from the IEA Civic Education Project* (pp. 111–136). Amsterdam: The International Association for the Evaluation of Educational Achievement.
Shaker, P., & Heilman, E. (2008). *Reclaiming education for democracy: Thinking beyond 'No Child Left Behind'.* New York: Routledge.
Sherman, H. (2010). *The roller coaster economy: Financial crisis, great recession, and the public option.* London: M. E. Sharpe, Inc.
Stevens, E., & Wood, G. (1995). *Justice, ideology, and education: An introduction to the social foundations of education* (1st ed.). Toronto: McGraw-Hill.
Tupper, J., Cappello, M., & Sevigny, P. (2010). Locating citizenship: Curriculum, social class and the 'good' citizen. *Theory and Research in Social Education, 38,* 298–327.
Westheimer, J., & Kahne, J. (2004). What kind of citizen? The politics of educating for democracy. *American Educational Research Journal, 41*(2), 237–269.
Winter, J. (2002). *Media think.* Montreal: Black Rose Books.
Wynne, E. (1985–1986). The great tradition in education: Transmitting moral values, *Educational Leadership, 43*(4), 4–8.
Yakabuski, K. (2010, August 27). Republicans caught in the 'honor' system. *The Globe & Mail.* Retrieved on 3 February 2011, from http://www.theglobeandmail.com/news/world/konrad-yakabuski/republicans-caught-in-the-honour-system/article1688432/
Young, I. M. (1997). *Intersecting voices: Dilemmas of gender, political philosophy, and policy.* Princeton, NJ: Princeton University Press.

Chapter 9
Neoliberalism: Laissez-Faire Revisited?

> *All aspects of life are transformed into economic issues, if not into commodities. Anything not commercialized before is now getting greedy looks. A culture of individualism and consumption is taking over to the detriment of collective responsibility and the pursuit of the common good.*
> *(Berthelot, 2008, pp. 33–34)*

Most Canadians have recently begun to worry over their social safety net. Pension plans and the federal employment insurance system are in increasingly precarious positions (Keenan, 2009). The reaction over President Obama's proposed health-care reforms indicate that there is much unease among Americans regarding their social safety net, as well. Movements such as The Tea Party suggest that there is a restlessness throughout the United States, that there is much concern over how the economy may be working for the elites but it is certainly not working for regular Americans. In both countries all sectors of the civil society – such as public schools, hospitals, and libraries – are in need of more funding. Yet, recently the biggest recipients of public funding in the United States have been the banks and other financial institutions.

This chapter was written during the first half of 2010, which was less than two years after the biggest economic crisis had hit Western economies since the Great Depression. Many commentators thought that this crisis signaled the beginning of the end of the highly touted "globalization" project, and by corollary, the political economic paradigm that it is built upon, *neoliberalism*. After all, it seemed that many people were pointing to the *deregulation* of the financial industry as the main reason for the crisis. Deregulating whatever the corporations want to make profits from is a major feature of this new set of economic arrangements associated with neoliberalism and globalization. But does the crisis mean the beginning of the end of this neoliberal period? Are citizens ready to take some of the power away from the corporations?

The people most affected by neoliberalism's assault on public institutions in the United States, the middle and working classes, often seem to be divided on what to do about deteriorating conditions. The vociferous reactions to President Obama's healthcare reforms and the related town hall meetings attest to this (Urbina, 2009).

P. Orlowski, *Teaching About Hegemony*, Explorations of Educational Purpose 17, DOI 10.1007/978-94-007-1418-2_9, © Springer Science+Business Media B.V. 2011

Many seemed to be confused about President Obama's plans for a public healthcare option, a service that exists in *every* other Western nation. The segment of the American population opposed to healthcare reform might be an example of what Gore Vidal (2004) describes with this comment: "We hate this system that we are trapped in, but we don't know what our cage looks like because we have never seen it from the outside" (p. 29). One question this chapter attempts to address is whether the current cage is anything different from what has trapped early generations of human beings living in industrial states. If so, in what ways does it differ?

Since the 1990s, media watchers and public policy analysts have noted ubiquitous use of three related terms: neoliberalism, neoconservatism, and globalization. Left unchallenged, the forces behind these "new" perspectives and ideas have the power to increase hardships on middle- and working-class families in the United States and Canada, as well as in most countries around the world. These forces saturate the collective unconsciousness of the public in diverse fields with discourses trumpeting the virtues of deregulation as support for freedom. The problem is that these discourses do not address what kind of freedom nor for whom. Moreover, the neoliberal doctrine has saturated the thinking in many fields, always to the detriment of those fields (Harvey, 2005). For example, the power behind these social forces has significantly weakened our public education systems and our democratic processes. Chapter 8 focused on our waning democracies. This chapter focuses on neoliberalism and its influence on the public's sense of powerlessness. Clearly, the two are connected. This chapter will also address these concerns.

But are these concepts really new? In what ways are they new systems of thought? To what extent are they similar to what people have already experienced? It would be easy to consider neoliberalism to be a new form of liberalism, as this ideology was presented in Chapter 2. Similarly, it would not be surprising to find that many people might think of neoconservatism as an evolved version of the conservative ideology as it was described in the second chapter. However, the new terms are not simply extensions of their root ideologies. They should be understood as *reflections* of certain aspects of traditional liberalism and conservatism. Yet, they also represent a break from the past because of the ways in which they can influence the development of a new type of citizen, one who is self-reliant and who puts individual interests above the collective interests. Taken together, neoliberalism and neoconservatism explain why so many working-class people vote against their own best interests. It is time to unpack these ubiquitous contemporary terms.

The first time I had ever come across the term "neoliberalism" was on a poster advertising a conference about Latin America at a nearby university in the early 1990s. Neoliberalism was presented as something very negative, and speakers from Latin America were going to explain why. At the time, and at the risk of presenting myself as very naïve, I was puzzled because I assumed that neoliberalism would be much more preferable than political systems involving military dictatorships, of course, but also preferable to systems based upon conservative or neoconservative ideals. At the time, I did not understand that neoliberalism only applied to economic issues, not social issues. I subsequently learned that the "liberal" part of neoliberalism refers to liberalizing rules in order to move money around so that a relatively few people can make huge profits. Further, the first experiment of transforming a country into a neoliberal state took place in Chile in 1973 after General Augusto Pinochet overthrew the democratically elected government of Salvador Allende (Harvey, 2005, p. 7). The subsequent terror inflicted by the military upon Allende supporters is on its own reason enough for citizens of Latin American countries to despise the neoliberal agenda. The key components of this agenda are deregulation, privatization, union busting, and free trade deals with poor countries.

As a veteran teacher who had covered the Industrial Revolution to the 1930s many times in high school social studies, I was struck by the similarities between the social and economic conditions of the past with what has been happening in Canada in recent years. A similar economic model to the one currently touted in the media had fallen out of favor with all Western nations during the Great Depression of the 1930s. This system used to be called laissez-faire economics. Supporters of laissez-faire economics in the eighteenth and nineteenth centuries believed that the only role of the state was to protect property rights and the "natural order" of things. It is an economic doctrine that is hostile to the state intervening in economic affairs, with a preference for the *invisible hand* of the market to influence economic arrangements.

Most high school social studies students learn that inhumane conditions for workers and no social safety net were major features of laissez-faire economics. Government imposed regulations on industry were seen as impediments to financial profit for the capitalist class, and consequently, were unacceptable. This is similar to the conditions in many countries in recent decades. The crisis that befell most Western economies in 2009 focused once again on this very same issue, namely, the regulation of industry in general, and the financial industry in particular.

Since the 1980s, the hegemonic discourses that fill American and Canadian mainstream news stories on the economy always support tax cuts, deregulation, privatization, labor flexibility, the free market, and free trade. One particularly effective discourse is that neoliberalism will help everyone no matter their social class – the deregulated economy will create a rising tide and all of the boats, big and small, will rise with it. Neoliberalism's supporters contend that "advances in social life are attributable to the fostering of individual freedoms and encouraging entrepreneurship within a framework of strong private property rights, free markets, and free trade" (Tobin, 2011, para. 4). A discursive formation led by the notion that everyone will benefit from a deregulated economy allowing energetic entrepreneurs to create jobs and markets is powerful.

Under the banner of fiscal responsibility, neoliberal supporters in government and the media have been calling for funding cuts to public education in both countries. In Canada, entrepreneurial forces are pushing for the creation of a two-tiered healthcare system to replace its treasured universal public healthcare system. The main reason given for these perspectives is that it is no longer affordable to fund these public institutions through taxes. The public would have to get their information from sources outside of the mainstream corporate media to learn that these discourses are being trumpeted during a period in which the gap between the rich and the poor is increasing to grotesque proportions in both countries. It would be difficult for concerned citizens to learn that one of the major roles for the state, according to neoliberal doctrine, is to create markets in areas such as education and healthcare if they do not already exist (Harvey, 2005, p. 2).

Based on years of research, Richard Wilkinson and Kate Pickett (2010) contend that societies with a massive gap between the rich and the poor, such as in the United States, are not doing *anyone* any good, including the well-off. According to their research, "[t]he scale of income differences has a powerful effect on how we relate to each other" (pp. 4–5). The authors of this unique study claim that once countries reach a certain level of affluence, further rises in average income account for less increase in overall health and happiness until there is no increase whatsoever. It is *the degree of inequality* that provides the major influence on the psychological wellbeing of a nation's citizens. Yet, in countries adopting neoliberalism, economic policy continues to favor the affluent.

For several decades, the economic elites of the United States and Canada have dismissed any notion that they have been implicated in any kind of class warfare. Yet, when one considers increasingly massive gaps in wealth, there can be little doubt that neoliberalism is indeed "a project aimed at the restoration of class power" (Anijar & Gabbard, 2009, pp. 45–46). David Harvey (2005) states that "if it looks like class struggle and acts like class war then we have to name it unashamedly for what it is" (p. 202). According to Harvey, by 1996 the neoliberal agenda had created an economic super elite in which the net worth of the richest 358 people was equal to the world's poorest 2.3 billion people.

Since the 1980s, corporate media sources in both the United States and Canada have inundated citizens with a set of discourses that has further entrenched the economic power of the elites while greatly affecting the lives of everyone else, and for the most part, in negative ways. These discourses have evolved into an extremely powerful discursive formation that forms the underpinnings of neoliberalism. As it is concerned solely with economics, the neoliberal agenda provides the basis for a new class war, one that is attempting to replace the Fordist arrangement between capital and labor, and end the influence of Keynesian economics.[1]

Neoliberalism: Is This a New Political "Ideology"?

[T]here is no morality, no faith, no heroism, indeed no meaning outside the market. (Brown, 2003, p. 10)

Is neoliberalism a political ideology? I make the case that it is not. In Chapter 2, as you will recall, ideology was defined as consisting of three elements: a critique, an ideal, and agency (Schwarzmantel, 1998, p. 2). Each ideology has a response to the prevailing social conditions, either favorable or not, depending on how an individual's perspective agrees with the dominant ideology. Moreover, each ideology has an articulation of the ideal society. In the United States and Canada today, there does not seem to exist large segments of the public that adhere to the values of neoliberalism. For example, I have never heard anyone say that they would like to see as many things as possible commodified, or that public institutions should be privatized so that profits can be made by someone else. Indeed, it would seem that neoliberalism is touted by the economic elites and the media pundits who work for them, but not by very many people who benefit from strong public institutions, namely, the middle and working classes.

Although specific neoliberal strategies such as deregulation and privatization of the commons may be unacceptable to most citizens, this is not to suggest that the overall neoliberal project, as far as it is understood by the public, is not supported. This is because it is most often promoted in terms that resonate with people hoping to improve their economic wellbeing. Harvey (2005) provides an example of a positive description of neoliberalism:

> Neoliberalism is in the first instance a theory of political economic practices that proposes that human well-being can best be advanced by liberating individual entrepreneurial freedoms and skills within an institutional framework characterized by strong property rights, free markets, and free trade. (p. 2)

Harvey's description fits with the idea of a rising tide raising all of the boats regardless of size and quality. As the massive numbers of house foreclosures and personal bankruptcies in the United States demonstrate, not all of the boats rise; in fact, many of them sink. Moreover, less well known are the incendiary policies that go along with deregulation and privatization. These include roles for the state to protect the quality of money itself, to ensure that military, police, and legal infrastructures exist to guarantee the proper functioning of markets (by force, if necessary), and to secure private property rights. Lastly, the state must act to create markets in areas such as education, healthcare, social security, and environmental pollution. If citizens understood these aspects of neoliberalism, it is unlikely that the majority would support the entire project.

Ideology is about the "thought-production of human beings" (Giroux, 1981, p. 19). A political ideology contains "a specific set of assumptions and social practices" that leads to various "beliefs, expectations and biases" (p. 7). Yet, because neoliberal strategies such as deregulation and privatization do not appear to be accepted by most American and Canadian citizens, it would be inaccurate to say that neoliberalism leads many citizens to alter their beliefs, expectations or biases to conform to what they are hearing about in the media. Rather than promoting an ideal society that working people can get excited about, it is about assessing and assigning market values to all institutions and social actions. In these terms, neoliberalism cannot be considered a political ideology.

Moreover, all political ideologies function to provide the framework for political action designed to produce a version of the good society. Despite the proclamations in the corporate media that neoliberal policies increase choice, freedom, and efficiency, there seems to be very little support for this type of society among common citizens (Livingstone, 2007). Furthermore, the discussion in Chapter 2 emphasized that each political ideology had two sets of values or positions along a continuous spectrum, an economic scale and a social scale. Neoliberalism is only concerned with economic strategies, not social issues. It is clear, however, that it has detrimental effects upon social relations.

If Not an Ideology, Then What is Neoliberalism?

At the risk of employing confusing political terminology, neoliberalism is an economic *rationality*, rather than a political ideology (Brown, 2003). I believe the distinction is an important one. In the same manner that a person might rationalize, for example, not claiming on an income tax form the payment they received for painting someone's fence because they feel it is none of the government's business, neoliberalism is somewhere between a bold-faced lie and an honestly held truth. Do the beneficiaries of neoliberalism really believe that their economic policies will create a better society with more freedom for more people? Or do even these people understand that the so-called trickle-down theory does not really work in an era in which they can and often do deposit their wealth in overseas tax-free banking schemes? Neoliberalism is based upon a free market theory that is touted as the *only* option. Indeed, one of its early proponents was former British Prime Minister Margaret Thatcher who famously claimed that "there is no alternative" to the neoliberal agenda, which has since become known as the TINA discourse. Thus, it enables its adherents to feel good about their money despite the extreme poverty these policies created. Neoliberalism can be viewed as an elaborate form of self-deception, a rationalization rather than an ideology.

It is important, I believe, for educators to understand the historical trajectory that has led to the dynamics in the current stage of capitalism we find ourselves living in. This is the focus of the next two sections.

From Laissez-Faire *to State Interventionism in the Economy*

The foregoing discussion concluded that neoliberalism is not a political ideology per se. Yet, its roots can be found in the ideology known as classical liberalism. As mentioned in Chapter 2, the two cornerstones of classical liberalism are "the supreme value of the individual and the need for a political system that was suitable for an emancipated and rational population" (Schwarzmantel, 1998, p. 68). As such, emancipation and democracy are the progeny of liberalism. Initially, however, liberals were quite happy to engage in the pursuit of wealth through laissez-faire economic policy and the conquest of nature. An economic system based on free-market principles became dominant as the newly emerging bourgeoisie refined the economically successful but racist mercantile system that had existed for at least a century prior to these revolutionary times. Adam Smith's *Wealth of Nations* became the source of rational liberal principles. Smith's belief in free market capitalism was based in part on what he also thought to be the best way to free as many people as possible.

Unfortunately, as Karl Marx pointed out, there is an inherent contradiction in classical liberalism in that workers can never be free, while the capitalists can lower wages and increase the price of goods and services for more profits. With its support for laissez-faire economics, classical liberalism was opposed to state intervention in the economy.[2] Therefore, there was no institutional recourse for workers to improve their working conditions and their standard of living. Only during and after the Great Depression and the Second World War did classical liberalism give way to a more progressive version of liberalism. This reformed liberalism was based upon *Keynesian economics.*

In the 1920s, British macroeconomist John Maynard Keynes understood that the self-correcting aspect of capitalism, also known as the hidden hand of the market, was a myth. The common belief among economists in those years was that the cause of unemployment was workers' wages that were too high. This led to policies that continually lowered their wages, which, in turn, obviously led to a lowering of the standard of living for the British working classes. Keynes pointed out that with so little money in the hands of people, there was no demand for products, and this, in turn, led to a climate of little investing and, therefore, a flat economy. He argued that no matter how low wages fell, if there was no demand for products, employers would not begin to hire workers. Capitalists, Keynes argued, would be foolish to invest money in risky ventures when the prospects of making a profit were so low.

Once Keynes had demonstrated the fallacy of the self-correcting nature of capitalism, the stage was set for what was at the time unthinkable: he advocated for state intervention in the economy by pumping money into the system. The idea was to get the idle factories up and running with the labor of the formerly unemployed, who became the newly employed. Keynes' emphasis on placing unemployment front and center, rather than as a mere by-product of achieving a growing economy, became accepted by more and more economists. His theory demanded that the economy serve the interests of the people, not the other way around as it was with classical economics. Linda McQuaig (1998) states Keynes' important contribution to the role of government as follows:

> What Keynes essentially did was overturn the notion of human powerlessness, the notion that we are mere numbers in a supply-and-demand equation whose fate ... is determined by some remote natural law over which we have no control. Keynes showed that *through government, we can exert enormous control over our economy and therefore over our lives.* (p. 212, emphasis mine)

Moreover, what made Keynesian economics even more radical was that the strong role for government in a democratic system meant that an informed public could very well elect politicians who had the best interests of most people in mind, not the best interests of the elites. This, then, is the genius of Keynesian economics – even in a capitalist system, it is possible that a politically aware citizenry could take hold of the levers of power and make decisions to benefit themselves, and strive for the elusive civil society. And from the mid-1940s until the 1970s, Keynesian economics more or less provided the basis for state interventionism, a strong social welfare state, and an expanding economy throughout the West. An influential American economist, Keynesian disciple Robert Eisner, once remarked, "Neither God nor nature decreed that involuntary unemployment need always be with us" (cited in McQuaig, 1998, p. 30). Contrary to what Marx thought possible within capitalism, for three decades the standard of living for the working classes rose substantially in Western nations.

So, one would be wise to ask, what happened? Why have the economic theories of John Maynard Keynes become mostly obsolete in today's world? This is the point of entry for economists Friedrich von Hayek and Milton Friedman and their influence on global economic policy.

Neoliberalism Finds Fertile Ground

> [T]his return of ultra-liberalism with a vengeance is not a product of either chance or necessity. It was the subject of one of the most important intellectual battles of the 20th century. And it still is. (Berthelot, 2008, p. 31)

In 1944, two scholarly books were published by European economists about the best way for capitalism to proceed: *The Great Transformation* by Karl Polanyi, and *The Road to Serfdom* by Friedrich von Hayek. The first one provided the inspiration for the social democratic movement that rose to prominence in Western Europe after World War II. The importance of the second book would become apparent several decades later. It "became the manifesto of neoliberalism with Hayek as its intellectual guru" (Berthelot, 2008, p. 31). After a decade into the twenty-first century, it appears that Hayak's book has proven to be more influential than the one by Polanyi. But these things, too, can change.

Polanyi was convinced that citizens of Western nations did not want to go back to the economic theories that had influenced global economic arrangements throughout the nineteenth century and well into the 1930s. (This is what he was referring to with his usage of the term "transformation" in the title of his book.) He agreed with Keynes that the idea of a self-correcting market was an illusion at best, and at worst, a recipe for dystopia. Polanyi believed that *the profit motive was a poor choice to have as an organizing principle for any society.* He was very concerned that an economy should not be based exclusively on personal interest (Berthelot, 2008, p. 32). In fact, if market forces were the sole determinant of the fate of human beings, Polanyi reasoned, then the likelihood of a demolished society would be inevitable (Harvey, 2005, p. 167). Not everyone, of course, agreed with Polanyi's treatise on social democracy.

Hayak and his disciples disagreed with government intervention in the economy. Moreover, Hayak believed that "the pursuit of personal interest was for human nature what universal gravity was for physical bodies" (Berthelot, 2008, p. 33). Hayak called for cuts to social programs, repression of unions, deregulation, and privatization, precisely the cadre of policies much of the world has been inundated with since the 1980s and 1990s. But Hayak's book was published in 1944. Why did it take so long for his ideas to become influential?

After the Second World War, Western economies were expanding, and governments began to support the notion of a strong social welfare state for their citizens. This meant that economic theories dismissive of the common good and strong public institutions were not very popular. Neither were politicians who agreed with these policies. The theories of Keynes and Polanyi triumphed over Hayak's, whose ideas were relegated to the fringes of economic and political thinking. Eventually, however, conditions changed to the extent that these once fringe ideas started to garner more support among economists and politicians. Eventually, support for the dismantling of the social welfare state began to grow.

One of Hayak's most celebrated disciples was a colleague of his at the University of Chicago, Milton Friedman, the author of *Capitalism and Freedom* (2002), which was first published in 1982. It includes Friedman's argument opposing Keynes on the issue of unemployment. Friedman believed that unemployment has a natural state in each economy. He also saw that a portion of the populace unable to procure a job will help effectively keep the wages of the employed lower than with full employment. The economic elites began to listen (Eisner, 1994).

In the introduction to the second edition of *Capitalism and Freedom* (2002), Friedman explains how these ideas moved from the fringe to the mainstream:

> [O]nly a crisis – actual or perceived produces real change. When that crisis occurs, the actions that are taken depend on the ideas that are lying around. That, I believe, is our basic function: to develop alternatives to existing policies, to keep them alive and available until the politically impossible becomes the politically inevitable. (p. ix)

The "crisis" that gave the impetus for the acceptance of neoliberalism took place in Chile in 1970 (Harvey, 2005, p. 7). This was the year that this South American country had democratically elected as its leader the social democrat, Salvador Allende. In order to build more schools and hospitals, Allende's government nationalized all the copper deposits in the Andes, leading to the CIA-backed military coup d'etat of 1973 that ended Allende's life. The coup also replaced Allende as Chile's leader with General Augusto Pinochet. After the 1973 military coup d'etat, the next general election held in Chile occurred in 1990. This demonstrates the inherent disdain for democracy among neoliberal supporters.

The military coup d'etat in Chile gave Friedman his first opportunity to exploit a major national crisis. He became the economic advisor to General Pinochet, and shortly afterward brought some of his colleagues and students from the University of Chicago to Santiago, a group that subsequently became known as the Chicago Boys (Harvey, 2005, p. 8). Naomi Klein (2007) describes what took place:

> Not only were Chileans in a state of shock following Pinochet's violent coup, but the country was also traumatized by severe hyperinflation. Friedman advised Pinochet to impose a rapid-fire transformation of the economy – tax cuts, free trade, privatized services, cuts to social spending and deregulation. Eventually, Chileans even saw their public schools replaced with voucher-funded private ones ... [Friedman] coined a phrase for this painful tactic: economic "shock treatment." (p. 8)

Pinochet's Chile was presented to the world as an economic wonder, a run-down country that was very quickly transformed into a nation filled with boutiques and new cars. The glossy magazines, however, did not have any depictions of the newly formed shantytowns or the brutal military repression of Chile's citizens. Supporters of neoliberalism pushed the same strategies mentioned in the quote above as the best way, indeed the *only* way, to transform an economy so that it maximizes profits for entrepreneurial-minded individuals. The neoliberal project first proposed by

Friedrich von Hayak now found itself in very fertile soil, and adherents quickly began to flock to the trough.

Chile under General Pinochet was the first country to implement the neoliberal policies required to completely overhaul a nation's economy. Since then, many other countries have adopted neoliberal policies, often by coercion. Some of the so-called Third World nations have had these policies forced upon them through borrowing money from the World Bank and the International Monetary Fund (IMF), the world's two largest international loans agencies, both mostly controlled by the United States. Yet, most Western countries have also implemented neoliberal *domestic* policies of their own (Hill, 2009).

Since the 1990s, neoliberalism has attracted its share of critics in Canada and the United States . For example, in *Profit Over People: Neoliberalism and Global Order* (1999), American political philosopher and linguist Noam Chomsky clearly states his position: "Neoliberal doctrines, whatever one thinks of them, undermine education and health, increase inequality, and reduce labor's share in income, that much is not seriously in doubt" (p. 32). Moreover, Canadian social commentators such as McQuaig (1998) and Klein (2007), as well as Chomsky (1999), have made strong arguments showing that neoliberalism renders citizens almost "powerless" in economic decision making. This is particularly disturbing given that the doctrine that preceded it, Keynesian economic theory, enabled the public to influence public policy through democratic initiatives. The question that needs to be asked is this: How did the citizens of Western nations such as the United States and Canada come to accept an economic project that is antithetical to the notion of the common good? The next section addresses this very question.

Getting the Masses to Support the Neoliberal Project

> The angry workers, mighty in their numbers, are marching irresistibly against the arrogant. They are shaking their fists at the sons of privilege ... [W]hile the millionaires tremble inside their mansions, they are bellowing out their terrifying demands. "*We are here*," they scream, "*to cut your taxes!*" (Frank, 2004b, p. 109, emphasis mine)

Most Americans and Canadians have benefited from a strong social welfare state. This has especially been the case during the period from the late 1940s until the 1970s. There is no question that Keynesian economics, with its support for government intervention in difficult economic times, has more to offer the common person than what Hayak and Friedman proposed as an alternative. This would be the case even if neoliberalism was presented in the extremely positive light discussed earlier in this chapter. The mystery lies in why so many of these common citizens support politicians who want to deregulate industry and privatize or dismantle the social welfare state.

Like all neoliberals, Hayak and Friedman were not concerned with social issues. Theirs was solely an economic project. (This would explain how they could support the extremely brutal tactics employed by General Pinochet to quell Chileans opposed to neoliberal policies.) In this sense, neoliberalism, it might be argued, is an *amoral* enterprise. So where does its support come from? How do politicians in favor of increasing wealth for the wealthy while dismantling the commons get elected and even reelected? This is where neoconservatism enters the discussion. Neoconservatism is somewhat of a contested term. It first started appearing in American media reports in the mid-1990s (Klein, 2007, p. 17). Since then, right wing think tanks associated with Milton Friedman – such as the Cato Institute, Heritage Foundation, and American Enterprise Institute – have promoted what has become commonly referred to as a neoconservative world view that includes the use of the United States military to entrench the corporate agenda in foreign countries. One key neoconservative contribution to what we have been calling the neoliberal project on a global scale is their support for a strong military, which is clearly a major component of the American arsenal of tactics.

Another confusing feature of contemporary politics is the convergence of a political acceptance of Friedman's corporate agenda with the resurgence of American social conservatism. This resurgence began with Barry Goldwater's unsuccessful campaign for the American presidency in 1964. But it wasn't until the early 1970s when the movement really began to spread.

A secret memorandum written by a conservative, Lewis F. Powell, on behalf of the U.S. Chamber of Commerce in 1971 strongly suggested that wealthy conservatives needed to finance plans to influence a new generation of Americans toward conservative values. Powell expressed concern that critiques of the American economic system were becoming commonplace even in "perfectly respectable elements of society" such as the mainstream media and college campuses (Anijar & Gabbard, 2009, p. 39). To counter this trend, Powell urged corporations to "use think tanks to monitor schools and universities, the media, the courts, and politics for anti-business ideas, and aggressively target them for the distribution of pro-business and neoliberal ideas" (p. 40). Since then, Americans have seen the rise of these think tanks that support neoliberal economic policies while making connections to conservative values (Harvey, 2005). This has been a very successful strategy: get working-class Americans and Canadians to support politicians who pay some attention to traditional conservative values while deregulating the financial industry and privatizing as much of the commons as possible.

In *What's the Matter With Kansas* (2004), Thomas Frank explains how corporate executives and politicians, backed by corporate media pundits, managed to channel working-class anger over cultural issues into support for their corporate agenda. He calls this anger the "Great Backlash" and explains it as follows:

> The Great Backlash has made the laissez faire revival possible, but this does not mean that it speaks to us in the manner of the capitalists of old, invoking the divine right of money or demanding that the lowly learn their place in the great chain of being. On the contrary; the backlash imagines itself as a foe of the elite, as the voice of the unfairly persecuted, as a righteous protest of the people on history's receiving end. That its champions today control all three branches of government matters not a whit. That its greatest beneficiaries are the wealthiest people on the planet does not give it pause. (Frank, 2004, p. 6)

Although Frank does not use the term "neoliberalism," it is clear that he is pointing out a massive contradiction, namely, that this working-class movement fueled by support for traditional conservative values is doing great harm to the standard of living of these very same laborers and their families. The corporate beneficiaries will accept this needed support in exchange for media time (at least) for the neoconservative desire to reintroduce prayer into public school classrooms, to re-Christianize the state itself, and to uphold the traditional idea that marriage can only be between a man and a woman. It appears that what Frank called the "Great Backlash" in 2004 has evolved into the Tea Party in 2009 and 2010 (Yakabuski, 2010).

Neoconservatism and neoliberalism have a natural convergence in their common support for a strong military. For the neoconservatives, a strong military translates into being able to defend one's country. For neoliberals, a strong military means being able to force other countries to adopt the economic policies of Hayak and Friedman. The next section focuses on this latter impulse.

Is Today's Globalization the Same as Yesterday's Colonization?

Economic restructuring has proceeded hand in hand with neoliberal policies and a massive offensive to transform the world into a single market. (Berthelot, 2008, p. 25)

As a market analyst remarked of a particularly good quarter for the earnings of the energy services company Halliburton, "Iraq was better than expected." That was in October 2006, then the most violent month of the war on record, with 3,709 Iraqi civilian casualties. Still, few shareholders could fail to be impressed by a war that had generated $20 billion in revenues for this one company. (Klein, 2007, p. 16)

Anyone who paid attention during their high school social studies or history classes understands that colonizing other peoples often brought great wealth to the colonizers. Indeed, European nations that engaged in usurping the resources from other peoples' land saw their own economic status improve considerably. In what is now Canada and the United States, the British and French forced Aboriginal peoples onto reserves to block them from living on their traditional lands. They used the labor of African slaves to work these lands. Most Americans and Canadians understand that both countries have this colonial past. And most students I have come across over the years see this aspect of our nation-building periods as exceptionally brutal and unjust.

Indeed, several decades of multicultural education has had some positive effect, at least in the ways many people view the past. In my teaching experience there has been a significant percentage of students who recognize the horrors of the colonial past, but most feel that everyone must get past that now. These students are unaware of the lingering and powerful effects of the colonial legacy toward people of Aboriginal and African ancestry. They are not conscious of systemic racism or the privileges of "whiteness" in contemporary society (McIntosh, 1988; Roediger, 1999).

Yet, does the typical American or Canadian hold negative views toward globalization in the contemporary context? Some people have learned about grossly unfair labor practices in sweat shops run by multinational corporations. In my experience, however, the term *globalization* does not connote the same negative feeling in students that *colonialism* does. This undoubtedly has something to do with the current hegemonic discourses trumpeting the virtues of globalization in the corporate media. As well, globalization has multiple meanings, some easier to take than others. The high school social studies curriculum has not yet caught up to these multiple meanings. In fact, it does not include prescribed learning outcomes that deal with globalization in any depth.

There are two prevalent, and oppositional, meanings of globalization. There is a hegemonic meaning of globalization that refers to global capitalism and its needs pertaining to trade, investment, and labor mobility. There is also another meaning of globalization that is based on human rights and includes the notion of a progressive, cosmopolitan citizen. In this chapter, globalization will refer to the first interpretation, that is, as a major global force for capitalist endeavors.

In this context, contemporary globalization refers to the process of persuading countries, through military force or loan arrangements, to adopt neoliberal policies. In short, globalization today demands that societies should be governed by the rules of trade and understood only in terms of its economic rationality. According to Berthelot (2008), "the much vaunted 'global village' is turning out to be a 'global pillage' " (p. 9). A brief look at the experiences some countries have recently gone through will explain why Berthelot refers to this stage of corporate capitalism as a *pillage*.

Neoliberal policies have been foisted upon several countries that have undergone major crises of some form or another (Klein, 2007; Harvey, 2005). The World Bank, the IMF, and the U.S. Treasury often arrange loans to nations in need of a major influx of money on the condition that they adapt their economies to maximize corporate profits. Taken together, these conditions are called a *structural adjustment*. Some of the conditions demanded of the debtor country are reminiscent of the old mercantile system of colonial times. These include increased export of raw materials and a required agricultural regime. Other conditions comprise the privatization of public institutions, the dismantling of social programs, pro-business labor laws, and of course, tax cuts for the wealthy and corporations (Berthelot, 2008, p. 26). Klein (2007) bluntly summarizes what happens to each one of these debtor countries: "the elimination of the public sphere, [and] total liberation for corporations and skeletal social spending" (p. 17). Most of these countries must also scrap environmental protection policies, especially if these policies inhibit profits for the corporations. Moreover, after the crisis the citizens all of these countries find themselves with a similar type of partnership holding onto the levers of power: a few mega-corporations and a group of extremely wealthy politicians (McLaren, 2005, p. 25). The injustice inherent in these scenarios is obvious.

After the collapse of the Soviet Union, the oil fields of Russia, once publicly owned, quickly became the domain of wealthy individuals and corporations. Russia's president at the time, Boris Yeltsin, was more than willing to accept the neoliberal conditions the IMF demanded rather than allow democratic initiatives to run their course (Klein, 2007, p. 263). Similarly, the NATO attack on Belgrade in 1999 enabled the expedient privatization of public resources (p. 11). During the 1980s and 1990s, many countries in South America, such as Brazil, Venezuela, Argentina, and of course, Chile, engaged in extreme cuts to social spending in order to receive loans from the international lending agencies. The exorbitant interest rates on these loans ensured that increased spending on public infrastructure would be rendered impossible. This was especially the situation while transnational corporations were the benefactors from the local resources. Further, labor practices in these countries, as in all countries involved with IMF and World Bank loans, were almost universally opposed to unions and union organizing (Berthelot, 2008).

If we look back to the colonial era, we find the dominant economic practices were very similar. The colonizers usurped the resources from the lands of the colonized peoples, without giving much back. Parallels can be gleaned between colonialism and today's globalization. Yet, there is a profound difference between the two international systems. Arundhati Roy (2004) explains:

> On the global stage, beyond the jurisdiction of sovereign governments, international instruments of trade and finance oversee a complex system of multilateral laws and agreements that have entrenched a system of appropriation that puts colonialism to shame... The World Trade Organization, the World Bank, the International Monetary Fund, and other financial institutions like the Asian Development Bank, virtually write economic policy and parliamentary legislation ... As a consequence of this reform, in Africa, Asia, and Latin America, *thousands of small enterprises and industries have closed down, millions of workers and farmers have lost their jobs and land.* (emphasis mine)

Roy's succinct description of what happens to desperate and broke Third World countries strongly suggests something of a Faustian agreement. In exchange for the loan, the cost seems to be the soul of the nation itself. Many citizens of Western nations, who have been educated for several decades about the injustices and unethical behaviors of past colonial practices, would not accept these international arrangements. After all, these loan conditions are destined to keep the debtor countries mired in poverty for a very long time.

A question arises about the ability of citizens to stop their government from making deals so that corporations receive large sums of money from nations that are barely able take care of their own people. As Stiglitz (2003), the former senior vice president and chief economist at the World Bank, explains, the United States "pushed a market fundamentalist set of reforms, in any way we could, paying little attention to how what we did undermined democratic processes" (p. 25). This would explain why the most successful counter attacks to neoliberalism seem to be occurring in Latin America, a part of the world where people saw firsthand the devastation wrought by Friedman's theories.

Are American and Canadian citizens ready to resist the neoliberal juggernaut? After all, they have also experienced these policies for at least a couple of decades. The next section addresses this situation.

Neoliberalism On the Home Front

> A fully realized neoliberal citizenry would be the opposite of public-minded, indeed it would barely exist as a public. (Brown, 2003, p. 15)

Much has been made in recent years about the low voter turnout in many Western nations. In Chapter 8, the discussion explored citizenship and our waning democracies in Canada and the United States. The reasons for our waning democracies include low voter turnout, voter apathy, uninformed voters, media spin, announced poll results during election campaigns, the Prime Minister's notwithstanding clause (which is similar to the President's veto), no-paper voting machines, and the first-past-the-post voting system (rather than proportional representation, which was described in Chapter 8). I also emphasized that a strong democracy has more than two parties to choose from in order to decrease the potential of corporate influence.[3] It is quite possible, however, that many of these factors may be attributed to the effects of neoliberalism on Americans and Canadians.

In the current period we find ourselves living in, one dominated by neoliberal economics, the *individual* has become hyper-emphasized. Wilkinson and Pickett (2010) explain the effect of this on society itself: "Instead of a better society, the only thing that almost everyone strives for is to better their own position – as individuals – within the existing society" (p. 4). Related to this is the appearance of a powerful discourse addressing the rise of unemployed people, city panhandlers, and home foreclosures. This discourse stresses the victim's own shortcomings as the reason why they are in such dire straits. In other words, these social problems are *not* seen as political issues with political solutions.

McQuaig (1998) points to the "powerlessness" that many people feel today, which she refers to as "the cult of impotence." This clearly points to a major reason why fewer people engage in the democratic process, but it is not because people do not care anymore. In fact, this line of thinking implies that *people really do care* about the society they live in, and have heart-felt concerns about their public education system and other aspects of the social welfare state. The problem lies in what many citizens perceive to be their inability to evoke change. For example, many Americans may not have noticed any changes in federal government educational policy since President Obama has come into office. Obama's policies still support state-wide testing, charter schools, and the voucher system, ideas that especially came to the fore under the George W. Bush administration. (All of these policies are features of the neoliberal assault on public education.)

Furthermore, if the public cannot see very much difference in the economic policies of Republicans and Democrats, many will not bother to vote. If they do vote, they will do so based on the *social* policies of each party on issues like gay marriage. This situation enables right-wing media outlets such as Fox News to have an even greater influence on American society through the so-called Culture Wars strategy (Martin, 2010). The Culture Wars strategy has proven to be so successful for American conservatives that the Conservative Party of Canada has attempted to import it to Canada by creating a Fox News North TV station (Taber, 2010).

The situation also demonstrates a major difference between neoliberalism and the ideology of liberalism. After all, as was pointed out in Chapter 2, democracy was spawned in the modern world out of liberalism. As well, human rights were a major part of the democratic initiative. Yet, the so-called Patriot Act, which was signed into law by the George W. Bush administration on October 26, 2001, highlights just how easily and quickly hard fought for gains in areas such as civil rights can disappear.[4]

Ironically, neoliberalism is best able to function in the way that the elites want when there is formal electoral democracy. In this situation, however, there must also be obstacles blocking citizens from accessing information or engaging in public forums that lead to meaningful participation in the decision-making process. These conditions describe what has been going on in both the United States and Canada in recent years. According to American media critic Robert McChesney, "[N]eoliberal democracy in a nutshell: trivial debate over minor issues by parties that basically pursue the same pro-business policies regardless of formal differences and campaign debate" (cited in Chomsky, 1999, p. 9). The basic premise of neoliberalism, namely, the corporate agenda, is not up for debate in this kind of democracy. A generation of corporate public relations people working the media has created an almost sacred aura around neoliberalism and its byproducts of an unregulated financial industry and unfettered capitalism. It is no wonder that another byproduct of neoliberalism is an apathetic and cynical citizenry without much of a political consciousness. Many citizens now see the role of governments as making policies that advance corporate interests in many areas of public and private life.[5]

Yet, there may be an even greater danger to democracy in these neoliberal times than apathy and a sense of powerlessness among the public. This is in the manner in which neoliberalism constitutes the identity of the ideal citizen. Brown (2003) contends that the American individual is being re-made as "calculating rather than rule-abiding" (p. 16). This conception of the ideal citizen is *to the right* of the personally responsible citizen promoted by traditional conservatives. It influences individuals to strive for their own needs, wants, and ambitions. It renders the concept of the public to be subservient to the needs of capitalism. In other words, we are clearly in a period of regression in terms of supporting the common good. From this perspective, it is obvious that the progressive economic ideas of Keynes and Polanyi do not play a major part in the minds of these kinds of citizens.

Another frightening aspect of neoliberalism is that, rather than let nature take its course with these market values, "it develops institutional practices and rewards for enacting this vision" (Brown, 2003, p. 4). This explains why politicians and journalists who support the corporate agenda push for laws and policies that will clear the way for huge profits to be made by individuals or corporations. It also explains why corporate leaders who manage to navigate the political system so that ideal neoliberal conditions are attained are handsomely rewarded with massive financial bonuses, and sometimes the source of the money is the taxpayer. In a provocative article called "The Quiet Coup," Simon Johnson (2009), who was the chief economist of the International Monetary Fund from 2007 until 2008, explains how the financial industry has taken hold of the levers of political power in the United States.

Bearing all of this in mind, it is obvious that progressives cannot count on the corporate media to help rectify the situation. Indeed, the corporate media work as an exceptionally powerful and effective hegemonic device in the service of neoliberal ideals. Once again, it falls upon teachers to deconstruct this onslaught on our public institutions. But this is not going to be an easy task, as our public education systems have also been under attack from this neoliberal juggernaut.

Neoliberalism and Its Implications for Public Education

A tendency to blame public schooling, school districts, principals and teachers is pervasive and consistent with neoliberal frameworks that embrace the need to hold individuals responsible for educational productivity. (Tobin, 2011, para. 7)

In 1976, educators Samuel Bowles and Herbert Gintis published their highly seminal work, *Schooling in Capitalist America*. This book highlighted the school's role in reproducing the class structure in the United States in order to fulfill the requirements of capitalism. Resistance theorists subsequently incorporated the notion of human agency into the mix, pointing to the opportunities for destabilizing the school's supportive role for the economy. Even so, this position is still a long way off from what John Dewey and Social Reconstructionists wanted to see for the role of the school, namely, to develop critical thinking and active citizens. Yet, there is reason to be concerned that the thesis Bowles and Gintis developed is once again a concern to people worried about schooling in our liberal democracies.

McLaren (2005) states this concern in blunt terms: "neoliberal educational policy operates from the premise that education is primarily a subsector of the economy" (p. 31). Harvey (2005) takes this point even further: "[I]f markets do not exist (in areas such as land, water, education, health care, social security or environmental pollution) then they must be created, by state action if necessary" (p. 2). Every citizen who values public education, to name but one important part of the commons under threat, must pay attention. After all, the public school system has been instrumental in improving the standard of living for most people in Canada and the United States.

The debate about the proper role of the public school is rooted in historical struggles around the school curriculum itself, as discussed in Chapter 4. Put succinctly, this debate centers around viewing students as human capital in need of training for their future jobs versus educating future citizens in possession of critical thinking skills so they will be able to actively participate in a democracy. Clearly, the neoliberal position in this debate is to influence school policy in favor of the human capital model.

American educators Karen Anijar and David Gabbard (2009) have examined neoliberalism's effects on the American public school system. Their overall assessment is that neoliberalism is having a very deleterious effect on what was once a cherished public institution of middle- and working-class Americans. They point out the clever use of language manipulation employed by neoliberals. For example, the *voucher system*, which is much more prevalent in the United States than in any other country, is described in media campaigns as an idea based on the discourse of *democracy and freedom*. Harvey (2005) explains that the "idea of freedom, long embedded in the U.S. tradition, has played a conspicuous role in the U.S. in recent years" (p. 5).

Calling the voucher school an instrument for freedom is in stark contrast to how numerous critics see it, namely, as a strategy designed to bring a slow death to the public school system. Moreover, neoliberals refer to the public school system as the "government school" system (p. 24).[6] Moreover, Anijar and Gabbard contend that the frequently heard discourse of "failing schools" in America is a "manufactured crisis" that has led many members of the American public into believing that vouchers "provide a pragmatic utilitarian solution" to this so-called problem (p. 24). The corporate media use this "crisis" as an opportunity to create political spectacle.

Charter schools have a similar function as voucher schools, according to Anijar and Gabbard, with the added "bonus" of profit-making possibilities. It is important to note that when comparing similar types of students with similar backgrounds, charter schools perform worse than traditional public schools (p. 28). Indeed, many of the charter schools in the United States are religious schools that do not have to adhere to the standards and intense accountability imposed on public schools (p. 26). Clearly, this is a very difficult issue for progressives to address, especially with a hostile media. Yet, in order to save the "slow death" of public education, this debate must begin in a public forum setting.

The situation in Canada is not much brighter, although neoliberal educational policies appeared almost a decade after American schools experienced them. Yet, when they did appear they did so with a vengeance under the federal Liberal governments of the 1990s (Davidson-Harden, Kuehn, Schugurensky, & Smaller, 2009). With the exception of teacher accountability, the most noticeable effect of the neoliberal agenda is in the appearance of corporate advertising in the public school system because of funding shortfalls.

The Canadian revenue-sharing system includes a transfer payment scheme in which the federal government collects taxes and divides it among the ten provinces for public education and public healthcare funding. In order to combat the federal deficit, the Liberal government stopped sending the transfer payments in the mid-1990s, which meant that approximately $5 billion was taken away from the provinces annually, money that was to go toward the public education and healthcare system (Davidson-Harden et al., 2009, p. 51). Many of the provincial governments of the time, such as the Conservative governments of Ontario and Alberta, used this as an opportunity to make further cuts, thereby opening the door to privatization in both spheres. The neoliberal effect in Canada has resulted in "tighter controls over, but less funding for, public sector social institutions" (p. 62). The situation is ripe for corporate intrusion into public schools and the cherished healthcare system. In the spirit of entrepreneurial opportunism, Canadian corporations took advantage of the situation in much the same way as their American counterparts have done.

In recent years, corporate intrusion in the public school system has taken several forms: vending machines (mostly selling junk food), cash donations for advertising space, and in the United States, the appearance of Channel One News almost every day.[7] The corporate sector appears to have a fairly straightforward plan: fight for tax cuts, which results in school funding cuts, and the shortfall is made up by the corporations flush with extra money from the tax cuts. The only difference is that advertising targeting students now appears in our public schools. This is clearly *not* what we want to see in a civil society.

The funding cuts for public schools have had another deleterious effect: school districts find themselves in competition with each other over the lucrative international student market. Schools that are already doing better financially from fundraising ventures and higher socioeconomic neighborhoods tend to attract more foreign students, leading to an even greater discrepancy between schools. Of course, all of these issues would disappear if public education was adequately funded. Funding cuts to public education, however, are only part of the neoliberal agenda to control the K to 12 public school system.

The Neoliberal Attack on the Teaching Profession

One of the goals of this book is to encourage educators to eschew neutrality and develop an enacted curriculum based on the real-life experiences of the students and their families. Yet, it is becoming increasingly difficult for teachers to supplement the official curriculum with lessons specifically designed around relevant issues. This is because of the major emphasis in recent years on state- and province-wide testing in both the United States and Canada. I can attest to how teacher accountability around provincial exams inhibits the creativity of the teacher in employing constructivist approaches to pedagogy. After all, I only stopped teaching in the high school classroom in 2006 – neoliberal discourses to increase teacher accountability had already been around for several years by the time I left.

A major neoliberal strategy to weaken public education has been an almost complete dismissal of teacher autonomy and professionalism. Standards-based educational reforms, including state-wide testing, are part of the campaign to increase teacher accountability. The No Child Left Behind legislation enacted by the Bush administration in 2001 linked these standards and state-wide exam scores to school funding (Mathison & Ross, 2008). In Canada, the school system is under the jurisdiction of provincial governments, but every province and territory now uses some form of large-scale testing (Klinger & Luce-Kapler, 2007, p. 31). The rationale for this is the assumption that educational goals and outcomes are best developed by bureaucratic elites rather than teachers. Such reasoning has led to a loss of teacher autonomy and sense of professionalism, resulting in low teacher morale (Au, 2009; Cuban, 2008; Mathison, Ross, & Vinson, 2006; McNeil, 2000).

The decision that teachers must make today is whether to employ critical pedagogy to teach in authentic, meaningful ways, or to teach to the tests so that their students obtain higher scores. According to Mathison and Freeman (2008), many teachers will "sacrifice their professional integrity in order to help every child be as successful as she or he can be on the tests" (p. 86). Although this may be perceived as altruistic behavior, a disturbing byproduct is the increasing trend for teachers to leave the profession entirely rather than to work in an environment where their professional judgment on pedagogical matters has been outright dismissed.

There are many more problems associated with standards-based educational reforms and state-wide testing. These externally produced exams increase student anxiety (Klinger & Luce-Kapler, 2007; Landry, 2006). As well, there is a clear narrowing of the curriculum that decreases the potential for critical thinking, let alone critical pedagogy (Au, 2009; Vinson & Ross, 2001; McNeil, 2000). State-wide testing of the entire curriculum also makes it much more difficult for teachers to develop context-based or culturally relevant pedagogy, thereby leading to a less successful and a less *meaningful* school experience for students not from White middle-class backgrounds.

There is another relatively recent development in the neoliberal assault on public education, and that is the publication in major newspapers of school rankings based on state- or province-wide exam scores. This tactic is occurring more frequently in both Canada and the United States. In British Columbia, for example, the pro-corporate Fraser Institute publishes the provincial exam scores for every public and private school in the province in the major newspapers.[8] Invariably, the published exam scores lead parents to believe that a private school education is superior to an education in a public school. Private schools often have higher exam scores because of parental commitment and because most of them can cherry-pick their students, an option not open to public schools. Yet, even for parents committed to public education, the published school-by-school exam results tend to treat students and their parents as educational *consumers*.[9] It is even becoming more commonplace to have "realtors provide copies of school report cards to potential clients to sell them a home in a district with high test outcomes" (Landry, 2006, p. 31). This is one more example of the neoliberal impetus to commodify everything so that some people can make a financial profit.

In the 1960s and 1970s, reforms in public education often focused on improving conditions for teachers, with the assumption that this would translate into better learning conditions for students. This is not the situation anymore, however. Current reforms include increases in levels of report writing, monitoring, and surveillance. As well, some places in the United States have implemented policy that links teacher pay to their individual performance. Teacher unions, of course, have argued against this tactic because of the difficulties in measuring very important aspects of what a teacher actually does in the classroom. In other words, it is the hope of teachers that many people will not consider test scores and football championships as very important indicators of a good education for their children. Right-wing politicians and their supporters in the media, however, have been able to blunt the critical analysis from teacher unions. They have engaged in a long campaign of *teacher bashing*. This has coincided with a general attack on trade unions and their members in both countries, but the attacks seem to be more venomous toward teachers.

The time seems to be running out for teachers and supporters of public education to fight back. Yet, not everything is so bleak as much of this chapter suggests. There are signs that the neoliberal agenda is showing some serious signs of faltering.

Resistance to Neoliberalism: Where Hope Resides!

[I]t is the profoundly anti-democratic nature of neoliberalism backed by the authoritarianism of the neoconservatives that should surely be the main focus of political struggle. (Harvey, 2005, p. 205)

[E]very advance in history, from ending slavery and establishing democracy to ending formal colonialism, has had to conquer the notion at some point that it was impossible to do because it had never been done before. (McChesney, Introduction, Chomsky, 1999, p. 15)

This chapter paints a fairly bleak picture of the damage that neoliberalism has already done to the public commons on many fronts. An economic theory considered to be without credibility less than half a century ago has become the basis for how Western nations ignore the social dimension of humanity. Berthelot (2008) states the results in blunt terms: "[E]verywhere, inequalities are on the increase" (p. 34).

Yet, neoliberalism is not natural or ontological. It has only been put into practice for less than 40 years. For this reason alone, we should have hope that these very regressive policies can be placed into the dustbin of history where they belong. After all, challenging the elites on this issue cannot be any more difficult than ending slavery or establishing democracy and social, economic, and cultural rights in all Western nations.

In order to secure the proper conditions on the domestic front, neoliberalism needs deregulation policies, a "free" market, and institutions such as the World Trade Organization (WTO). In terms of persuading other Western nations to buy in, free trade agreements are the main mechanism. In order for governments of Third World countries to be persuaded to create the optimum conditions for neoliberalism, the World Bank and the International Monetary Fund (IMF) do the main bulk of the work. But the massive protests in Seattle during the WTO Conference in December 1999 indicate a turning point in terms of the political awareness of middle- and working-class Americans and Canadians. Since then, large protests have greeted every WTO meeting and gathering of G8 and G20 political world leaders. Moreover, there is also evidence that the IMF itself is in financial difficulty (Clark, 2009).

Also on the international scene, there has been a burgeoning resistance to combat the deleterious effects of neoliberalism in spheres including and beyond public education. In fact, resistance to neoliberalism and the type of globalization advocated by the IMF and World Bank is rapidly increasing throughout many parts of the world. The most successful counter attacks to neoliberalism seem to be occurring in Latin America.

The leader of this independence movement is Hugo Chavez, who was first elected President of Venezuela in 1999. Chavez calls this movement the *Bolivarian Revolution*, which is a socialist-light interpretation of the philosophies of the nineteenth century Venezuelan independence leader, Simon Bolivar. In 2006, Bolivia elected an indigenous president, Evo Morales, and Equador elected Rafael Correa, both of whom are adamantly opposed to neoliberal policies. In large countries such as Brazil, Argentina, and in the country where neoliberalism was first installed, Chile, citizens suffered greatly at the hands of military dictatorships. It is important for *all* citizens to understand that in these countries "the triumph of neoliberalism cannot be separated from the ferocious dictatorships propped up by the United States" (Berthelot, 2008, p. 34). Many of these military dictatorships were replaced with governments that gutted whatever public institutions and social structures existed in order to adhere to the neoliberal requirements of The World Bank and the IMF (Klein, 2007). Consequently, the typical commoner in these countries has no further interest in having a government make a deal with either of these international lending agencies.

There also appears to be a strong swell of resistance to neoliberalism sweeping across continental Europe. In May 2010, in order to receive a major financial bailout from the European Union, the government of Greece passed legislation that included gutting pensions plans, the public service, and social spending (Erlanger, 2010). The protests of Greek working- and middle-class citizens that followed stemmed from anger over why they should have to bear the brunt of poor economic decisions made by the political and capitalist classes over the past decade or so. Since the Greek protests, the labor movements in France, Spain, and Portugal have also vociferously expressed their discontent over the ways in which their respective governments have handled the economic crisis. Possibly as a preemptive measure, the Canadian business-friendly *MacLean's* magazine responded to these protests with a cover story headline that screamed "Europe Throws a Tantrum: A pampered continent protests the rollback of its lavish welfare state" (Gillis & Macdonald, 2010, p. 38). The hegemonic role of corporate media is blatantly clear here.

The neoliberal attacks on public education illuminate the vulnerability of one of the greatest victories made by working-class and middle-class Americans and Canadians over the course of the twentieth century – free public schooling for their children. Teachers across North America, however, have *not* been sitting back with passive acceptance of the current undermining of public education. Indeed, they have been resisting the neoliberal agenda whenever and wherever possible.

As one example of teacher resistance, the teachers in the province where I taught for 20 years, British Columbia, have been engaged in a long battle with the B.C. government around educational funding. Among other regressive reforms, the limits on class size have been removed, as have many teaching assistant positions for special needs students. By the fall of 2005 the B.C. public school teachers had not been allowed to engage in collective bargaining for several years. The B.C. government was poised to impose yet another 3-year contract onto the approximately 40,000-member strong teachers' union, The British Columbia Teachers' Federation (BCTF). When the BCTF threatened to strike, the government quickly passed a law declaring teaching to be an essential service and, therefore, making any strike action illegal. Rather than accept yet another imposed contract, the teachers voted overwhelmingly to ignore the last-minute law that made teaching an essential service. After a two-week job action, they were able to stop this assault on public education and its front-line workers.[10] Moreover, a contract was subsequently negotiated that included a significant bonus settlement and much better working conditions.

Social studies teachers and teacher educators are in an excellent position to make the next generation of citizens aware of the deleterious effects of neoliberalism on civil society. They can and should teach about these conflicts and the resistance to these forces. Of course, teachers must be careful in this endeavor. In Chapter 8, I describe pedagogical strategies involving ideology critique, critical media literacy, the reframing of hegemonic discourses, and assigning projects that support active citizenship. I have found all of these to be effective in developing an acute political consciousness during these dangerous times. There is not a clear thinking person in Canada or the United States who wants to see the commons and public institutions disappear. After all, when there appears to be a trend across the land to dismantle "every aspect of human life and attitudes and thought that involve social solidarity," the stakes are very high indeed (Chomsky, cited in Anijar & Gabbard, 2009, p. 21). The classroom is another place where hope resides.

Questions to Ponder

1. In 1999, four ships carrying Chinese migrant workers appeared on the shores of British Columbia. The public and media hysteria reminded historians of the "yellow hordes" discourse of a century earlier as fear seemed to grip many people about these "queue jumpers." As it turned out, almost all of these migrant workers came from province of Fujian, which is also where over a hundred export processing zones employ 18 million workers, the vast majority work for extremely low wages under horrific working conditions. Read the 1-page editorial written by former teacher Seth Klein that can be found at: http://www. policyalternatives.ca/editorials/1999/09/editorial764/?pa=47.
   After you have read it, discuss the following questions:

   (a) Why does Klein consider the vociferous reaction of many Canadians to the plight of the Chinese migrants to be "ugly" and "hypocritical"? Where do you stand on this issue?
   (b) Why does Klein consider the argument that Canada's immigration laws are to blame for the appearance of the Chinese migrants to be an "absurd proposition"? Where do you stand on this issue?
   (c) How do you think the Canadian government should handle such situations in the future?
   (d) Does the 2010 Arizona law around illegal immigrants describe a similar situation? Explain.

2. Why is neoliberalism considered an economic *rationality* rather than a political ideology?
3. What are the main tenets of neoliberalism?
4. Is neoliberalism similar to laissez-faire economics? Explain.
5. Discuss the idea that globalization today is a contemporary form of colonialism. Do you agree? Explain.
6. Why is neoliberalism an obstacle to a strong democracy?
7. The last section of this chapter pointed to a few places where people have stood up to the forces trying to impose neoliberal policies upon them. Try to find other examples of *resistance* to neoliberalism:

   (a) in the United States.
   (b) in Canada.
   (c) in Europe.
   (d) in poor countries.

Notes

1. *Fordism* refers to a form of productive organization once considered typical of advanced capitalism in which workers receive high wages and opportunity to be consumers in exchange for intensified work regimes. This began with Henry Ford's automobile production lines. As well, more will be said about Keynesian economics in a subsequent section.
2. There were exceptions to the rule. Classical liberals supported the idea of state intervention in order to break up monopolies. As well, the state was expected to protect the private property of individuals and businesses.
3. In Canada, corporations support the Conservative and Liberal parties, but are less likely to support the social democratic NDP and Bloc Quebecois or the environmentalist-friendly Green Party. In minority government situations, the corporate influence is less.
4. It is noteworthy that the Patriot Act was passed overwhelmingly in both houses of Congress by Republicans and Democrats. A revised version, which did very little to address civil liberty concerns, was signed into law on March 10th and 11th 2006.
5. The protests that have appeared at every gathering of political leaders like at G8 or G20 summits or World Trade Organization members since Seattle in 1999 indicates that there is still a significant number of citizens who are able to discern what is happening under neoliberal policies. The populist movement in the US known as The Tea Party also includes many citizens angry at what they see happening to their country. Yet, it would appear that there is a definite lack of clear political consciousness in the latter group, especially those who support former Republican Vice-Presidential candidate Sarah Palin's economic policies.
6. Calling any public institution a "government institution" seems to be a common ploy in the United States, as witnessed by opponents to President Obama's 2009 plan for healthcare reform that included a public option, which they referred to as "government healthcare." This strategy plays into right wing populist anti-government sentiments.
7. Channel One News is controversial largely due to the commercial content of the show. Critics claim that it is a problem because it forces children to watch ads, wastes class time, and exists only because of funding cuts. Supporters argue that the ads are necessary to help keep the program running so schools can lease TVs, DVD players, and satellite dishes to schools. In 2006, the American Academy of Pediatrics reported that children who watched Channel One remembered the commercials more than they remembered the news.
8. Many of my former teaching colleagues described decreasing morale among staff and students as a result of a low ranking in the Fraser Institute's School Report Card. See http://www.fraserinstitute.org/reportcards/.
9. The idea of ranking schools has spread to other aspects of education. For example, the Institute of Scientific Information (ISI) was developed in 1958 in Philadelphia to create a database of over 4,000 scientific journals. With the database, ISI creates products for sale, which is clearly in keeping with the capitalist notion of consumerism.
10. In order to hear the perspectives of teachers, school board trustees, parents, and teacher educators, see http://blogs.ubc.ca/newproposals/2005/11/teachers-strike-forum-videos/.

References

Anijar, K., & Gabbard, D. (2009). Vouchers, charters, educational management organizations, and the money behind them. In D. Hill (Ed.), *The rich world and the impoverishment of education: Diminishing democracy, equity and workers' rights* (pp. 21–50). New York: Routledge.

Au, W. (2009). Social studies, social justice: W(h)ither the social studies in high-stakes testing? *Teacher Education Quarterly, 36*(1), 43–58.

Berthelot, J. (2008). *Education for the world, education for all: Québec education in the context of globalization* (D. Clandfield, Trans.). Ottawa, ON: Canadian Centre for Policy Alternatives.

Bowles, S., & Gintis, H. (1976) *Schooling in capitalist America: Educational reform and the contradictions of economic life*. New York: Basic Books.

Brown, W. (2003). Neo-liberalism and the end of liberal democracy. *Theory & Event, 7*(1), 1–23.

Chomsky, N. (1999). *Profit over people: Neoliberalism and global order*. New York: Seven Stories Press.

Clark, A. (2009, September 19). IMF approves $13bn gold sale to aid poor states. *The Guardian*. Retrieved on 9 August 2010, from http://www.guardian.co.uk/world/2009/sep/19/imf-sells-gold-bullion

Cuban, L. (2008). *Hugging the middle: How teachers teach in an era of testing and accountability*. New York: Teachers College Press.

Davidson-Harden, A., Kuehn, L., Schugurensky, D., & Smaller, H. (2009). Neoliberalism and education in Canada. In D. Hill (Ed.), *The rich world and the impoverishment of education: Diminishing democracy, equity and workers' rights* (pp. 51–73). New York: Routledge.

Eisner, R. (1994). *The misunderstood economy: What counts and how to count it*. Boston: Harvard Business School Press.

Erlanger, S. (2010, May 2). Deflation could stall efforts to revive Greece. *The New York Times*. Retrieved on 15 July 2009, from http://www.nytimes.com/2010/05/03/world/europe/03austerity.html?ref=global

Frank, T. (2004a, April). Lie down for America: How the Republican Party sows ruin on the Great Plains. *Harper's Magazine*.

Frank, T. (2004b). *What's the matter with Kansas?* New York: Henry Holt & Co.

Friedman, M. (2002). *Capitalism and freedom* (2nd ed.). Chicago, IL: University of Chicago Press.

Gillis, C., & Macdonald, N. (2010, November 8). Europe loses its cool: A pampered continent protests the rollback of its lavish welfare state. *Maclean's*, 38–41.

Giroux, H. A. (1981). *Ideology, culture, and the process of schooling*. Philadelphia: Temple University Press.

Harvey, D. (2005). *A brief history of neoliberalism*. Oxford, UK: Oxford University Press.

Hill, D. (Ed.). (2009). *The rich world and the impoverishment of education: Diminishing democracy, equity and workers' rights*. New York: Routledge.

Johnson, S. (2009). The quiet coup. *The Atlantic monthly*. Retrieved on 28 October 2010, from http://www.theatlantic.com/magazine/archive/2009/05/the-quiet-coup/7364/

Keenan, G. (2009, October 18). Bankrupt companies, pension promises destroyed, *The Globe & Mail*. Retrieved on 31 January 2010, from http://www.theglobeandmail.com/report-on-business/retirement/bankrupt-companies-pension-promises-destroyed/article1322007/

Klein, S. (1999, September 1). Reaction to Chinese migrants exposes globalization's double-standard. *Canadian Centre for Policy Alternatives*. Retrieved on 4 March 2009, from http://www.policyalternatives.ca/editorials/1999/09/editorial764/?pa=47

Klein, N. (2007). *The shock doctrine: The rise of disaster capitalism*. Toronto: Alfred A. Knopf Canada.

Klinger, D., & Luce-Kapler, R. (2007). Walking in their shoes: Students' perceptions of large-scale high-stakes testing. *The Canadian Journal of Program Evaluation, 22*(3), 29–52.

Landry, D. (2006). Teachers' (K-5) perceptions of student behaviors during standardized testing. *Curriculum and Teaching Dialogue, 8*(1), 29–40.

Livingstone, S. (2007, May). Representing citizens and consumers in media and communications regulation. *The Annals of the American Academy of Political and Social Science, 611*(1), 51–65.

Martin, L. (2010, August 19). Is Stephen Harper set to move against the CRTC? *The Globe & Mail*. Retrieved on 18 March 2011; from http://www.theglobeandmail.com/news/politics/lawrence-martin/is-stephen-harper-set-to-move-against-the-crtc/article1677632/

Mathison, S., & Freeman, M. (2008). Teachers working with standards and state testing. In S. Mathison & E. W. Ross (Eds.), *The nature and limits of standards based reform and assessment* (pp. 81–91). New York: Teachers College Press.

Mathison, S., & Ross, E. W. (Eds.). (2008). *The nature and limits of standards based reform and assessment*. New York: Teachers College Press.

Mathison, S., Ross, E. W., & Vinson, K. (2006). Defining the social studies curriculum: Influence of and resistance to curriculum standards and testing in social studies. In E. W. Ross (Ed.), *The social studies curriculum: Purposes, problems, and possibilities* (3rd ed., pp. 99–114). Albany, NY: State University of New York Press.

McIntosh, P. (1988). *White privilege and male privilege: A personal account of coming to see correspondences through work in women's studies.* Wellesley, MA: Centre for Research on Women.

McLaren, P. (2005). *Capitalists & conquerors: A critical pedagogy against empire.* Lanham, MD: Rowman & Littlefield Publishers.

McNeil, L. (2000). *Contradictions of school reform: Educational costs of standardized testing.* New York: Routledge.

McQuaig, L. (1998). *The cult of impotence: Selling the myth of powerlessnesss in the global economy.* Toronto: The Penguin Group.

Polanyi, K. (1944). *The great transformation: The political and economic origins of our time.* New York: Farrar & Rinehart.

Roediger, D. R. (1999). *The wages of whiteness: Race and the making of the American working class* (rev. ed.). New York: Verso.

Roy, A. (2004). Tide? Or ivory snow? Public power in the age of empire. *Democracy Now.* Retrieved on 18 March 2011, from http://www.democracynow.org/static/Arundhati_Trans.shtml

Schwarzmantel, J. (1998). *The age of ideology: Political ideologies from the American revolution to postmodern times.* New York: New York University Press.

Stiglitz, J. (2003). *The roaring nineties: A new history of the world's most prosperous decade.* New York: W.W. Norton.

Taber, J. (2010, June 10). 'Fox news of the north' nabs its first host? *The Globe & Mail.* Retrieved on 9 June 2011, from http://www.theglobeandmail.com/news/politics/ottawa-notebook/fox-news-of-the-north-nabs-its-first-host/article1599162/?cid=art-rail-bureaublog

Tobin, K. (2011). Global reproduction and transformation of science education. *Cultural Studies of Science Education, 6.* doi:10.1007/s11422-010-9293-3.

Urbina, I. (2009, August 8). Health debate turns hostile at town hall meetings. *The New York Times.* Retrieved on 9 June 2011, from http://www.ocala.com/article/20090808/ZNYT04/908083014

Vidal, G. (2004, September 1). *Imperial America.* New York: Nation Books.

Vinson, K., & Ross, E. W. (2001). In search of the social studies curriculum: standardization, diversity, and a conflict of appearances. In W. B. Stanley (Ed.), *Critical issues in social studies research for the 21st century* (pp. 39–71). Greenwich, CT: Information Age Publishing.

Von Hayek, F. (1944). *The road to serfdom.* New York: George Routledge & Sons.

Wilkinson, R. & Pickett, K. (2010). *The spirit level: Why equality is better for everyone.* London: Penguin Books.

Yakabuski, K. (2010, August 27). Republicans caught in the 'honor' system. *The Globe & Mail.* Retrieved on 3 February 2011, from http://www.theglobeandmail.com/news/world/konrad-yakabuski/republicans-caught-in-the-honour-system/article1688432/

Chapter 10
Some Final Reflections: Dare the Schools Teach for a Fair Social Order?

Educators and the general public typically do not understand that the solutions to many of the educational challenges facing subordinated students are not purely technical or methodological in nature, but are instead rooted in typically unacknowledged discriminatory ideologies and practices. (Bartolome, 2008, p. ix)

The above quote underlies my opinion about what is missing from most public debates about the schooling of youth from marginalized social groups. A major problem is a general lack of political awareness among the public, undoubtedly related to a lack of understanding of political ideology and inherent vested interests. In this book, I have described approaches that have been at least somewhat successful in raising the political consciousness of high school students and preservice teachers. Taken together, the pedagogy I have described is a hybrid of anti-racism, a contemporary neo-Marxist analysis, with the emphasis on the material well-being of *all* citizens, and an elementary poststructuralism; hence, the focus on language, discourse, and discourse analysis. I believe that if other teachers were to adopt similar pedagogical strategies, the school could once again be seen to possess the potential to be an equalizer, as a cherished vehicle that would enable a citizenry to challenge social injustice and grotesque greed.

It may seem ironic to some readers to ask of the same institution that has been instrumental in structuring inequality around axes of race, culture, class, and gender to deconstruct these very same hierarchies. Indeed, at the end of the nineteenth century, the renowned sociologist Emile Durkheim stated that education "can be reformed only if society itself is reformed." He believed that education "imitates and reproduces" society but does "not create it" (Durkheim, 1897/1951, pp. 372–373). Several decades later, social reproduction theorists agreed with Durkheim on one major point, namely, that the schools were merely reproducing people to fill the needs of capitalism (Bowles & Gintis, 1976). This is a very pessimistic prognosis of the potential for schools to effect significant progressive change. But if there are serious concerns about social problems and political apathy among many citizens, what options are there? After all, it is unrealistic to expect corporate media sources to develop a critical perspective, especially on economic issues.

P. Orlowski, *Teaching About Hegemony*, Explorations of Educational Purpose 17, DOI 10.1007/978-94-007-1418-2_10, © Springer Science+Business Media B.V. 2011

I contend that the most efficient manner to instill a critical political consciousness in the citizenry is the high school classroom. There are legions of critical educators who would take exception with Durkheim's position, as well as the position taken by the social reproduction theorists. Their message to Durkheim is that perhaps the schools can lead the change that society needs to become more socially just. To the reproduction theorists, they can point to the research that indicates the role of student or teacher agency that disrupts the status quo. In other words, there is potential for the school to effect positive change.

During the first decades of the twentieth century, the renowned American philosopher of education, John Dewey, considered the school to be the best institution to carry the noble goal of developing critical thinking citizens. Around the same time as Dewey, American Social Reconstructionists such as Harold Rugg (1921) and George Counts (1932) called for the schools to be the main instruments in building a new social order based on social justice principles. Both conservatives and liberals of the day tried their best to dismiss and discredit these progressive or critical left thinkers (James, 1995). Since that time, much has been written about the purpose of schooling. Neoliberal attacks in the media are focused on teacher accountability, school choice, state or provincial exam scores, and a host of other topics. Neoliberal supporters recognize the potential for profit in public education. Public education, among other aspects of the social welfare state, is clearly under attack.

There are other problems to overcome. The public does not fully comprehend the role that political ideology in the school curriculum and in the attitudes of the teachers has on the academic achievement of students from less privileged backgrounds. If you were a member of a marginalized group, from a minority or the working class or both, would you prefer a policy that promoted culturally relevant pedagogy or one that promoted state-wide exams and school rankings? How would you feel about the 2010 Arizona legislation that bans multicultural education?

Despite neoliberal attempts to undermine one of the greatest civic victories of Western society, namely, free education for the masses, there are still significant numbers of teachers and teacher educators who support the progressive aims of Dewey and the Social Reconstructionists. In every teacher education course I teach, I begin by posing the following question: Should schools be used to maintain the status quo or to challenge the status quo? Many preservice teachers enter the profession believing that they can make a difference, that change is possible. This book is definitely in agreement! Yet, I am not so naïve to think that this is an easy task.

The obstacles in using the school to challenge the status quo are enormous. I am once again reminded of what a veteran high school social studies teacher once said to me when I asked if he would consider altering or supplementing the curriculum to help make it more relevant for students from marginalized groups. For purposes of ease, I have once again printed his response:

> Teaching is not a vehicle to promote your agenda. You have a job, when you sign that piece of paper, to teach the curriculum. You are not there to create an army of followers.

Clearly, this teacher believes that schools should not try to challenge the status quo. And there are many people in our society who would agree. Yet, because I am very aware of social inequities and injustice, I do not want schools to simply maintain the status quo. The teacher quoted above seems to consider the formal state-sanctioned curriculum to be devoid of bias, to be politically neutral. I hold no such illusions, and hope that readers of this book will come to see that the curriculum, for the most part, is a hegemonic device in the service of the status quo.

Teaching About Hegemoy is a textbook for teaching social studies that does not pretend to be politically neutral either. Rather, it promotes a progressive agenda for teaching about issues of race and class rooted in critical pedagogy. It is a call to use the classroom to strengthen our waning democracies. This book describes an approach that demonstrates the pedagogical possibilities to help create a more progressive citizenry, to help people understand approaches to organizing a society around the needs of people rather than the needs of capital. The imperative for progressive educators to teach for a socially just society has been increased with the push for neoliberalism in so many aspects of social life and consciousness. In response, many sites of resistance are getting primed to take on this corporate agenda. Public education should be at the forefront of this resistance.

Reflecting on the changing social conditions of one's own life is a good place to begin. Reflecting on one's social location and the privilege or oppression that this has brought to one's life is also an important step in understanding social power. Yet, in order to effectively do so, it is crucial that more and more people gain an understanding of how political ideology shapes the way we view our world. I am often struck by the sophisticated political awareness of many Europeans I have met over the years. By contrast, I am always disappointed by the lack of political awareness of many Canadians and Americans. In Canada, the corporate media is quick to call the social democratic NDP a *socialist* party, knowing that such a label conjures up Cold War sentiments of fear among many voters. Perhaps this does not make much difference anyway because I am often struck by how many Canadian and American adults do not know what is meant by the term social democracy.

To further this line of reasoning, I point to a recent example in the United States. Most of us can recall that during the American presidential election of 2008, several Republicans, including Vice-Presidential candidate Sarah Palin, Missouri Congressman Todd Akin, and Ohio Senator George Voinovich, called Democrat Barack Obama a socialist (Hertzberg, 2008). I do not know whether these politicians from the Republican Party really do believe that President Obama is a socialist. Nor am I aware of their own understanding of what socialism and social democracy means. But one thing is certain: these Republicans knew that they could frighten a large segment of the American electorate to believe that President Obama is bringing socialism to their country. Therein lies a major problem with American and Canadian democracy: there is a distinct lack of understanding of political ideology among the general populations of both countries.

The public gets its information and understanding of the world around them from a variety of sources: the family, the church, friends, and especially the media and the K-12 school system. The corporate media have corporate interests, plain and simple, and as such, they have been trumpeting neoliberal discourses for several years now. Therefore, it is up to progressive educators to educate the students so that they grow up to be politically aware and not duped by a false consciousness. The school, and the social studies classroom in particular, have a responsibility to help their students understand political ideology.

Because there is a significant percentage of school teachers who do not understand political ideology well enough to teach about it, it is imperative that teacher education programs ensure that this situation changes. There are two options here: either make courses in political ideology, feminism, labor studies, and anti-racism mandatory entrance requirements, or embed these courses into the program itself. Assuming that many Faculties of Education opt for the latter alternative, this book may be valuable for the purpose of helping students understand political ideology and their own biases. More importantly, the omission of ideology in debates of public concern increases the likelihood of the privileged furthering their interests through the use of various hegemonic discourses. We have witnessed this in the current neoliberal and neoconservative assaults on public education in the United States (Shaker & Heilman, 2008) and in Canada (Berthelot, 2008; Ungerleider, 2004).

More than understanding ideology, students must also comprehend *how* and *why* certain ideologies are supported by the elites and *how* and *why* other ones are discredited. This can only be gleaned from an understanding of hegemony itself. A nation's students, and by corollary its citizens, must see that the ruling social relations are not the natural order, but are a social construction, an example of power enacted. This applies to race and social class, of course, but also to issues of gender, sexuality, and culture.[1] I also do not want to suggest that teaching about the connections between ideology, discourse, and material well-being should be limited to classrooms of minorities and working-class youth. The research by Wilkinson and Pickett (2010) demonstrates that *everyone benefits* with a shrinking wealth gap.

I agree with the educators in the Weis and Fine's study (2001) who contend that classroom "counterpublics," to borrow a phrase from Nancy Fraser (1997), or a pedagogical focus on public responsibility, intellect, and resistance, can lead to the creation of counterhegemonic discourses. These discourses, in turn, have the potential to help develop a "public understanding across lines" of race and social class (Weis & Fine, 2001, p. 499). For several years I taught social studies in a west side Vancouver secondary school in which most students came from middle-class and upper middle-class homes. Placing ideology critique at the center of the social studies and civic studies courses at this school was well received by the students. Moreover, I never heard complaints from any of the other educational "stakeholders" about creating space for counterhegemonic discourses.

As I mentioned more than once in the book, the difficulty in countering hegemony is that one of its effects is in setting the limits and outer boundaries of social thought. This is why I focus on the deconstruction of hegemonic discourses through critical discourse analysis. Of course, there are economic right-wing ideologues who will likely always see the world from the standpoint of the privileged whether they themselves are privileged or not. Yet, my experience tells me that most teachers, such as most of the ones in studies I have been involved in, do not necessarily support hegemonic discourses; rather, they do not understand how these discourses work against the interests of most Americans and Canadians. Teachers need to be taught how the repetition of hegemonic discourses, if left unchallenged, often becomes part of the body politic. Blaming the poor for their plight by calling them lazy, ungrateful, or stupid for making poor choices is one example. Blaming the auto workers' unions for the woes of General Motors is another. In fact, it is when certain seemingly unrelated hegemonic discourses come together to form a discursive formation that the difficulty in resisting the onslaught greatly increases. It is important for all progressive educators to bear in mind Leonardo's (2003) contention that discourse is how "ideology is understood, perpetuated or challenged" (p. 207). There is much in this rather short phrase for teachers to ponder.

Teachers need to understand that the formal curriculum itself is a document laced with discourses capable of wielding enormous social power, especially in the race-blind and class-blind discourses inherent in liberalism. This book makes a case for a curriculum that does not emphasize the individual to the extent that it does today. Teaching about the importance of the individual in terms of human rights is a very good idea; teaching about the individual in a way that divorces the connection to others in society is not. Prescribed Learning Outcomes (PLOs) that address race–class intersections in the past and present would provide students with what I think is an accurate dynamic in current race relations in the United States and Canada today. It is obvious to many that most immigrants are often forced to accept low paying, unskilled jobs near the bottom of the social, political, and economic hierarchies of both countries. This is unfair in itself, but it is even more unfair when one considers that a significant portion of immigrants are very educated and highly skilled.

Specifically regarding social class, I would like to see PLOs that help students understand the construction of the social welfare state, including the public health-care system in Canada and in other Western nations. After all, an ignorant citizenry is in no position to stand up to the current neoliberal attacks on these hard fought victories that have helped Western nations take a few steps toward realizing the progressive slogan, *the emancipation of all*. The American public would be better prepared to resist hegemonic discourses touted in the corporate media that suggest universal healthcare is a major first step toward a socialist or communist state. PLOs should also address the widening gap between the wealthy and the poor in both countries, progressive versus regressive tax reform, the effects of globalization and free-trade deals on full-time employment and worker security, and Orwellian double-speak such as the need for a *flexible* labor market and, for Canadians at least, *two-tiered* healthcare.

Any Orwell-inspired PLOs might best be addressed by developing an entire unit on critical media literacy. Better yet, an entire *course* in critical media literacy would go far in removing the blinders on hegemonic discourses around issues of race and social class. This in itself would enable the school to better fulfill its potential of strengthening democracy and citizenship. Also for the purposes of strengthening democracy, students should understand that it is these struggles won through the agency of oppressed groups that have led to progressive legislation such as the 8-hour work day and 40-hour work week. I think it would be a good idea for a possible unit of lessons that track the lack of personal power in feudal society to the expansion of the franchise that began during the Enlightenment and connect this to current trends in voter apathy. On several occasions, lessons I have designed over the years with the specific aim of deconstructing the voter apathy discourse have led to discussions around consumerism, pop culture, declining class awareness, and the unwillingness of politicians to take on the corporate agenda. It is not all that difficult to imagine a politically aware teacher moving the discussion toward a class consciousness that manages to bridge race and gender to effectively deal with a growing White defensiveness embodied in movements such as The Tea Party.

Like all critically minded educators, I would like to see PLOs in state-sanctioned curricula reflect the needs of a complex multicultural society immersed in a global economy. For example, a PLO that addresses globalization and links current sweatshop labor practices to the old economic slave-based system in the Americas would likely prove effective. Another PLO should address the wages of Whiteness as described by both Roediger (1999) and McIntosh (1988). Although it is a contentious stand, I also agree with the notion of addressing racial hierarchies in *non-Western* cultures. It has been all too common for me to listen to students tell of racist episodes they have experienced that do not involve White people (Orlowski, 2001).

Critical left educators should not hold their breath waiting for the formal curriculum to include these kinds of progressive prescribed learning outcomes. This should not be a major problem, however, because, as was discussed in Chapter 4, an adept teacher should be able to bring at least some of these topics into the classroom regardless of whether they are in the official document. This enacted curriculum arises from the passions, interests, and experiences of students and teachers. Together, a very culturally relevant curriculum can form a significant portion of the topics covered in the classroom. This would apply to classrooms filled with minority and working-class youth, of course, but I think that students from more privileged backgrounds would find such topics interesting, as well. There is a very real concern, however, that teachers breaking free of the prescribed curriculum might find themselves in some difficulty with administrators, colleagues, or parents who do not want these topics covered. Yet, I do believe there are prescribed learning outcomes, such as ones that promote a *multiple perspectives* approach, that teachers can use to defend themselves in such situations.

The second half of the book applies much of the theory contained in the first half into the classroom. It also explores how ideology affects the curriculum and the attitudes of teachers. Anecdotal evidence from both students and teachers indicate that ideology very much informs their attitudes, whether or not they are conscious of this. This book is the first time my teaching experience and my research have been put together. The goal has been to better understand how to incorporate critical pedagogy into the classroom. *Teaching About Hegemony* is the realization of this goal.

In my own experience as a high school social studies teacher, I have noted the pedagogical success of focusing on discourse so that students better understand history. As an example, in teaching Canadian history, I begin by focusing on the taxonomy of racial discourses that Frankenberg (1993) so clearly described. This helps the students make much better sense of the past. An emphasis on how systemic racism replaces institutional racism once the racist laws are repealed leads students to see how the past affects the present. Aboriginal and Black peoples' concerns are better understood by students with this approach, regardless of cultural background.

Chapter 6 pointed out that issues of social class, which are vitally important to almost all Americans and Canadians, are virtually completely absent from the typical social studies classroom. Regardless of the class backgrounds of the high school students or the preservice teachers, I have found that virtually all of them appreciate learning about matters of social class. Regardless of their own background, students come to understand the importance of a class analysis, which is a crucial part of political consciousness. Pedagogy involving discourse analysis described in the section of Chapter 8 on critical media literacy goes a long way toward teaching for a political consciousness.

I have included the critique of liberal discourses around Aboriginal issues in Chapter 7 because I believe it is important for students to understand that much of liberal rhetoric is power blind. American readers may want to ask themselves if a similar dynamic is at work around the liberal rhetoric and education of African American and Mexican American students. I do not believe that an oscillation between liberal and conservative control of the curriculum is enough to evoke systemic societal change. The culture of poverty discourse first proposed by the liberal Oscar Lewis (1961) has been co-opted by conservative commentators to the point that this discourse has been rendered unhelpful to those groups caught in its trap. In other words, the cultural-deficit discourse must be deconstructed in teacher education courses.

The focus of Chapter 8 is to suggest an approach I have used to teach for a political consciousness and, therefore, a stronger democracy. Once again, ideology critique forms the basis for this approach. Without an understanding of ideology, the systems of representative democracy in both countries are reduced to individuals and groups desiring power for the sake of power. The neoliberal onslaught on civil society was the focus of Chapter 9. Teachers simply must understand the effects of commodifying as much as possible solely in economic terms. After all, our civil society is at risk if they do not.

Of course, I believe that most Canadians and Americans believe that a civil society is more appealing than any of the alternatives. Strengthening democracy through the development of an informed and active citizenry, one that understands what is in its best interests, should be the goal of social studies. Preservice social studies teachers should be introduced to seeing the world through a lens informed by the race cognizance and the class-power discourses. If done within the framework of an ideology critique that separates social issues from economic issues, the chances for pedagogical success greatly increase. Americans and Canadians need this language to help analyze current social, political and economic relations. They will be better prepared to understand why some media pundits disparagingly call the American Democratic Party and the Canadian Liberal Party *left wing*. They are positioned on the left only so far as social issues are concerned. Both parties have supported the neoliberal corporate agenda for several decades.

I am an optimist in that I see great transformative possibilities in the role of the school, especially in the social studies classroom. To claim neutrality by teaching strictly to the formal curriculum cannot be mistaken for being objective. This level of naivety is unacceptable. We need to have the blinders removed so that hegemony can be understood on a very deep level. It is imperative that all teachers entering the field of social studies understand one very important axiom: *all teaching is political.*

Question to Ponder

1. After reading this book, has your opinion changed at all on this question: Should the schools maintain the status quo or challenge it? Explain.

Note

1. This book only addressed discourses about race and social class. Framing the book around these two social variables is not to suggest their primacy as axes of oppression. Rather, these are the areas in which I have done almost all of my research.

References

Bartolome, L. I. (Ed.). (2008). *Ideologies in education: Unmasking the trap of teacher neutrality.* New York: Peter Lang Publishing.

Berthelot, J. (2008). *Education for the world, education for all: Québec education in the context of globalization* (D. Clandfield, Trans.). Ottawa, ON: Canadian Centre for Policy Alternatives.

Bowles, S., & Gintis, H. (1976) *Schooling in capitalist America: Educational reform and the contradictions of economic life.* New York: Basic Books.

Counts, G. (1932). Dare progressive education be progressive? *Progressive Education, 9,* 257–263. Reprinted (1982) as *Dare the school build a new social order?* by New York: John Day.

Durkheim, E. (1897/1951). *Suicide: A study in sociology.* New York: Free Press.

Frankenberg, R. (1993). *White women, race matters: The social construction of Whiteness.* Minneapolis: University of Minnesota Press.

Fraser, N. (1997). *Justice interruptus: Critical reflections on the "postsocialist" condition.* New York: Routledge.

Hertzberg, H. (2008, November 3). Like, socialism. *The New Yorker.* Retrieved on 16 September 2010, from http://www.newyorker.com/talk/comment/2008/11/03/081103taco_talk_hertzberg

James, M. E. (Ed.). (1995). *Social reconstruction through education: The philosophy, history, & curricula of a radical ideal.* Norwood, NJ: Ablex Publishing Corporation.

Leonardo, Z. (2003). Discourse and critique: Outlines of a post-structural theory of ideology, *Journal of Educational Policy, 18,* 203–214.

Lewis, O. (1961). *The children of Sanchez: Autobiography of a Mexican family.* New York: Random House.

Martell, G. (2008). Building education action: Toronto – grass roots policy and a political network. In G. Martell & E. Shaker (Eds.), *Breaking the iron cage: Resistance to the schooling of global capitalism* (pp. 1–18). Ottawa, ON: Our Schools Our Selves.

McIntosh, P. (1988). *White privilege and male privilege: A personal account of coming to see correspondences through work in women's studies.* Wellesley, MA: Centre for Research on Women.

Orlowski, P. (2001). Ties that bind and ties that blind: Race and class intersections in the classroom. In C. E. James & A. Shadd (Eds.), *Talking about identity: Encounters in race, ethnicity, and language* (pp. 250–266). Toronto: Between the Lines.

Roediger, D. R. (1999). *The wages of whiteness: Race and the making of the American working class* (rev. ed.). New York: Verso.

Rugg, H. O. (1921). Reconstructing the curriculum: An open letter to Professor Henry Johnson commenting on Committee Procedure as illustrated by the Report of the Joint Committee on History and Education for Citizenship. *Historical Outlook, 12,* 184–189. Reprinted in W. C. Parker (Ed.), (1996). *Educating the democratic mind.* Albany, NY: State University of New York Press.

Shaker, P., & Heilman, E. (2008). *Reclaiming education for democracy: Thinking beyond 'No Child Left Behind'.* New York: Routledge.

Ungerleider, C. (2004). *Failing our kids: How we are ruining our public schools.* Toronto: McClelland & Stewart, Ltd.

Weis, L., & Fine, M. (2001). Extraordinary conversations in public schools. *Qualitative Studies in Education, 14,* 497–523.

Wilkinson, R., & Pickett, K. (2010). *The spirit level: Why equality is better for everyone.* London: Penguin Books.

Index

A

Aboriginal
    graduation rates (high school), 10,
        128–129, 134–139, 142–144, 158
    issues in education, 96, 128, 130, 134
    issues in society, 83–86
    students, 10–11, 127–146
Adbusters, 45
Allende, S., 168, 173, 179
Althusser, L., 65, 129
American Civil Rights Movement, 48, 77
American Enterprise Institute, 181
Anijar, K., 174, 181, 187–188, 193
Anyon, J., 45
Apple, M. W., 7–9, 38, 42–46, 60–64, 87,
        104–105, 108, 141
    Ideology & Curriculum, 7–8, 104
Archibold, R. C., 65
Arizona legislation, 91, 198
Armstrong, J., 128, 162
Aronowitz, S., 22
Au, W., 189

B

Barman, J., 43, 64, 68–69, 123, 128, 136
Barthes, R., 42
Bartolome, L. I., 20, 127, 197
Battiste, M., 128
BCTF, *see* British Columbia Teachers'
        Federation
Beers, D., 43
The Bell Curve, 94
Berliner, D., 4
Bernstein, B., 109
Berthelot, J., 171, 178, 182–184, 191, 200
Bisbort, A., 3
Bloc Quebecois, 34, 123, 194
Bolivarian revolution, 191
Bolivar, S., 191

Bolshevik revolution, 64
Bourdieu, P., 109
Bowles, S., 46, 61, 115, 187, 197
Brandes, G. M., 141, 155–156
Brantlinger, E., 135
British Columbia Teachers' Federation, 42,
        192
Brown, W., 174, 176, 184, 186
Burke, E., 28
Burrows, M., 166
Bush, G. W., 6, 21, 29, 41, 44, 46, 51, 101,
        108, 149, 151, 153–154, 158–159, 162,
        168, 185, 189

C

Canadian Auto Workers (CAW), 105
Canadian Commonwealth Federation (CCF),
        104–106
Cappello, M., 156
Carter, J., 100, 145
Casanova, U., 4
Cato institute, 181
CAW, *see* Canadian Auto Workers (CAW)
CCF, *see* Canadian Commonwealth Federation
        (CCF)
Channel One News, 188, 194
Charter schools, 60, 185, 188
Chavez, H., 191
Cheney, D., 3, 62–63, 161
Cheney, L. V., 62, 90
Chomsky, N., 24, 35, 161, 168, 180, 186,
        190, 193
Christianity, 40, 43, 85
Citizenship
    the good citizen, 11, 154–157
    informed citizenry, 3, 107, 161
Citizenship Act (Canada), 150
Civil disobedience, *see* Protest
Civil rights, 29, 48, 50, 77, 153, 185

Clark, A., 191
Clarke, G. M., 150
Class consciousness, *see* Social, class consciousness; Working-class, issues
Clear Skies Act (U.S.A.), 162
Clinton, B., 35
Communism, 87, 102–103, 160
Connell, R. W., 39, 62
Conservatism, 5, 8, 13, 20–21, 23, 27–30, 35, 41, 59, 69, 83–84, 87, 90–91, 102–103, 108, 110, 114–115, 118, 120–121, 154–156, 160, 163, 172, 181
in education, 59
Conservative Party of Canada, 185
Constructivist pedagogy, 57
Consumerism, 45, 195, 202
Cookson, P. W., 60
Cornbleth, C., 57, 66, 119
Corporate media, *see* Media
Corporation, The (a film), 45
Correa, R
Counterhegemony, *see* Hegemony, counterhegemony
Counts, G., 14, 35, 51, 93, 152, 198
Crabtree, C., 63
Critical left
in education, 45–46
teachers, 45–46, 120
Critical pedagogy, *see* Curriculum; Critical left
Cuban, L., 61, 189
Cultural deficit discourse, *see* Discourse
Culturally relevant pedagogy, *see* Curriculum, culturally relevant
Cultural studies, 4, 9, 21, 47, 91
Culture of poverty, 110, 115–117, 120, 136, 203
Curriculum
in British Columbia, 104
color blind, 88–89, 139–142
common, 56–59, 141
culturally relevant, 7, 89, 202
enacted, 6–7, 55–73, 109, 114, 116–117, 119, 120, 122–123, 152–154, 156, 189, 202
essentialist, 85, 93, 139
Eurocentric, 7, 56, 58, 77, 90–91, 143
formal, 7, 9, 12–13, 57, 61–64, 66, 71, 107, 114, 116–117, 119, 120–121, 127, 129, 141, 159, 201–202, 204
as a hegemonic device, 7, 65, 106
history of, 7–8, 58–59
ideology, 5–8, 63, 104
Curtis, B., 9, 60, 109–111, 115

D
Davidson-Harden, A., 188
Davidson, P., 100, 188
Deconstruction, *see* Discourse, critical discourse analysis
de Cosmos, A., 43
Democracy
American, 25, 151–154, 167
flaws in democratic systems, 11, 149, 157–158, 164–166
Democratic party of the United States, 5, 21, 32–35, 106, 123, 168, 203
Derrida, J., 38
de Tocqueville, A., 11, 24–25, 29, 151–153
de Tracy, D., 19
Dewey, J., 7, 11, 14, 35, 51, 58–59, 62, 107, 151–152, 154, 187, 198
Dickason, O. P., 132, 136
Discourse
blame-the-victim, 45, 50, 131, 139
color blind discourse, 8, 10, 37, 48, 80, 87–90, 127, 131, 133, 139–140, 142
counterhegemonic discourses, 3, 11, 42, 44–46, 50, 57, 61, 66, 80, 90, 153, 159, 200
critical discourse analysis, 4, 6, 9, 15, 38–39, 200
cultural deficit discourse, 8, 10, 85, 94, 110, 116, 118, 127, 135–139, 143–144, 203
culture of poverty, *see* Cultural deficit discourse
discursive formations, 6, 25, 40–43, 51, 63, 99, 106, 173–174, 201
essentialist discourse, 37, 83–86, 90, 93–94, 96, 115, 120, 123, 134–135, 139, 146
genetic deficit, *see* Curriculum, essentialist
liberal discourses, 10–11, 50, 59, 94, 96, 110, 127–146, 189, 199, 203
neoliberal discourses, 50, 189, 199
race cognizance discourse, 89, 94, 131, 138–144
racial discourses, 8, 25, 82–90, 93–94, 110, 131, 134, 145, 202
teacher bashing, 190
Discursive formations, *see* Discourse
Dissent, *see* Protest
Dominion Institute of Canada, 63
Donahue, J., 50
Douglas, T., 105
Dunne, M., 73, 81, 109, 116

Dunn, R., 63
Dunsmuir, R., 68–69, 89
Durkheim, E., 197–198

E
Eageton, T., 19
Eisner, R., 177, 179
Emerson, D., 35, 165–166
Enlightenment, the, 19, 22–24, 30, 50, 60, 87,
    102, 149–151, 201
Enron, 123
Environmentalism, 30
Erlanger, S., 192
Ethnography, *see* Sociology

F
Fairclough, N., 37
False consciousness, 44, 159, 163, 166, 200
Fanon, F., 80
Fascism, 29, 160
Feminism, 1, 4, 20, 30, 35, 40, 42, 58,
    163, 200
Financial industry, 12, 26, 34, 50, 100–101,
    158, 171, 173, 181, 186
    deregulation of, 158, 171
Fine, M., 200
Foner, E., 152
Foucault, M., 22, 39, 42, 44
Fox News, *see* Media
Frankenberg, R., 8, 82
Frank, T., 152, 158, 180–182
Fraser Institute, 190, 194
Fraser, N., 11, 21, 151, 153–154, 200
Freeman, M., 189
Free trade, 34, 45, 101, 104, 107, 123, 163,
    173, 175, 179, 191, 201
Freire, P., 66
French revolution, the, 22, 26, 32
Friedman, M., 12, 41, 100, 178–182, 184

G
Gabbard, D., 174, 181, 187–188, 193
Gazeley, L., 73, 81, 109, 116
Gender, 2–3, 6–7, 14, 31, 35, 45–47, 50–51,
    57, 59, 63, 65, 70–72, 89, 91–93,
    107, 122, 131, 150, 162, 166, 197,
    200, 202
Genetic deficit discourse, *see* Discourse
Giddens, A., 21
Gillis, C., 192
Gintis, H., 46, 61, 115, 187, 197
Giroux, H., 19–20, 43–45, 61, 175

Globalization, 4, 12, 77, 100, 163, 171–172,
    182–184, 191, 193, 201–202
Goldwater, B., 181
Gorski, P., 110–111
Goulet, L., 144
Graf, G., 65, 87, 105
Gramsci, A., 42, 44–45, 158
    organic intellectuals, 44, 66, 158–159
Granatstein, J., 56, 63, 90–91, 141
Grant, C., 93, 111, 152
Great Depression, 12, 27, 100, 107, 120, 171,
    173, 177
Green party of Canada, 34, 168, 194
Green party of the United States, 33, 35,
    46, 168
Greenspan, A., 25–26, 100
Guskin, S., 135
Guthrie, W., 66–67, 120

H
Habermas, J., 22
Hale, G., 85
Halliburton, Inc, 3
Hall, S., 40
Harper, S., 41, 165
Harvey, D., 41, 172–175, 178–179, 181,
    183, 187, 190
Hayes, C., 82
Healthcare, 2, 9, 21, 25, 32–34, 48, 101, 103,
    105–106, 122, 123, 151, 164, 168, 171,
    173–175, 188, 194, 201
Healthy Forests Restoration Act (U.S.A.), 162
Hegemony
    counterhegemony, 3, 6, 44, 158–159
    hegemonic device, 3, 7, 25, 40, 44–45, 61,
        65, 88, 92, 106, 131, 159, 186, 199
    hegemonic norm, 8–9, 49, 80, 84, 107
    hegemonic strategy, 3, 9, 49, 63, 66, 78, 87,
        105–108, 120, 134, 162
Heilman, E., 162, 200
Heritage foundation, 181
Herman, E., 161, 168
Herrenvolk labor, 68
Herrnstein, R. J., 94, 96, 110, 115
Heteronormativity, 4, 44
Hill, D., 180
Hirsch, E. D. Jr., 56, 59, 90–91, 141
Hobsbawm, E., 27, 106
Holocaust, 77
Huffington, A., 154
Hughes, A., 150
Hursh, D., 129, 155
Hyslop-Margison, E., 160

I

Ideology & Curriculum, see Apple, M. W.
Ideology
  in curriculum, 5–8, 63, 104
  ideology critique, 13, 38–39, 50, 100–102,
    158, 160–162, 166, 192, 200, 203
  in teacher attitudes, 149, 154
IMF, *see* International Monetary Fund (IMF)
Immigrants, 48, 65, 69, 72, 78, 91, 193, 201
Immigration, *see* Immigrants
Indian Act (Canada), 87, 90, 96
Industrial revolution, 22, 26–27, 105–106,
    119, 173
Institute of Scientific Information (ISI), 194
International Monetary Fund (IMF), 180,
    183–184, 186, 191
International Workers of the World, 72
ISI, *see* Institute of Scientific Information (ISI)
I.W.W, *see* International Workers of the World

J

James, C. E., 60, 128, 142
James, M. E., 198
Jensen, A. R., 94, 96, 110, 115
Jim Crow laws, 79
Johnson, S., 15, 186
Juarez, B., 82

K

Kahne, J., 11, 154–156, 167
Kelly, D. M., 15, 60, 116, 141, 150, 155–156
Keynesian economics, *see* Keynes, John
    Maynard
Keynes, John Maynard, 12, 41, 100, 177–179,
    186
  Keynesian economics, 41, 100, 107, 174,
    177, 180, 194
Kincheloe, J., 4, 8–9, 11, 91–93, 111, 145,
    154–156
King, Martin Luther, Rev., 37
Kirkpatrick, D., 162
Klein, N., 100, 168, 179–183, 191
Klein, S., 193
Kliebard, H., 58–59, 71, 123
Klinger, D., 189
Knights of labor, 68–69
Krugman, P., 26
Kuehn, L., 188
Ku Klux Klan, 63

L

Labor, *see* Working-class; Unions
Laclau, E., 22

Ladson-Billings, G., 56, 66, 128, 140–141, 144
Laissez faire economics, 4, 12, 22, 24, 100,
    173, 176, 193
Lakoff, G., 11, 162–163
Landry, D., 189–190
Lareau, A., 109
Laut, A., 69–70
Laxer, J., 99, 101–102, 105–107, 150
Leier, M., 64, 69–70
Lemke, J., 38
Leonardo, Z., 37–39, 50–51, 201
Leroy, C., 81
Levine, D. U., 116, 118
Lewis, A., 49, 94
Lewis, O., 110, 203
Liberalism, 5, 8, 20–21, 24–31, 41, 50, 60, 87,
    92, 102–103, 108, 110, 114, 120–121,
    128, 131, 140, 143, 154, 156, 160, 168,
    172, 176–178, 185, 201
  in education, 60, 103, 121, 128, 131, 140,
    154, 160
Liberal party of Canada, 32, 34, 161, 203
Libertarianism, 22, 25–26
Limbaugh, R., 91
Lindbloom, C. E., 152
Lippman, W., 168
Livingstone, D. W., 9, 60, 109
Livingstone, S., 175
Luce-Kapler, R., 189
Ludlow Massacre, 7, 66–67, 120, 123
Lukacs, J., 108

M

Macdonald, N., 192
Mackey, E., 10, 48, 128–129, 132–133, 136,
    140–144
Majd-Jabbari, M., 135
Manicom, A., 62
Martin, L., 50, 185
Marxism, 58
Marx, K., 19–21, 26–27, 50, 103,
    176–177
Mathison, S., 189
McCain, J., 161
McCarthyism, 63, 168
McChesney, R., 186, 190
McGovern, G., 153
McIntosh, P., 96, 182, 202
McLaren, P., 183, 187
McLeod, I., 105
McLeod, T., 105
McNeil, L., 189
McQuaig, L., 177, 180, 185

Media
  corporate, 1–3, 6, 8, 11, 31–32, 40, 45–46,
    50, 52, 72, 109, 145, 149, 153, 159,
    161, 163, 167–168, 173–175, 181, 183,
    186, 188, 192, 197, 199, 201
  critical media literacy, 12, 43, 158,
    161–164, 166, 192, 201, 203
  Fox news, 20, 29, 46, 101, 153, 159, 163,
    185
  as a hegemonic device, 3
Meritocracy, 8, 32, 35, 59–60, 65, 87, 90, 92,
    94, 99, 110, 115–116, 132, 139, 150
Meyerson, H., 105
Mill, J. S., 24, 151
Modernity, 4–5, 22–25, 28–31, 160
Morales, E., 191
Mother Jones, 67
Mouffe, C., 22
Multicultural Act (Canada), 128
Multicultural education, 1, 8, 49, 90–91,
    95–96, 111, 144, 182, 198
Multiculturalism, 1, 8, 28, 30, 35, 90–94, 96,
    109, 111, 128–129, 131–132, 133, 143
  forms of, 8, 91, 93
Murphy, J. M., 161
Murray, C., 94, 96, 110, 115

N
Nader, R., 46
NAFTA, see Free trade
Nash, G. B., 62–63
National Endowment of the Humanities, 63
Nationalism, 23, 28–29, 104, 127
NDP, see New Democratic Party of Canada
Neoconservatism, 41, 172, 181–182
Neoliberalism, 4, 12, 22, 26, 35, 41, 50,
    100–101, 171–194, 199
  in education, 4, 12, 172, 180, 187–189
New Democratic Party of Canada, 21, 32,
    34–35, 42, 106, 123, 168
Ng, R., 67–68
Nixon, R., 41
No Child Left Behind Act (U.S.A.), 162

O
Oakes, J., 60–61, 111
Obama, B., 25, 101, 145, 153, 157, 171, 185,
    194, 199
OECD, see Organisation for Economic
    Co-operation and Development
Ogbu, J., 128
One Big Union, see International Workers of
    the World

Organic intellectuals, see Gramsci, A.
Organisation for Economic Co-operation
    and Development, 101
Orientalism, see Said, E.
Orlowski, P., 2, 9, 15, 20, 79, 81–82, 99, 103,
    117, 127, 158, 202
Ornstein, A. C., 116, 118
Osborne, K., 58, 61, 71, 111

P
Palin, S., 145, 194, 199
Palmer, B., 64, 68–69, 105–106
Parti quebecois, 123
Passeron, J. C., 109
Patriarchy, 163
Patriot Act (U.S.A.), 29, 153, 185, 194
Pickett, K., 99, 174, 185, 200
Pinochet, A., 168, 173, 179–180
Plato, 55, 58, 61, 150
Polanyi, K., 12, 178, 186
Political consciousness, see Social, class
    consciousness
Political ideology, see Ideology
Postmodernity, 22, 29–31, 39, 58, 77, 94, 135
Poststructuralism, 197
Privatization, 12, 21, 24, 48, 50, 102–103, 173,
    175–178, 183, 188
Progressivism, 22, 31, 168
Protest, 30, 49, 65, 68, 100–101, 154, 156,
    165–166, 181, 191–192, 194
Province-wide testing, see Teacher
    accountability
Public education, 1, 11–12, 34, 40, 43–46, 48,
    51, 56, 58, 60, 62, 65, 71, 103–104,
    109, 120, 122, 131, 144, 151–152,
    172–173, 185–192, 198–200
  funding of, 1, 34, 43, 105, 120, 171, 173,
    188, 189, 192, 194
Public ownership, 10, 102, 122

R
Race
  /class/gender intersections, 7
  /class intersections, 7
Racial discourses
  color blind, 8, 25, 90, 94, 131, 134
  essentialist, 8, 90, 94, 131, 134
  race cognizance, 8, 90, 94, 134
Racial hierarchies, 43, 78, 83–84, 89,
    94, 202
Racism, 7–8, 15, 41–42, 48–49, 63, 67–70,
    77–96, 134–135, 182, 197, 200, 203
  forms of, 8, 78–82, 94, 134

Radicalism, 20–21
    See also Critical left
Ravitch, D., 56, 90
Reagan, R., 22, 26, 35, 59, 100–101
Reproduction theory, 61
Republican party of the United States, 5, 33,
    101, 153, 199
Residential schools, *see* Aboriginal, issues in
    education
Reuther, W., 105
Riley, T., 129
Rock Springs Massacre, 72
Roediger, D. R., 68, 96, 182, 202
Rorty, R., 28, 153
Ross, E. W., 120, 129, 155, 189
Rothstein, R., 111
Roy, A., 184
Roy, P. E., 68–69
Rugg, H. O., 14, 35, 51, 93, 152, 198
Rushowy, K., 49
Rushton, J. P., 94, 96, 110, 115

S
Sadovnik, A., 60
Said, E., 47, 92
St. Denis, V., 127, 139
Santa Cruz, N., 55, 82, 91, 141
Schick, C., 127, 139
School choice, 1, 198
Schooling, purpose of, 6–7, 55–73, 198
Schugurensky, D., 188
Schwarzmantel, J., 20, 23–26, 28–29, 31, 160,
    174, 176
Sears, A., 150, 160
Semel, S., 60
Sevigny, P., 156
Shaker, P., 162, 200
Sherman, H., 161
Sleeter, C. E., 20, 93, 111, 152
Smaller, H., 9, 60, 109, 188
Smith, A., 24, 35, 176
Smith, D., 82
Social
    class consciousness, 1, 9, 11, 67, 99–104,
        106, 122–123, 202
    democracy, 5, 22, 27, 48, 103, 168, 178,
        199
    positionality, 6, 46–48, 51, 56
    reconstructionists, 51, 93, 111, 152, 167,
        187, 198
    reproduction, 46, 197–198

welfare state, 6–7, 9, 32–33, 40, 48, 50, 65,
    100, 102, 106–107, 116–117, 120, 122,
    177–178, 180, 185, 198, 201
Socialism, 5, 21–23, 26–31, 69, 102–103, 154,
    160, 199
Sociology
    ethnography, 2, 4, 15, 78
    informing curriculum, 9
Spencer, H., 85, 94
State-wide testing, *see* Teacher accountability
Steinberg, S., 8, 91–93, 111, 145
Stevens, E., 152
Stiglitz, J. E., 26, 184
Stoler, A. L., 83
Streaming, *see* Tracking
Symes, B., 81

T
Taber, J., 185
Tan, J.-Y., 68–69
Tax cuts, *see* Taxes
Taxes, 9, 38, 117, 153, 158, 164, 173,
    180, 188
Teacher accountability, 55–58, 71, 142,
    188–189, 198
    state-wide testing, 55, 185, 189
Teacher attitudes, 116, 118, 134–139
Teacher expectations, 118, 123
Teacher professionalism, 60, 120–121,
    189–190, 198
Teacher unions, 40, 56, 190
Tea party, 9, 29, 41, 78, 101, 129, 158–159,
    171, 182, 194, 202
Thatcher, M., 176
Tobin, K., 173, 187
Tracking, 59–61, 81, 111
Trade union movement, *see* Unions
Treaster, J. B., 100
Trickle-down theory, 176
Tupper, J., 156
Tyack, D., 61

U
UAW, *see* United Auto workers
Ungerleider, C., 129, 200
Unions, 1, 40, 56, 64, 67, 69–70, 100, 105–106,
    114, 117, 178, 184, 190, 201
United Auto workers, 105, 163
United Nations, 87
Universal Declaration of Human Rights, 87
Urbina, I., 171
U.S.A. Patriot Act, 29

V
Values
  economic, 51
  personal, 91, 156
  political, 78, 91, 168, 175
  teacher, 47, 129, 152, 164
Vidal, G., 172
Vinson, K., 189
Volcker, P., 25, 100
Von Hayek, F, 12, 178
Voucher system, 185, 187

W
Walker, T. J. E., 101, 106
Wall Street, 12, 62, 100–101
War, 3, 8, 14, 35, 37, 48, 59, 62, 64, 78–79,
  87, 90, 94–95, 102, 104–107, 117,
  122–123, 162, 166, 168, 174, 177–178,
  182, 199
Weis, L., 200
Weissman, R., 50
Westheimer, J., 11, 154–156, 167
White defensiveness, 20, 69, 78, 129, 202
Whitehorn, A., 106
Whiteness, 8–9, 49, 80, 82, 84, 96, 130, 145,
  182, 202
White supremacy, 25, 37, 40–41, 43, 69, 83–84
Whitson, T., 45–46
Wilkinson, R., 99, 174, 185, 200

Williams, R., 43, 82, 92, 130, 162
Willis, P., 61
Wilson, E. O., 93, 112
Wilson, W., 67
Winter, J., 162
Wobblies, *see* International Workers of the
  World
Wood, G., 152
Working-class
  consciousness, *see* Social, class
  consciousness
  issues, 92, 104, 106–107, 109, 116–119,
  121
  pedagogy, 56, 144, 202
World Bank, 180, 183–184, 191
World Trade Organization, 184, 191, 194
WTO, *see* World Trade Organization
Wynne, E., 155

Y
Yakabuski, K., 158–159, 182
Yeltsin, B., 183
Young, I. M., 11, 30, 151, 154
Young, R. J. C., 83

Z
Zinn, H., 57, 66–67, 72, 105, 120
Zizek, S., 20, 24, 42

Printed by Printforce, the Netherlands